D0075766

TRANSCENDENCE AND THE SACRED

BOSTON UNIVERSITY STUDIES IN PHILOSOPHY AND RELIGION

General Editor: Leroy S. Rouner

Volume Two

Volume One
Myth, Symbol, and Reality
Alan M. Olson, Editor

Transcendence and the Sacred

Edited by

Alan M. Olson

and

Leroy S. Rouner

UNIVERSITY OF NOTRE DAME PRESS
Notre Dame & London

WILLIAM MADISON RANDALL LIBRARY UNC AT WILMINGTON

Copyright © 1981 by
University of Notre Dame Press
Notre Dame, Indiana 46556

Library of Congress Cataloging in Publication Data

Main entry under title:

Transcendence and the sacred.

(Boston University studies in philosophy and religion; v. 2)
Includes indexes.
1. Religion — Philosophy — Addresses, essays,
lectures. 2. Transcendence (Philosophy) — Addresses,
essays, lectures. I. Olson, Alan M. II. Rouner,
Leroy S. III. Series.
BL51.T62   291   81-50456
ISBN 0-268-01841-3   AACR2

Manufactured in the United States of America

BL51
.T62

Contents

228316

Foreword

Boston University Studies in Philosophy and Religion is a joint project of the University of Notre Dame Press and the Boston University Institute for Philosophy and Religion. The series includes an annual volume of papers edited from the lecture series of the Institute as well as other occasional volumes dealing with critical issues in the philosophy of religion. In preparation are volumes on meaning and truth in nineteenth-century philosophy and religion, and on foundations of ethics.

The Boston University Institute for Philosophy and Religion is sponsored jointly by the School of Theology, the Department of Philosophy, the Department of Religion, and the Graduate School of Boston University. As an interdisciplinary and ecumenical forum it does not represent any philosophical school or religious tradition. Within the academic community it is committed to dialogue on questions of value, truth, and ultimate meaning, which transcends the narrow specialization of academic life. Outside the university community it seeks to recover the "public tradition" of philosophical discourse which was a lively part of American intellectual life in the early years of this century, before the professionalization of both philosophy and religious studies.

Our themes are purposely broad and inclusive. Our essays focus on analyses of specific issues, and we encourage our authors to make an autobiographical connection with their analysis. We also emphasize the need for comparative studies, since our global survival is threatened by religious and ideological conflict. Humane scholarship in world religions makes a small but significant contribution to mutual understanding among the world's various believers.

The Institute program receives support from several sources. We are especially grateful to the United Methodist Board of Higher Education and Ministry, and to the Associate General Secretary of the Division of Higher Education, Dr. James Barrett. The Board's recent contributions have made it possible for us to expand our program considerably.

It is our hope that these volumes may be a resource for critical reflection on fundamental human issues both within the academic community and beyond.

Leroy S. Rouner, Director
Boston University Institute
for Philosophy and Religion

This volume is dedicated to JOHN N. FINDLAY, Borden Parker Bowne Professor of Philosophy at Boston University, whose lectures to the Institute for Philosophy and Religion have combined elegance with wit, technical craftsmanship with a sly imagination, philosophical substance with lightness of heart.

Acknowledgments

The editors wish to express their appreciation to the authors of these essays for their cooperation, and to members of the Institute staff for their help, especially to Irena Makarushka, who prepared the manuscript for the publishers, and most of all to Barbara Darling Smith, who was responsible for technical editing. The people at the University of Notre Dame Press are now friends as well as publishers, and we count ourselves fortunate indeed to have them as colleagues. Ann Rice has guided the book through the publication process with patience and good cheer, while Jim Langford's enthusiasm and imagination continue to be one of our major resources.

Contributors

J. G. ARAPURA is Professor of Indian and Comparative Philosophy in the Department of Religious Studies at McMaster University in Ontario. Born and educated in India, he received his doctoral degree from Columbia University in 1955. He is the author of numerous articles and his books include *Religion as Anxiety and Tranquillity* (1972). Currently he is working on a definitive philosophical study of Vedānta called *Vedānta and Its World*, in which he seeks to raise ultimate questions through the medium of Advaita Vedānta and to see all Indian systems in its light.

J. N. FINDLAY is University Professor and Borden Parker Bowne Professor of Philosophy at Boston University. His books include *Meinong's Theory of Objects* (1933), *Hegel: A Re-Examination* (1958), *Values and Intentions* (1961), *Language, Mind and Value* (1963), *Meinong's Theory of Objects and Values* (1963), *The Discipline of the Cave* (1966), *The Transcendence of the Cave* (1967), *Ascent to the Absolute* (1970), *Axiological Ethics* (1970), *Plato: The Written and Unwritten Doctrines* (1974). He has just finished *Kant and the Transcendental Object*. Mr. Findlay received his B.A. and M.A. at Transvaal University College, South Africa. He was a Rhodes Scholar and received a B.A. First-Class Honours in Literae Humaniores at Balliol College, Oxford; M.A. (Oxford), 1930. He received his doctorate from the University of Graz, Austria, 1933. He is a Fellow of the British Academy and a Fellow of the American Academy of Arts and Sciences.

HANS-GEORG GADAMER was born in 1900 and took his doctorate at the age of twenty-two under Paul Natorp at the University of Marburg. After World War II he was Rector of the University of Leipzig, before resigning to become Professor Philosophy at Frankfort. He eventually succeeded Karl Jaspers as Professor of Philosophy at Heidelberg, where he continues as Professor Emeritus. He is also occasional Visiting Professor of Philosophy at Boston College. Professor Gadamer's early work dealt with Plato's dialectical ethics. He is best known today for his *Truth and Method* (1975) and *Philosophical Hermeneutics* (1976). He is currently writing a history of the intrepretation of Plato.

FREDERICK G. LAWRENCE is the editor of *Lonergan Workshop* and Director of the Lonergan Workshop at Boston College. He received his doctorate from the University of Basel in 1976 and is currently Associate Professor of Theology at Boston College. His numerous articles and essays include "Self-knowledge in History in Gadamer and Lonergan" (1972), and "The Horizon of Political Theology" (1978). Mr. Lawrence has also translated Henrich Ott's "Questioning, Presentiment and Intuition in the Theological Thought-Process," which appeared in *Foundations of Theology* (1971).

ROBERT LEE has taught at Amherst College, the University of Tennessee, and Boston University. Currently he is Wilson-Craven Professor of Religion at Southwestern University. He received his doctorate from Harvard in 1974. Writing extensively on Japanese religion and culture, he is presently working on an NEH Group Research project called "Buddhism in Japanese Civilization" at the Center for East Asian Research, Harvard University.

ALAN M. OLSON is Assistant Professor of Religion and Chairman of the Department of Religion at Boston University. He is the editor of *Disguises of the Demonic: Contemporary Perspectives on the Power of Evil* (1975); the editor of the previous volume in this series, *Myth, Symbol, and Reality* (1980); and the co-editor of this volume. Professor Olson is the author of *Transcendence and Hermeneutics* (1979), and co-authored *The Seeing Eye: Hermeneutic Phenomenology in the Study of Religion* (1981) with Theodore Brenneman and Stanley Yarian. Mr. Olson received his doctorate from Boston University in philosophy of religion and systematic theology. He is presently writing a book on "Mysticism and Modern Philosophy."

PHEME PERKINS is the author of several books including *The Gospel of St. John* (1975), *Reading the New Testament* (1978), *The Gnostic Dialogue: The Early Church and the Crisis of Gnosticism* (1980) and *Hearing the Parables of Jesus*, to be published in 1981. Ms. Perkins received her doctorate from Harvard and is Associate Professor of Theology at Boston College.

LEROY S. ROUNER is Professor of Philosophical Theology and Director of the Institute for Philosophy and Religion at Boston University. He has edited several volumes on the philosophy of William Ernest Hocking, including the Hocking Festschrift, *Philosophy, Religion and the Coming World Civilization*. He is the author of *Within Human Experience* (1969), *The Discovery of Humankind* (1975), and a recently completed book on the philosophy of community. Mr. Rouner taught for five years at the United Theological College in Bangalore, India, and has written numerous articles and papers on comparative religious philosophy. He is General Editor of Boston University Studies in Philosophy and Religion.

PETER SLATER is Chairperson of the Religion Department at Carleton University. He was born in England, educated in

Canada, and received his doctorate from Harvard University in 1964. His most recent book is *The Dynamics of Religion: Meaning and Change in Religious Traditions* (1978). Mr. Slater is the recipient of numerous grants and has contributed articles to leading journals of religious studies. He was also elected President of the Canadian Society for the Study of Religion in 1978.

HUSTON SMITH was born in Soochow, China, and took his doctorate at the University of Chicago in 1945. Currently he is Thomas J. Watson Professor of Religion and Adjunct Professor of Philosophy at Syracuse University. His books include *The Religions of Man* (1958) and *Forgotten Truth: The Primordial Tradition* (1976). Author of over forty articles, he has also produced three film series on world religions for National Educational Television. Mr. Smith has been the recipient of many honorary degrees and awards including the E. Harris Harbison Teachers Award (1964) and the Bronze Medal at the New York International Film and Television Festival (1968).

ROBERT A. F. THURMAN is the author of *The Holy Teaching of Vimalakīrti* (1976), *Golden Speech: Life and Wisdom of Tsong Khapa* (1978), as well as numerous articles and essays in the field of Buddhist studies. He is also the editor of the *Sanskrit/Tibetan/Chinese Lexicon on Technical Terms* and has translated a significant number of Buddhist texts. Having studied at Namgyal College in India, he was ordained as *bhikṣu* in 1965, and received his doctorate in Buddhology from Harvard in 1972. Recipient of many awards, Mr. Thurman was Senior Fellow at the American Institute for Indian Studies in 1979–80 and is now teaching at Amherst College.

EDITH WYSCHOGRAD is Associate Professor of Philosophy at Queens College of the City University of New York and is Director of the Religious Studies Program there. She received her doctorate from Columbia University in 1970. Her writings include *Emmanuel Levinas: The Problem of Ethical Metaphysics* (1973). She is the editor of *The Phenomenon of Death: Faces of Mortality* (1974). Last year Ms. Wyschograd worked on a study called *Mass Death and Human Finitude: A Critique of Hegel, Heidegger and Sartre* at the National Humanities Center of the University of North Carolina.

Introduction:
The Challenge of Cross-Cultural Studies in Philosophy of Religion

ALAN M. OLSON

ONE OF THE SIGNIFICANT developments in philosophy of religion during the past few years has been the resurgence of cross-cultural studies. Given the disastrous legacy of Vietnam, the Cambodian genocide, and the startling Islamic revival in the Middle East, some of this interest may be viewed as the predictable academic response to situations of chronic neglect. Viewed constructively, however, the cross-cultural emphasis may also signal the dawn of a new era in which we attempt to understand more accurately and sensitively those intellectual traditions that are not directly a part of Judaeo-Christian life and thought.

Comparative studies in philosophy and religion, of course, are not new. Indeed, comparative or "analogical" approaches to understanding, as John E. Smith rightly suggests, are both necessary and inevitable, especially when one's subject is religious experience and meaning.[1] And the new epoch of cross-cultural studies has a great deal to learn from the rich tradition of comparative studies that emerged through the pioneering work of Max Muller, E. B. Taylor, James Frazer, Wilhelm Schmidt, and others during the late nineteenth and early twentieth centuries, a tradition that has been refined and extended through such notable figures as G. van der Leeuw and Mircea Eliade. One of the critical lessons to be learned from this work, as Eric Sharpe indicates, is

1

that comprehensive knowledge is impossible. Hence, a surmounting of this uncritical assumption is the precondition for comparative studies to enter into its maturity.[2] Unfortunately, this necessity has not always been appreciated in the past, at least not when the comparativist assumes a total comprehension of the starting point. When this is the case, as it tended to be in the previous epoch, then comparative studies can easily degenerate into a kind of academic imperialism in which the scholar moves toward the *other* from a position of privileged perspective that is either overtly or covertly aprioristic.

The term *cross-cultural* is designed as a self-conscious attempt to disavow any and all privileged positions and perspectives, whether cultural, confessional, ideological, or methodological. In the past scholars have frequently generalized the so-called Hindu or Buddhist points of view on matters theological and philosophical. Today such generalizations will inevitably elicit the response, "Just which Hindus or Buddhists are you talking about?" as we begin to appreciate that Eastern philosophical and religious traditions are just as polymorphous as their Western counterparts. Thus our task today, as Clifford Geertz has suggested, "is not to explain religion, but to find it"; hence the project of what he terms "the thick description."[3] Few scholars today are any longer so bold as to presume that "all paths lead to the same goal" or that one path "is superior to all others." The most we can do is to acknowledge, with Heidegger, that "there are several paths in the same forest"[4] and even here to use the word *same* cautiously.

This sense of prudential openness provides the horizon for this inquiry into the various meanings of *transcendence* and *the sacred* in multi-cultural contexts. On one hand, the essays in this collection manifest the common conviction that if the symbolic terms *transcendence* and *the sacred* no longer have "cash value," as William James put it, then human existence is much less than we have understood it to be traditionally. Thus the ancient saying of Euripides still speaks, "Ye gods, alas, why call on things so weak for aid? Yet there is something that doth still cry out when one of us hath woe!" But on the other hand, the essayists here represented have refrained from the temptation of simply collapsing into comprehensive formulae the variegated nuances and meanings of transcendence and the sacred in their specific contexts and manifestations. This second volume in "The Boston University Studies in Philosophy and Religion" is the result.

The essays in Part I, "Reflections on Method in Comparative Studies," suggest that, while there are many obstacles to be surmounted in cross-cultural studies, the potential rewards are equally great. The lead essay by Huston Smith is informed by a profound sense of loss in the face of the domination of the Western religious and philosophical tradition by only a few of its actual sources. He would seek to retrieve the meaning of Western philosophy as a "great religion" so that it might be added to Judaism, Christianity, and Islam as one of the principal spiritual resources of the Occidental world.

It goes without saying that Smith is not the first to reflect on the perplexity of *philosophia perennis* in a post-Hegelian world. Smith's question gathers momentum from the cogent observation of Hannah Arendt that the post-Kantian loss of the "supersensible" really means that we have lost the "sensible" as well. It is a lament that was first echoed, perhaps, by the poet Hölderlin when he contemplated the loss of a measure against which we can anymore measure ourselves. And Smith indicates that he also is not willing to settle for what he terms the "epistemology of prometheanism" that seems to dominate our age, an epistemology in which what is held to be "true" must be capable of being verified by experimental and empirical means alone. Such an attitude, he implies, is tantamount to the death of transcendence and the sacred.

It is Smith's intention to rehabilitate the spiritual dimension of Western philosophy by reconnecting the Italianate tradition of ancient Greek philosophy (Pythagoras, Heraclitus, Socrates, etc.) with its Vedantic and Buddhist counterpart in *jñāna yoga*. His strategy is not to import into the Western tradition something that is not there already, but simply to alert us to the fact that we have in our midst a rich tradition of *gnosis* that may still speak to us if we will but listen. It might also be noted that this tradition of *gnosis* is not to be confused with the Gnostics against whom the early Christians battled so furiously. The kind of knowing that Smith is speaking about cannot be confined historically, since it has its origin in a far more primordial apprehension of Truth. Nevertheless, it is all too evident, he notes, that this primordial sensibility has been systematically abused and denigrated by the major religions of the West and by modern philosophy as well. It is a denigration that Smith sees arising out of the Western separation of devotion and work from wisdom and meditation. In the East, by contrast, *bhakti* and *karma yoga* are viewed as integral parts of the larger way of *raja* and *jñāna yoga*. If Western religions had maintained this complementarity, Smith suggests, the endlessly divisive question of Tertullian, "What has Athens to do with Jerusalem?" would not have become so deeply rooted in our theological traditions. Therefore, if we look beyond — or behind — the dogmatic overlay occasioned initially by the threat of the Arian gnostics so many years ago, perhaps we can begin to recognize more clearly the reality of the "jnanic/gnostic" strand in Western philosophy as a "great religion." Smith's analyses of Western philosophy under the categories of community, cult, ultimate concern, the self, theophany, intuition, and ontology are designed to begin to do this.

Peter Slater presents us with the outline of a method whereby we can more effectively understand experiences of transcendence and the sacred both past and present. It is his concern to develop "a new dialectics" that can effectively move beyond the old dichotomies of vertical and horizontal modes of transcendence and adumbrate the appositional values of Christian "order" and Buddhist "harmony." Such a method must be attuned, he insists, to the meaning of the "way" or "process" within which transcendence and the sacred are experienced rather than located as objects of reference. Slater suggests that the process method was, in fact, the way transcendence and the sacred were understood prior to Augustine. Augustine, for him, is something of a watershed in terms of the manner in which transcendence and the sacred have been understood ever since. After Augustine, Slater contends, the "transcending process" no longer had as much to do with "conversion" or transformation into a new philosophy of life, as with an initiation into an organized religious institution. In short, with the rise of medieval Christianity, the dynamics of transcendence as a process is progressively displaced by sacred referents clearly and definitively established and mediated by dogmatic theology. Thus it is against the dichotomy of transcendence and the sacred as it is understood by many in the West that Slater poses a method that is cognizant of the relativities of all models of explanation — whether Eastern or Western — and that abstains from seeking "the absolutely perfect sacred canopy" within which one can safely adjudicate the claims of all religions.

Slater's position, of course, bears some similarity to and dependence upon process thought generally. Indeed, in arguing for the primacy of the relation rather than the relata in the task of understanding transcendence and the sacred, his position bears some resemblance to the "relational ontology" of Harold Oliver.[5] This approach, of course, is not without its own difficulties, for, as I have shown in another context,[6] transcendence and the sacred have traditionally been understood in terms of both "act" and "being" and must admit both criteria. It is simple enough to comprehend transcendence as self-transcendence or human act. But transcendence in relation to what? Traditionally, it is in relation to the sacred or Being. If *Being* is an uncoinable term, however, and if the sacred is simply the product of cultural relativity, why call it "self-transcendence" or "process" at all and not simply "change"?

These questions and others are explored and extended by Edith Wyschogrod. It is her thesis that "apart from a civilizational perspective, the inquiry into transcendence remains an empty speculative exercise which fails to acknowledge the wider sphere of metaphysical commitments from which its terms have been derived, since such inquiry is rooted in contexts extending beyond those it immediately discloses." What she understands by the "civilizational perspective" is not a comprehensive understanding and explanation of everything that exists within a given civilization. On the contrary, her task is rather one of focusing on the dialectically reciprocal constitution of transcendence and its expressions — a constitutive process that simultaneously mediates and is mediated by those expressions — and this can be done only on the basis of a recognition of the limits of our understanding of this very process. It is from the awareness of *limit* that she judges the traditional explanations of transcendence as "myths of fixed

origin" (Derrida), whether they are derived from the otherworldly view, or a Whiteheadian immanent-process point of
view, or the apophatic, mystical approaches that would protect
and guard transcendence and the sacred from any and all objecti-
fying intrusions.

Her strategy, following Heidegger and Derrida, is to discern
the "traces" of transcendence and the sacred. Such traces are
never to be viewed as objects or processes, nor are these traces the
origins of anything. The "trace," she says, is not the effect of
which transcendence is the cause. The trace, rather, marks the
disappearance of the origin through a reciprocal, back-and-forth
oscillation which permits the emergence of both trace and origin.
In other words, Wyschograd envisions a dialectical but nonpro-
gressive relation between trace and origin. This notion is ampli-
fied through a direct quotation of Derrida: "The trace is not only
the disappearance of the origin . . . it means that the origin did
not even disappear, that it was never constituted except reciprocally by a non-origin, the trace, which then becomes the origin of
the origin."

Derrida's notion of the trace, of course, draws a good bit of
its inspiration from Heidegger's dialectic of disclosure and con-
cealment (*Anwesenheit*). But it is also a notion that has antece-
dent expressions in the higher mystics of both the Western and
Eastern traditions. One thinks, for example, of the injunction of
Plotinus and of Dionysius the Aeropagite regarding that "Eternal
Spring that knows no origin" and the pretense of those "who
would know by ordinary knowing Him who has made the dark
his hiding place," and also of the collapse of *saṁsāra* and nirvana
in Nāgārjuna's notion of "universal relativity." But irrespective of
what one's personal views of the trace might be, Wyschograd
sketches an approach that is self-consciously aware of the methodological limits inherent in any cross-cultural study of transcendence and the sacred. Such a focus on limits, the limits of both delineating and appropriating the meaning of any particular trace,
has dramatic implications for the traditional models and approaches to comparative studies, whether the East-West model
and its "ideal types," the problems method and related paradigms
with its "core questions," the theological foil approaches with its
"manageability" and not-too-hidden agenda, the comparison of

modes of inference approach, or the paradigms of linguistic determinism. Indeed the civilizational perspective envisioned by Wyschograd probably has as its single largest contribution the proviso of "precautions" as it sets out, as in the manner of Michel Foucault, "to discover the rules, the discursive policies, of what can and what cannot be said within the confines of a given system."

The essays in Part II, "Brahmanism, Buddhism, and the Gnostic Way," are sensitive to these rules, policies, and limits in the process of delineating the meanings and claims of transcendence and the sacred within four specific religious and philosophical contexts. While the fourth essay on Gnosticism by Pheme Perkins does not fall into the same geographical arena as the others, it presents the difficulties faced by *esoteric* religions vis-à-vis predominantly *exoteric* religions of the ancient Occidental world. As such this essay, in addition to treating a topic much in the public eye these days, provides a natural transition to the final section of essays dealing with Western experience.

The essays by John Arapura and Robert Thurman are both analytical and apologetical. Both Arapura and Thurman provide a clear and incisive philosophical understanding of transcendence and the sacred, and both proceed to argue respectively for the superiority of the Vedantic and Mahayanist points of view. The essay by Robert Lee, on the other hand, is descriptively analytical and may be viewed rather as a contra-apologetical warning against the inclination of the comparativist to seek a "post-Cartesian, post-Kantian enlightenment." Therefore, Lee confines himself to a historical and sociological reconstruction of the manner in which the terms *transcendence* and *the sacred* have themselves changed within the single case represented by Japanese Kamakura Buddhism, changes that are due to influences and developments that very frequently escape the attention and interests of philosophers and theologians. As such it is especially attentive to the warnings of Wyschograd regarding the "civilizational perspective" and the "limits" of both cross- and intra-cultural modes of analysis and comparison. It also focuses on what Slater has described as the "processes" of transcendence and the sacred rather than fixing the ultimate meaning of these terms trans-culturally.

Professor Arapura develops his question regarding "Tran-

scendent Brahman" and "Transcendent Void" both historically
and phenomenologically. Like Kant and Husserl he views the nature and problem of transcendence as arising from the structured
orientation of consciousness itself. And like Huston Smith, Arapura also laments the loss of reference in the movement of the
transcending process and the reduction of the meaning of transcendence to something strictly immanent. Arapura maintains,
however, that this loss of reference is not characteristic of Hinduism or even Buddhism and proceeds to indicate how, and under
what conditions, Eastern philosophy may be of some help in the
recovery of a sense of the sacred in the West.

Arapura's earlier work focused cross-culturally on *faith* as
the "anxiety pole" of the Western religious consciousness, and on
dharma as the "tranquility pole" of the Eastern consciousness.[7] In
this essay he uses the same approach in terms of the Vedantic conception of Brahman or "Origin" and the Buddhist conception of
nirvana or "Voidness." Both Hinduism and Buddhism, according
to Arapura, start from the common awareness that an abyss or
chasm separates ordinary consciousness from its highest state.
The difference between them, however, has to do with what the
highest state of consciousness signifies in terms of reference. For
the Buddhist, as Thurman indicates, this highest state of consciousness (*samādhi*) signals the collapse of questions of sense and
reference because they are precisely the questions that ultimately
stand in the way of Enlightenment. Indeed, it is to the end of facilitating this collapse that the radically negative dialectic of
Nāgārjuna known as *dṛṣṭi* is deployed in the attempt to move beyond the temptations of ontology.

Arapura's view of Brahman has more in common with Western religious ontologies of positive remainder than with classical
Indian forms of Buddhism. This can be seen in the willingness of
Arapura to draw an analogy between Brahman and the Platonic
understanding of *logos* and the long-standing Western notion that
"nothing comes out of nothing" (*ex nihilo nihil fit*), for by completely comprehending the abyss, he argues, Brahman has removed the possibility of its being absolutized as the transcendent
Void and hence has surpassed it. If this were not the case, he as-
serts, the "blissful" character of nirvana would be "nonsense" and

the Buddhist conception of *śūnyatā* ('emptiness' or 'voidness')
would be reduced to an epistemological meaning devoid of soteriological significance. The key to this conclusion, he maintains,
consists in recognizing that even though Buddhism uses logic
against logic in denying any kind of fundamentality to the Void,
it is precisely logic that is used! In other words, the transcending
process of consciousness toward its highest possible state is based
on a "structural possibility" that itself presupposes the reality of
logos, and for Arapura this seems to be a reality identical with
Brahman.

For Thurman the use of logic or a metaphysics of the concept that drives toward fundamentality of any kind whatsoever is
what distinguishes the Mahāyāna "Middle Way" from all other
religious and philosophical traditions. It is precisely logic that
must itself be renounced as that which represents the ultimate
barrier to *samādhi* in its most radical and complete form. He argues, against Arapura, that the experience of nirvana does not
have anything to do with soteriology. He leaves us with succinct
metaphors of transcendence as the "diamond" of clarity and differentiation, with the sacred as the "lotus blossom" of concrete
immediacy. Experience alone, and not any logic of the concept,
can tie them together. Indeed, in the view of Bodhisattva, a successful correlation of transcendence and the sacred as "method"
and "truth" respectively is manifest through "compassion" and
not through metaphysical cogency. As he puts it eloquently, "The
diamond of the transcendent sustains these living beings in their
ordinariness, and the raindrops of the sacred strengthen them to
rise above it." Therefore, there is nothing in the strictly transcendental model of analysis that can lead to a synthesis of the two
terms of transcendence and the sacred, method and truth. The final implications of his position approximate what Gadamer suggests through his development of the Aristotelian notion of
phronesis — namely, the praxis of moral wisdom.[8] The reader may
also discern these connections in the essay by Fred Lawrence in
Part III.

In his essay on Japanese Buddhism, Robert Lee tries to avoid
any philosophical or theological resolution of transcendence and
the sacred. While his purpose is one of focusing on the "tran-

scending process," as in the case of Slater, it is not with a view to the justification of any kind of process ontology. His strategy is to isolate the historical and sociological relativities of understanding within a specific context and to become aware of precisely those processes that constitute the "civilizational" perspective, as in the case of Wyschograd. Even though Lee agrees with Arapura and Thurman that the terms *transcendence* and *the sacred* largely have to do with the respective tasks of differentiation and integration, he makes no ontological claims regarding the status of these terms, whether each is in isolation from or in relation to the other. Thus he deals with what Bellah terms a "submerged transcendence" which manifests itself in different ways relative to what Hans Mol calls the "sacralization process." On this view there is a "sacralizing" process that strives toward "personal integration" and, conversely, a "desacralizing" process that strips away or erodes religious and personal identity. Since these processes are always changing and never the same during any period of history, it is well-nigh impossible, he warns, to locate with any precision meta-historical meanings of transcendence and the sacred.

Some of the same concerns occupy Pheme Perkins. She suggests that the Gnostic conception of the sacred (God) has much in common with the Eastern understanding of the primordiality of Being (what Lee calls *hongaku*). Gnosticism has its natural antecedents in the ancient Wisdom traditions of religion. However, such traditions meet considerable difficulties in the face of the practical concerns of the mainstream religions of the West. These religions are institutionally hierarchical and eschatologically oriented. Her analyses of selected Gnostic texts shows them falling rather indecisively "between" the genres of *mythos* and *logos*. Because the Gnostics cultivated a literary corpus of mixed metaphor for the express purpose of "serving" rather than "avoiding deception," the Gnostics ultimately became the victims of their own deception. Perkins therefore avoids the implied "sexual politics" thesis in the recent arguments of Elaine Pagels[9] by arguing that the Gnostics were not so much the victims of a male-dominated power struggle as the victims of themselves.

One of the striking features of the essays in Part III, "Modes of Transcending: Will, Mind, and Praxis," is their biographical quality. The article by J. N. Findlay is avowedly autobiographical, and Hans Gadamer's biographical analysis of "The Religious Dimension in Heidegger" is also semi-autobiographical in some respects, as is Leroy Rouner's attempt to focus on the dynamics of personal experience as a means of overcoming some of the restrictions in the orthodox Protestant understanding of transcendence and the sacred. Finally, the essay by Frederick Lawrence makes a case for the centrality of "story" and its relation to praxis as a means of breaking through what he views as the Western "privatization" of religious meaning in the modern period.

While this biographical feature was not planned as the leitmotiv of this section, the fact that it turned out to be so is itself significant, for it bears testimony to the manner in which the meanings of transcendence and the sacred for Westerners have so long been caught up in the personal struggles of faith and doubt. As such the essays in this section probably manifest less certainty but more urgency regarding the precise qualities of transcendence and the sacred and their corresponding realities. This is partially the case because philosophy and religion, transcendence and the sacred, have suffered a series of radical demarcations one from the other in the West. But it is also because the dominant strand of ethical monotheism in Western religions places such a severe constraint on the parameters and possibilities whereby one may advance definitive claims regarding the nature and reality of transcendence and the sacred.

The essay by Leroy Rouner places these difficulties into bold relief. He notes the absolute distinction made in the orthodox Protestant tradition between the Creator and the created, or what Kierkegaard fashioned as the "infinite qualitative difference between the temporal and the eternal." As the model that emerged out of medieval Europe after the breakdown of medieval metaphysics, Christianity was faced with what Rouner characterizes as a conception of transcendence and the sacred that is utterly disproportionate to immanent experience, namely, a God of absolute power who is viewed, in fact, as having the ability to save us from "the world powers of nature and history" — which is to say *from* experience! One thinks of the famous line of Bultmann concerning belief "in spite of" our experience,[10] for since

there is here no possibility of an *analogia entis* between the immanent and the transcendent, the powers and abilities of human experience and understanding tend to be reduced to "the will of
obedience." Herein lies what William Barrett refers to as "the
desperate and uncompromising thing" faith is after the Protestant
Reformation, namely, "the willful belief of the unbelievable,"[11]
or what Alasdair MacIntyre more recently has referred to as "the
will to believe in belief."[12]

It is for this reason that Rouner turns to William James as
one possible attempt to break out of this impasse through a careful examination of experience itself. There are, he contends, "live
options" arising out of ordinary experience that may enable us "to
be at home in a confusing and sometimes chaotic world." It is,
therefore, the pragmatic strategy that permits James, according
to Rouner, to confine his judgment regarding the nature and reality of transcendence and the sacred to "what he knows" and to refrain from extending his claims beyond what one can "reasonably
know." But there are problems with this approach, and Rouner
notes them — not least the problem of radical evil and the inability of the pragmaticist to account adequately for its presence in
the world. And there are also other problems which, as our three
remaining essayists contend in their respective ways, can be
avoided either simply by not accepting the dualistic implications
of Western religious thought, or by actively seeking to bring about
the deconstruction or demontage of the prevailing neo-Kantian
epistemology whereby these problems have both arisen and are
being compounded.

The former strategy is taken by J. N. Findlay, who virtually
embodies the project of "Western philosophy as a great religion"
as it is suggested by Huston Smith. Professor Findlay clearly indicates in this moving, witty, and confessional essay that he simply
does not feel obliged to accept the ontological problem that is inherent to the Judaeo-Christian-Islamic theological legacy. His
view of the *philosophia perennis* is larger, taking its clues from the
"three paradigmatic instances" of transcendence and the sacred
manifest in Jesus, the Buddha, and Socrates.[13] For Findlay, these
instantiations of the Absolute are acknowledged not by wagers
based on blind leaps of faith, but through practical, empirical

grounding in value theory or axiology. The essay provides a rare opportunity to see how Findlay has moved to an "apical vision" of transcendence and the sacred: a journey that leads us through family history, Theosophy, idealism, the critical influence of Russell and Wittgenstein, and finally to his present position by way of Brentano, Meinong, and Husserl. It is a testament of one man's experience and understanding of the realities we so haltingly and inadequately name *transcendence* and *the sacred.*

That language and concept finally are inadequate to account for the experience and meaning of transcendence and the sacred is a position shared, of course, by Heidegger. Indeed, Findlay and Heidegger are similar in their refusal to fall into line with the prevailing philosophical currents of skepticism in the twentieth century. But these thinkers are very different in the way each has resisted the demise of the spiritual and the humane in twentieth-century philosophy. One of these differences has to do with the decidedly hermeneutical stance of Heidegger (and Gadamer also) over against the great traditions of German idealism and confessional theology. While this religious aspect of Heidegger has been much misrepresented through what Gadamer terms "highly superficial" readings of his so-called atheism, Gadamer has made it clear that this "over-against-ness" is not to be viewed as hostile rejection but a constructive "coming-to-terms-with."[14] In this essay Gadamer indicates that Heidegger, like Luther, recognized that the only way "back to the ground of metaphysics" was through Aristotle. The critical difference, of course, is that whereas Luther simply went "around" Aristotle to the Bible, Heidegger goes "through" Aristotle and ultimately into the region of Being's Truth understood as *Alētheia* in the pre-Socratics. What Luther and Heidegger share, according to Gadamer, is a sense of the weight and implication of the *deus absconditus.* The meaning of transcendence and the sacred is necessarily "hidden," and its appearance as revelation or "event" can never be fixed by any onto-theology. But this observation is not a romanticism of the primordial, and this is precisely what separates Heidegger from those who, according to Gadamer, would mistakenly label him either an atheist or an archaicist. One of the ways to avoid this temptation, according to Gadamer, is to appre-

ciate the impact of Nietzsche's "audacity" on Heidegger's development of the "forestructures" of being-in-a-world. It is Nietzsche's
notion of man as "everwaiting" Being combined with Hölderlin's
fascination with a dialectics of absence that is a strange kind of
presence which results in a thinking "on" rather than "about" Being. Hence, the essence of Heidegger's understanding of transcendence and the sacred is "anticipatory," not primordialistic or revi-
sionistic: an active-contemplative dwelling with the mystery of
that which "worlds."

Is the "religious dimension" of Heidegger excessively priva-
tistic? I suspect that Gadamer, in the final analysis, would con-
cede that it is, even though he does not say so in this essay. But
Gadamer has contended elsewhere that one of the unfortunate
legacies of transcendental idealism is precisely the subjectiviza-
tion of religious meaning.[15] Thus it is entirely fitting that Frederick Lawrence, in our final essay, should take an approach to the
meaning of transcendence and the sacred as "interruption" that
eventually establishes an intriguing link with Gadamer's notion
of *phronesis*.

It is the contention of Professor Lawrence that the "mystery"
inherent in transcendence and the sacred is to be found neither in
the conceptual *loci* of traditional theology nor in consciousness
per se. His purpose is to lead theology beyond the impasse he sees
in the contemporary period where, quoting Muggeridge, "the
Freudians are looking for their Marx, and the Marxists for their
Freud." Indeed, it is precisely to challenge the existentialist immanentalism implicit to this state of affairs — namely, the "unquestioned questions" raised so routinely by modern humanity — that
Lawrence raises his notion of transcendence as "interruption"
(*Unterbrechung*).

Lawrence's position turns on the political theology of Johann
Metz in an attempt to develop a constructive supplement to the
transcendental Thomism of Karl Rahner, which is informed by
the dynamics not only of being "hearers" of the Word but of being
"doers" also. To do this, Lawrence focuses on the apocalyptic implicit in the Christian story as the means to differentiate "praxis
theology" from the historical praxis of neo-Marxist critical theory.
For Lawrence the key to this differentiation lies in disclosing the

nature of the "master metaphor" of critical theorists as being one of "evolution" and "progress" exclusively based upon "anthropodicy." It is precisely against what he regards as the uncritical immanentalism of this view that Lawrence raises his not un-Barthian notion of "interruption" as the shortest and most effective definition of Christianity. Through this analysis he shows that the project of critical theory is based ultimately upon an "ideology of the winners" informed by the value of survival as the greatest good. For Lawrence, it is against this "flattened continuum" of time that Jesus, and apocalyptic generally, stand as a radical interruption by forcing us to confront the realities of death, suffering, and evil as meaningful subversions of this immanentalism. Hence the dangers, for Lawrence, of historical memory—not as something that permits us to escape from history, but as the means of discovering that one's identity is actually a relative baseline or context of unfolding action and suffering within a narrative or story. On this model transcendence and the sacred are displaced from an idealistic or privatized-subjective locus and reaffirmed precisely as those concepts which provide for dynamic narrative and constructive social action. In other words, transcendence and the sacred are "relocated," to use Slater's term, in a manner akin to Gadamer's conception of *phronesis*, as the active working synthesis of knowledge and ethics. Thus, transcendence as "interruption" provides Lawrence with the means of "sublating" theories of emancipation through a "sacred story of redemption." For Lawrence this "interruption" is identified with the Christian "belief in the resurrection of the dead and hope in our passing through death to life," since it is, for him, a belief that "frees one to live a life of self-transcendence that goes against the grain of self-affirmation or self-aggrandizement."

In a larger sense, however, it might be said that the virtue of which he speaks is *humility*. But this humility is not superficial effacement of self which is itself a subtle form of self-aggrandizement. It is rather a humility signaling a transformation of the self as evidenced in and through the practice of life and never in separation from it. Such a notion may be said to be shared universally by the higher religions of the world as requisite to any authentic comprehension of transcendence and the sacred.

NOTES

1. John E. Smith, *The Analogy of Experience* (New York: Harper & Row, 1973).

2. Eric Sharpe, *Comparative Religion* (New York: Charles Scribner's Sons, 1975), pp. 144–171.

3. Clifford Geertz, *The Interpretation of Cultures* (New York: Basic Books, 1973).

4. The statement was made by Heinrich Ott, at one of the meetings of the 1978–79 series of the Institute for Philosophy and Religion, on "Transcendence and the Sacred."

5. Harold Oliver, "Relational Ontology and Hermeneutics," in *Myth, Symbol, and Reality*, ed. Alan M. Olson, Boston University Studies in Philosophy and Religion 1 (Notre Dame, Ind.: University of Notre Dame Press, 1980). See also Oliver's forthcoming treatment of this problem, *A Relational Metaphysic* (The Hague: Martinus Nijhoff, 1981).

6. Alan M. Olson, *Transcendence and Hermeneutics* (The Hague: Martinus Nijhoff, 1979), pp. ix–xxiii.

7. John G. Arapura, *Religion as Anxiety and Tranquility: An Essay on Comparative Phenomenology of Spirit* (The Hague: Mouton, 1972).

8. Hans-Georg Gadamer, *Truth and Method* (New York: Seabury Press, 1975), pp. 274–305.

9. Elaine H. Pagels, *The Gnostic Gospels* (New York: Random House, 1979).

10. Rudolf Bultmann, *Jesus Christ and Mythology* (New York: Charles Scribner's Sons, 1958), p. 84.

11. William Barrett, *Irrational Man* (New York: Doubleday & Co., 1958), pp. 20–25.

12. Alasdair C. MacIntyre and Paul Ricoeur, *The Religious Significance of Atheism* (New York: Columbia University Press, 1969), p. 21.

13. J. N. Findlay, "Religion and Its Three Paradigmatic Instances," in *Religious Studies* 2 (1975): 215–227.

14. Hans-Georg Gadamer, *Hegel's Dialectic* (New Haven: Yale University Press, 1976), pp. 100–116.

15. Gadamer, *Truth and Method*, pp. 39–90.

PART I

Reflections on Method in Comparative Studies

1

Western Philosophy as a Great Religion

HUSTON SMITH

IN A STRIKING BUT as yet unpublished paper titled "Philosophia as One of the Religious Traditions of Mankind," Wilfred Cantwell Smith argues that the Greek legacy in Western civilization deserves to be ranked as one of the world's great religions. We couldn't recognize this earlier, he says, because our notion of religion was too tightly tied to Judaism and Christianity. A century of work in comparative religion has now loosened this parochial mooring; it has enabled us to bring the entire human heritage into view, lining up its components in our mind's eye, arraying them side by side, and according reasonable justice to each. This, in turn, has given us a better understanding of what a religious tradition looks like — what it is that makes it such. Among other advantages, this new understanding doubles back to "proffer a substantial reinterpretation of Western data," including the realization that

> it is legitimate and helpful to consider . . . the Greek tradition in Western civilization, rationalist-idealist-humanist, within the generic context of various [other] religious traditions of mankind. It is neither absurd, nor trite, to reinterpret it as one of our planet's major religious traditions: different, of course, from each of the others yet comparable, and understood most truly when so contrasted and compared.

Like so many of Professor Smith's insights, I find this one exciting, although I propose to develop it differently from the way

19

he projected in his paper. First let me say why I think a fresh look at our Western philosophical heritage is in order.

World views are shaped by their sponsoring epistemologies, which in turn are shaped by the motivations that prompt these epistemologies. We naturally want to know the kinds of things that will carry us to where we want to go.[1] Modern science has hit on an epistemology — roughly, the scientific method — that has enormously augmented our capacity to control the physical world. In catering to this particular human impulse — our will to power — with an effectiveness which epistemologies that service other human needs have not been able to equal, the scientific method has, in effect, carried the day. Tailored as much to the scientific method as common sense will allow — occasionally, as in behaviorism and positivism, somewhat more than common sense allows — modern epistemology is essentially promethean: X counts as knowledge if it holds promise of facilitating control. Like the scientific method which is its model, this epistemology is limited. It follows that the conception of the world that it sponsors is proportionately limited, for the view that appears through a restricted viewfinder is necessarily a restricted view.

This, *in nuce*, is my reason for unrolling again the scroll of our philosophical past: driven by the universal dream of knowing the way things are, I do not like settling for a partial ontology. This unrolling is my main object in the essay; but because it runs counter to the current institutionalized assumption that we have advanced philosophically more than we have wandered down a blind alley, I feel the need to document, if only minimally, my opposite impression.

I

World views derive from epistemologies, which in turn derive from motivations. That the driving motivation of modern science is to control is, I take it, too obvious to need documenting. The epistemology that has fashioned our modern outlook derives from this same animus: we wove its net with the hope that the kind of knowledge it would lift from the sea of being would be the kind that would augment our effectiveness in dealing with life as a whole, *effectiveness* being defined here in its problem-solving sense. I shall limit myself to a single witness for each of the two remaining links in my propaedeutic chain: Ernest Gellner for epistemology, and Hannah Arendt for its consequent ontology or world view.

I choose Gellner for epistemology because, being a sociologist as well as a philosopher, his perceptions carry more than private weight. I am not saying, of course, that he is infallible or even necessarily right — only that, as a philosopher-sociologist who trains his sociological equipment on philosophy as a discipline, his findings lay claim to more than private standing. Gellner focuses on the way Western philosophers have come to see things rather than on the way he himself sees them.

What is this way? Gellner admits that at first glance there seems to be no "way" in the singular; what greets us is, to use the title of the opening section of his *Legitimation of Belief*, "The Pluralist Chorus." But beneath this surface variety — even cacophony — a trend can be discerned. Most generally, it is the trend toward acceptance of epistemology as contemporary philosophy's focal task; more specifically, it is an "emerging consensus" that, to be recognized as legitimate, beliefs must now pass two tests, or "insistences" as he calls them. "There is the empiricist insistence that faiths . . . must stand ready to be judged by . . . something reasonably close to the ordinary notion of 'experience'. . . . Secondly, there is the 'mechanistic' insistence on impersonal . . . explanations."[2]

Gellner proceeds to ground these two insistences in the prometheanism I have charged with calling the tune for modern Western epistemology:

> We have of course no guarantee that the world must be such as to be amenable to such explanations; we can only show that *we* are constrained to think so. It was Kant's merit to see that this compulsion is in us, not in things. It was Weber's to see that it is historically a specific kind of mind, not human mind as such, which is subject to this compulsion. What it amounts to is in the end simple: if there is to be effective

knowledge or explanation *at all*, it must have this form, for any other kind of 'explanation' . . . is *ipso facto* powerless.[3]

"We have become habituated to and dependent on effective knowledge, and hence have bound ourselves to this kind of genuine explanation," Gellner continues. The view of the world it produces is inevitable—I am speaking now for myself, to make the transition from Gellner to Arendt, from epistemology to ontology. Empiricism and mechanism being ill-suited to deal with transcendence and the unseen, the epistemology of prometheanism necessarily delivers a naturalistic world. "What has come to an end," Hannah Arendt writes toward the close of her life, "is the . . . distinction between the sensual and the supersensual, together with the notion, at least as old as Parmenides, that whatever is not given to the senses . . . is more real, more truthful, more meaningful than what appears; that it is not just beyond sense perception but *above* the world of the senses."[4]

That says it: our (promethean) motivation has elicited our (mechanistic-empiricist) epistemology, which in turn has brought forward a naturalistic metaphysics. Now the price of focusing attention on one thing is, of course, inattention to other things: when a botanist peers down his or her microscope at a leaf cell, the leaf as a whole disappears. This simple analogy alone should cause us to have second thoughts about our prevailing naturalism, so obviously is it a product of a partial epistemology. But one of the tolls that has been exacted from us on the road we have traveled is interest in truth for its own sake. Preoccupied with "effective knowledge" (Gellner's term), we have grown forgetful of Being; the self-centeredness that prompts prometheanism in the first place carries right through to the end. If motivations forge epistemologies that forge ontologies, these ontologies in turn forge anthropologies, meaning, by this last word, lives as conditioned by the worlds in which they live.

What is the feel of the life that naturalism has generated? As early as two centuries ago, Gellner points out, Kant saw "the inescapable price of this Faustian purchase of real [*sic*] knowledge. [In delivering] cognitive effectiveness [it] exacts its inherent moral, 'dehumanizing' price. . . . The price of real knowledge is that our identities, freedom, norms, are no longer underwritten by our vi-

sion and comprehension of things. On the contrary we are doomed
to suffer from a tension between cognition and identity."[5] A hundred years later, Hannah Arendt continues, Nietzsche deepened
Kant's analysis. Picking up on the point we have already cited
from her, that the distinction between the sensual and the supersensual has been brought to an end, she proceeds as follows:

> Meanwhile, in increasingly strident voices, the few defend-
> ers of metaphysics have warned us of the danger of nihilism
> inherent in this development; and although they themselves
> seldom invoke it, they have an important argument in their
> favor: it is indeed true that once the suprasensual realm is
> discarded, its opposite, the world of appearances as under-
> stood for so many centuries, is also annihilated. The sensual,
> as still understood by the positivists, cannot survive the
> death of the supersensual. No one knew this better than
> Nietzsche who, with his poetic and metaphoric description
> of the assassination of God in *Zarathustra*, has caused so
> much confusion in these matters. In a significant passage in
> *The Twilight of Idols*, he clarifies what the word *God* meant
> in *Zarathustra*. It was merely a symbol for the suprasensual
> realm as understood by metaphysics; he now uses instead of
> *God* the word *true world* and says: "We have abolished the
> true world. What has remained? The apparent one perhaps?
> Oh no! With the true world we have also abolished the ap-
> parent one."[6]

Kant for the eighteenth century, Nietzsche for the nineteenth
— for the twentieth I shall choose a sociologist at my own university, Manfred Stanley:

> It is by now a Sunday-supplement commonplace that the so-
> cial, economic and technological modernization of the world
> is accompanied by a spiritual malaise that has come to be
> called *alienation*. At its most fundamental level, the diagno-
> sis of alienation is based on the view that modernization
> forces upon us a world that, although baptized as real by
> science, is denuded of all humanly recognizable qualities;
> beauty and ugliness, love and hate, passion and fulfillment,
> salvation and damnation. It is not, of course, being claimed

that such matters are not part of the existential realities of human life. It is rather that the scientific world view makes it illegitimate to speak of them as being "objectively" part of the world, forcing us instead to define such evaluation and such emotional experiences as "merely subjective" projections of people's inner lives.

The world, once an "enchanted garden," to use Max Weber's memorable phrase, has now become disenchanted, deprived of purpose and direction, bereft — in these senses — of life itself. All that which is allegedly basic to the specifically human status in nature comes to be forced back upon the precincts of the "subjective" which, in turn, is pushed by the modern scientific view ever more into the province of dreams and illusions.[7]

Are we ready, now, to take another look at our philosophical past?

II

Professor Smith keeps the Greek philosophical heritage intact, seeing that heritage-as-a-whole as an alternative to the Western family of religions (Judaism, Christianity, and Islam) and the religions of non-Western civilizations. Using a diagram he does not himself introduce, we might visualize his demarcation of the major historical religious alternatives as follows:

Judaism	Chris-tianity	Islam	Philosophia: The Greek Heritage	Hinduism	Buddhism	The Chinese Religious Complex

I, on the other hand, want to take as my encompassing unit our Western religious tradition as a whole, in which the Greek component figures as one-fourth, the other three-fourths being Judaism, Christianity, and Islam. Moreover, only a fourth of Western philosophy enters the Western religious tradition: its modern half becomes too fastened to modern science to be religiously important, while half of its original, traditional half was likewise more occupied with worldly than with religious concerns.[8] Perhaps the layout on page 25 will convey my overview.

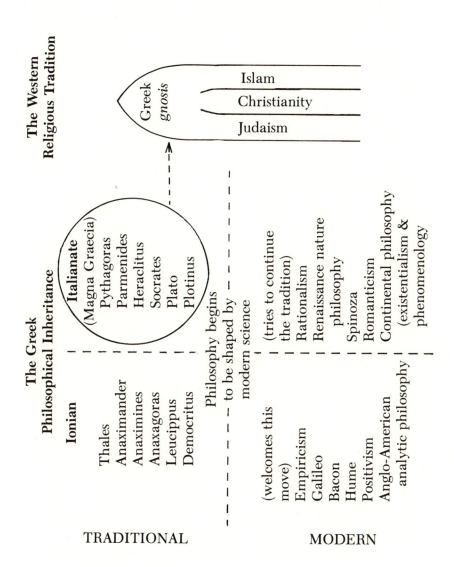

The Western
Religious Tradition

Islam

Christianity

Judaism

Greek
gnosis

The Greek
Philosophical Inheritance

Italianate

(Magna Graecia)
Pythagoras
Parmenides
Heraclitus
Socrates
Plato
Plotinus

Ionian

Thales
Anaximander
Anaximines
Anaxagoras
Leucippus
Democritus

Philosophy begins
to be shaped by
modern science

(tries to continue
the tradition)
Rationalism
Renaissance nature
philosophy
Spinoza
Romanticism
Continental philosophy
(existentialism &
phenomenology)

(welcomes this
move)
Empiricism
Galileo
Bacon
Hume
Positivism
Anglo-American
analytic philosophy

TRADITIONAL   MODERN

Explanations are at once required.

a. In placing Greek *gnosis* at the pinnacle of Western religion I do not mean that it is superior to Judaism, Christianity, and Islam. I mean only that when these Semitically originated communities came to conceptualize their deepest insights, a grammar for the purpose awaited them. It was, moreover, a grammar so advanced, so carefully tuned to the highest registers of the human spirit, that Christians, Muslims, and Jews alike embraced it. In Chomskian idiom, they found its grammar to be "generic" — we need think only of the equal enthusiasm with which Philo and Maimonides, Dionysius and Thomas Aquinas, Avicenna and ibn 'Arabi assimilated it. The zenith of the Western religious tradition is Greek in the sense that Greece provided its grammar and vocabulary, but the discernments this equipment was used to articulate were present in the Semitic religions from their start.

b. Analytic philosophers often point out that the novelties that have entered philosophy in our century do not token a break with its past: Aristotle, Anselm, Thomas Aquinas, and Duns Scotus, they contend, were analytic philosophers. Fair enough. But analytic philosophy's preponderantly critical attitude toward religion[9] makes me want to enter the same claim for religious philosophy. It too is solidly grounded in our philosophical past, continuing the Great Tradition.

c. Philosophers who are comparativists will see almost at once what I am up to, for it is in Vedantic idiom that my project can be stated most succinctly. This is not surprising, for the project would never have occurred to me had I not encountered India; it is from her that my controlling paradigm is lifted.[10]

I want to consider the Greek inheritance in philosophy as our Western version of *jñāna yoga*. It is common knowledge that India delineates four paths to God, of which *jñāna*, the path of knowledge, is one. Its chief alternative is *bhakti yoga*, the path of love or devotion, for the two remaining paths — those of work and meditation, *karma yoga* and *rāja yoga* respectively — tend to be assimilated by the first two.[11] India accommodates these two great spiritual options in a single tradition, called the *sanātana dharma* or *varṇāśrama*, depending on whether one is thinking of its theoretical or its practical side. But in the West these alternatives have not been partners in a single tradition. They look more like distinct separate traditions that for two thousand years have been trying to work out a modus vivendi.

Athens and Jerusalem, philosophy and religion, the Hebraic and Hellenic components of Western civilization: does the Indian experience have anything to say to us as we continue to work toward a harmonious marriage of these parents that have begotten us? To Indian eyes, Judaism, Christianity, and Islam appear basically as bhaktic or devotional paths which, because they don't provide much room for *jñāna* or *gnosis,* leave the latter housed with the history of philosophy. *Jñāna visits* the Western religions proper, who grant it temporary visas, we might say; but except for the duration of the medieval synthesis it isn't given citizenship.[12] We need only think of Spinoza, Eckhart, and al-Hallaj to be reminded of how restive Judaism, Christianity, and Islam can become when full-fledged gnostics appear in their midsts. Śaṅkara and Nāgārjuna had to contend with the Brahmins and Bhikkus of their traditions too, but in the end they were fully ensconced. Insofar as this essay has a programmatic thrust, it is to propose that the Western religious tradition open its gates comparably to the jnanic strand in its civilization, the strand that originated in Greek philosophy.

III

What is *jñāna* or *gnosis* (spelled with a small "g" to distinguish it from Gnosticism as a specific doctrine) as a religious category?

In *Farewell Happy Fields,* the first volume in her trilogy of memoirs, Kathleen Raine describes in some detail her father's Wesleyan Methodism in Ilford, England. On the verge of manhood he had undergone conversion to "a living faith," which remained thereafter unshaken and enabled him to live a life of many sorrows with deep confidence. He looked for no earthly happiness, for it was clear to him that in this world a human is "a stranger and sojourner." All he asked of his brief time on earth was to perform the tasks life placed before him, for task was precisely what life was—a task to be performed, sure of the reward of the faithful servant in the world to come. Ambition had no place in such a life; it was unimaginable to him, for he did not regard his life as his own but rather his Master's. What his Master willed for his life was that he spend it assisting in the titanic struggle of good against evil. This good was situated in social improvement and service rather than in nature, truth, and beauty. These latter he valued only for their "message," for moral purpose was everything—the question of salvation made it so. This relentless moralism forced a certain narrowness on his life. Still, the fineness of his moral sense infused his conduct with a beauty of its own.

A summarizing paragraph cannot do justice to Dr. Raine's account of this religious universe of her father, but that doesn't matter because it is not that universe itself that concerns us here. I have introduced it only as a foil to bring out what is of moment, namely, his wife's reaction to it. Fortunately Dr. Raine's own account is succinct enough to let her give it directly.

> My mother's evasion, after her marriage, of the religion of John Wesley was not different from her earlier evasion of John Knox; a withdrawal of attention, a failure of interest availed her more than argument and useless opposition. She had, besides, a habit of fainting in church; I never knew her to faint elsewhere, certainly not at the theatre, on the longest walk, or in the hottest greenhouse in Kew. My father I think never knew whether my mother had been "saved" or not; for she always agreed with everything he said. But at over eighty it was the *Upanishads* and the works of A. E. and G. R. S. Mead and even Israel Regardie that my mother would take down from my shelves, or travels in Tibet, or works on spiritualism; never have I seen her read any work of Christian devotion. The supernatural world was for her, as were her vivid nightly dreams, rather an escape from the moral world than, as for my father, a region of it. She confessed to me (she was in her mid-eighties then) that she was not "religious" and had always found the emotionalism of Methodism vulgar; "but I am very interested in the cosmos." Some time before this she had had a slight stroke and

thought she was dying. What was it like? I asked her; and my mother's eyes flashed like those of a hawk whose hood is lifted and she said, "I was very interested."[13]

She said she was not religious, but do we believe her? Her disinterest in the kind of religion she saw around her comes through to us (in her daughter's account) categorically, but the account shows something positive at work as well — that to which she was drawn as "religion's" alternative. She was interested, we are told, in the cosmos and in her near-encounter with death. *More* than interested, actually; in these she was "very interested" — the phrase is repeated for both topics. And the question for us becomes: Do we not sense in these interests themselves something religious? Her own protestations to the contrary count for nothing here, of course, since it's precisely the meaning of the word *religion* that is at stake. In part her *religiousness* (in our enlarged definition of the word) discloses itself in the objects that interested her, for death and the cosmos are religious themes in ways that ice cream and horse racing are not. But it is in the *way* those objects drew her that the character of her religious impulse, its jnanic character, is disclosed. In contrasting her mother's interest to her father's, Dr. Raine highlights its form. Her mother's interest was disinterested in a way her father's was not; it was the "disinterested interest" that is the hallmark of jnanic religion.[14] A wife's confession that she was "not 'religious' . . . but" has brought us to the distinctive feature of jnanic religion or gnosis. It is religion in the presiding mode of pure interest — pure, disinterested interest, to repeat the paradoxical formulation. Hypnotized by the strangeness of a new and unfamiliar beauty, the person is fascinated, engrossed, awestruck, transfixed. The jnanic vision is so totally its own reward that the question "What's in it for me?" doesn't even intrude. In pure cases there is no "me" in the picture at all.

I am not contending that self-transcending vision is the only important thing in religion or even in jnanic religion. Questions of action (what's to be done) and the meaning of one's own individual life inevitably enter and must be dealt with — justice interested the West's paradigmatic *jñāna* yogin, Socrates, only slightly less than did wisdom. I am, though, claiming that important as these other components are, to the *jñāna* yogin they are secondary to the religious object as it transcends finally not only oneself but humanity and the entire created universe. If we cannot recognize a position that fixes on the strange, transhuman beauty of being as it passes in awe-inspiring recessions from the natural world into the infinite; or, if acknowledging that such a position exists we nevertheless refuse to grant it full religious status, I should end my essay here. For if Western philosophy is religious, it is so in the mode I have tried to describe; and if that mode is not authentically religious, Western philosophy is not a great religion.

IV

The preceding section tried to identify the heart of the jnanic position. In this final section I shall argue the religiousness of this position as it appears in the West, primarily in the gnostic strand of Greek-originated philosophy. I have already observed that the bhaktic, devotional character of Judaism, Christianity, and Islam has obscured the fully religious character of this jnanic stance. My strategy toward removing that prejudice will be to enumerate seven properties we tend spontaneously to recognize as religious and show the extent to which our philosophical tradition has housed them. There is space here only to touch on these seven themes which elsewhere I hope to expand to the proportions of a book, but perhaps their simple enumeration can help us to see why Peter Brown could note toward the beginning of his biography of Augustine of Hippo that "for centuries now, the *idea* of philosophy had been surrounded with a religious aura."[15]

1. *Philosophy's communal nature.*[16] When Whitehead defined religion as what we do with our solitariness, he was voicing at most a half-truth. More obvious is its deep involvement with our social nature; as people associate around the things they prize, their lives get woven together: synagogues, churches, and the Islamic *ummah* (community) take shape. So it was with the schools of ancient Greek philosophy. The Epicureans, Stoics, Academics, Peripatetics, and Neo-Pythagoreans were not philosophical schools in the abstract sense in which we speak of schools

of thought today — positivist, idealist, pragmatic, and the like. They were also cultic communities, half ritual and half philosophy — more like colleges in the medieval, monastic sense than in the sense of even our residential colleges today. Like the *ashrams* of India and American communes today, they often sprang up around central founding figures such as Plato, Aristotle, Zeno the Stoic, Epicurus, or, later, Plotinus — individuals who were not just thinkers or professors but who were regarded as inspired men. Correlatively, their students were not students in the contemporary academic sense but more like disciples. They congregated around their masters because they wanted actually to live by their doctrines. The Pythagorean communities are the extreme case here, of course. Their students were more like candidates for the priesthood than candidates for a degree at a modern university.

2. *Its cultic features.* These follow in part from the communal features just noted. Mary Douglas contends that communities become such through the conscious or unconscious rituals that knit lives together more powerfully than does conversation. But my interest here is not in the rituals the Greek philosophers devised or adopted for their own communities. Such rituals existed; we know, to cite a single case, that "Plato's Academy was a religious association with its own divine worship, in which the cultus was of such importance that we find it explicitly laid down that one of its members should be appointed to prepare the sacrifice."[17] But the more important point, I think, is that the philosophers typically participated in the normal rituals of their communities. I see no reason to view this cynically, as if they did so for reasons of prudence or expediency. On the contrary, I take it as evidence that they saw themselves adding their insights to the religion of their people rather than using these insights to oppose that religion. (Their critique of the crass anthropomorphism and immorality of the Homeric pantheon doesn't counter that statement, for that way of imaging the divine was on its last legs for the populace as a whole.) This is not to say that the relations between priests and the philosophers were always harmonious. Being of different spiritual temperaments they at best felt somewhat awkward with one another, while at worst hostility could flame. Soc-

rates is the classic case, having been condemned in part on the charge of teaching atheism. But the other side of that coin is his denial of the charge. I venture the generalization that whereas exoterics (*bhaktis*) often felt threatened by esoterics (*jnanins*), not fully comprehending what the latter were up to, esoterics (the philosophers) generally saw their spirituality as continuous with that of the people, though of course they did claim to see more deeply into its meaning. The *Republic* opens with Socrates reporting, "I went down yesterday to the Pieraeus with Glaucon . . . that I might offer up my prayers to the goddess [Bendis]," and his last words as recorded in the *Phaedo* were, "Criton, we owe a cock to Asclepios [the god of healing]; pay it without fail."

3. *Its ultimacy.* In a well-known lecture, John Burnett argues that the core of Socrates' teaching is to be found at *Apology* 29D4 and 30A7ff., where stress is laid on the care of the soul and how to make it as good as possible:

> Men of Athens, I honour and love you; but I shall obey God rather than you, and while I have life and strength I shall never cease from the practice and teaching of philosophy. . . . I believe that no greater good has ever happened in the state than my service to the God. For I do nothing but go about persuading you all . . . not to take thought for your persons or your properties, but first and chiefly to care about the greatest improvement of the soul.

Quite apart from the word *God* that appears twice in this brief statement, it is impossible to miss its author's conviction of the urgency of his mission. If religion is ultimate concern, we sense it in statements like these by Socrates or we sense it nowhere. The schools of philosophy I referred to several paragraphs back arose during a time of skepticism; the ancestral order had dissolved and men and women were looking for an alternative way to get their bearings. To say that skepticism — rootlessness, rudderlessness — didn't satisfy them is too weak; they found it intolerable and reached for truth as for a lifeline. "To Pythagoras, philosophy was not an engine of curiosity, but a way of life and death."[18] *Our* popular imaginations may picture Epicurus as a man who had good times in beautiful gardens, but his disciples called him *soter*, "savior," for he did one of the greatest things for them that a teacher can do. He freed them from anxiety.

4. *Its involvement of the total self.* Let me lead into this point through an example that may seem trivial but which points to something important. In his treatise "On Cleanliness" Epictetus writes:

> By the gods, when the young man feels the first stirrings of philosophy I would rather he came to me with his hair sleek than dishevelled and dirty: for that shows a sort of reflection of the beautiful, and a longing for the comely, and where he imagines these to be, there he spends his effort. (*Discourses* 4.11)

To generalize from the case in question, Epictetus is saying that a candidate's capacity for philosophy does not turn on I.Q. alone. It roots down into regions of the person which, while they will definitely affect the mind's performance — will it be able to grow wise? — are not themselves strictly cognitive.

Few professors today could comfortably open their philosophy courses by saying, "If you hope to acquire not just knowledge but wisdom you must change your lives. You must try to tell the truth. You must cease to live in your skin-encapsulated egos with their petty wishes and try instead to identify yourself with the all-embracing Self. Seek God, pray." If on rare occasion a Western philosopher should now say something like this, it would probably be in a course on ethics or aesthetics, not metaphysics or epistemology. Yet this is the way wisdom philosophers (*jñāna* yogins) used regularly to speak. Socrates argued that if you want to keep your ability to philosophize intact it is better to suffer wrong than to do wrong. Plato taught that by using poetry and music the young should be schooled to approve what is to be approved and condemn what is to be condemned to the end that "when reason comes, he will greet her as a friend with whom his education has made him long familiar" (*Republic* 402A). Aristotle echoed that general point when he said that the young are not ready for ethical reflection, being able to understand no more than the grammar of words. In short, factual knowledge is one thing, wisdom and *gnosis* another. In the broadest sense of the word, the latter require virtue. For to borrow an image from Frijhof Schuon, light does not go through an opaque stone and barely illuminates a black wall. The knower must become like crystal or snow.

5. *Its theophanies.* Standard classifications link revelation to religion and reason to philosophy, but again the question is whether these accepted divisions cut where the joints are. For the jnanic philosophy we are dealing with does not proceed through reason alone. We have just seen that the reason it does employ ties in with deeper-lying components of the self, but the point now is that this reason is also fed by transcendent sources. In the *Meno* Plato tells us that wisdom comes to us somehow "by divine dispensation," and Parmenides clearly presents his theory "as a revelation, accorded to him by the Goddess who governs all things in person."[19] I pass over specifics like these to note three general areas where we catch sight of revelation infusing Greek philosophy.

a. The first of these places is in the mythic base out of which philosophy arose. In *The Presocratics*, Werner Jaeger points out that these thinkers capped the preceding mythic period quite as much as they launched a new beginning—Greek philosophy. And the myths they thus rounded off were held to be of nonhuman origin. It was not in merely human eulogy that Homer was called "the divine poet," for the mythic wisdom of the Greeks, like that of the Vedas, was held to be uncreated—eternal. Unlike the hypotheses of science, which come and go, it could never become obsolete, for it was believed to be not cumulative but a priori. As metaphysicians and poets alike testified, it was derived not from experiment but from inspiration. Plato said it came by *anamneses*, "recollection." It is not human but divine, belonging not to the ego but to the Self which is common to all. Today we might not speak of myths in quite these terms, but if we know our subject at all we recognize that myths are wholly different from fables deliberately fashioned by individuals to amuse or preserve a lesson learned. Myths are never intentionally made nor produced by individual authors. The least we can say is that they arise from the cumulative experience of countless generations and embody instinct and deep communal feeling.

b. If myth is collective revelation, revelations are also given to individuals. In the *Timaeus* 80B, Plato says that to our God-given vision and hearing the muses add harmony to those who can use it "intellectually . . . to assist the soul's interior revolution, to restore it to order and concord with itself." Etymologically, *revelation* derives from *re-velum*, 'the drawing back of a veil that conceals,' and Plato's Allegory of the Cave is as powerful an account of such disclosure as has ever been written. It is the account of the philosopher who is shown something others do not see and who is changed — and finds the universe changed — by the revelation.

c. Perhaps the most important kind of revelation is that which manifests itself in human form — an incarnation. Christ is the chief instance of this mode, of course, but he has his counterpart in Greek philosophy in the figure of Socrates. Socrates stands to Plato as Christ stands to St. Paul; we have the one through the other. It was Socrates who showed Plato the way. Plato's name barely occurs in his dialogues; for decades he effaced himself to leave the stage to his master. Compared with his fateful encounter with Socrates, everything else Plato encountered was episodic. His entire corpus is the effort to recapture the vision of Socrates and hold it up for others. How is it possible that there could have been a man of this stature? The question reaches its climax in Alcibiades' eulogy in the *Symposium*. Bernard Loomer once remarked that the eulogy makes the *Symposium* the New Testament of Greek philosophy, and establishes (almost by itself) the Platonic tradition in Western philosophy as one of the world's great religions.

6. *Its intuitive intellect.* In referring above to *jñāna's* involvement with the total self, I noted that it links reason to human sensibilities that are not cognitive in the strict sense of that word. It follows that in isolation from these deeper sources, reason is a distinctly limited instrument. In Indian philosophy *manas* is augmented by *buddhi*, which Zimmer translates as "intuitive awareness."[20] In Western philosophy reason is supplemented by intellection.

If we watch carefully we can all sense kinds of knowledge that flow from a source in us that is different from reason. We might call this supplementing faculty *insight*, or *intuition* if we don't read that word in its Bergsonian sense. We can even call it *imagination* if we are clear that in doing so we use the word in a way almost opposite to the way Spinoza used it, siding instead with the romantic poets who elevated imagination into a capacity for apprehending realities that can be reached in no other way. For Shelley imagination was "that imperial faculty," and Blake saw the person of imagination as the person of vision, opposed by the person of reason who sees with the corporeal eye only. We are obviously involved here with the doctrine of the intuitive imagination as the distinct organ of perception in the human soul, the "eye of the soul" as Plato called it. In the full-blown medieval doctrine of *intellectus*, the object that this eye perceives is the transcendent.

What lies behind these various locutions — Hegel's distinction between *Verstand* and *Vernunft* and Spinoza's between science and intuition could be added to them — is the fact that in metaphysical matters insight is decisive. This insight cannot be produced by assembling brute data or initiating chains of formal logic, or any combination of these. For the reigning epistemologies of our time this is a scandal, for it opens the prospect of studies that require a certain level of insight as their prerequisite as well as the possibility of issues that cannot be arbitrated by additional evidence. The most each side can do is appeal to its opponent to deepen powers of insight and nurture the intuitive intellect.

7. *Its ontology.* I have saved till last the ontology of the jnanic tradition in Western philosophy because I consider it decisive. Twice in these pages I have alluded to Tillich's definition of religion as "ultimate concern," but it is obvious that that phrase can be read either psychologically or ontologically. Read psychologically, religion is whatever happens to concern a person most, be it sex, ambition, or whatever. Ontologically approached, on the other hand, religion is involvement with what in fact *is* ultimate, ontologically ultimate. For the Western philosophy I have been examining, this ontological ultimate is radically transcendent, which does not keep it from being fully immanent too for those who have eyes to see. Denotatively, it is Anaximander's "boundless" or "infinite," Plato's "Idea of the Good," Plotinus's "One," and Spinoza's "Deus sive natura." It is the initial link in the Great Chain of Being that proceeds from it.

Having examined this chain at some length in my *Forgotten Truth: The Primordial Tradition*, I shall not detail it further here. I shall remark only that though reason cannot climb its links to any great height, to penetrate beyond reason into what the intuitive intellect alone can discern is the strongest drive of the gnostic's nature.

NOTES

1. "We use our criteria of rational acceptability to build up a theoretical picture of the empirical world. [Indeed] we must have criteria of rational acceptability to even have an empirical world. [As these criteria] reveal . . . our notion of optimal speculative intelligence . . . the 'real world' depends upon our values" (Hilary Putnam, in an unpublished paper on "Fact and Value").

Kathleen Raine makes the same point in a way that anticipates the argument that I am commencing: "Knowledge, in any culture, is only an agreed area of the known and the knowable; 'let X equal knowledge' is premised and the proofs follow. Every X can of course yield its results. But there is always an excluded knowledge; and as the crude beginnings of science were the excluded knowledge of pre-Renaissance Christendom, so theology and all the wisdom of the spirit is the excluded knowledge of a materialistic society. As R. P. Blackmur (apropos of Eliot and Yeats) wrote in 1957, 'The supernatural is simply not part of our mental furniture.' But reality does not change its nature because we are unaware of it; a fact which the scientists themselves would not deny" ("Premises and Poetry," *Sophia Perennis* 3:2 [Autumn 1977]: 60–61).

2. Ernest Gellner, *Legitimation of Belief* (Cambridge: At the University Press, 1974), p. 206.

3. Ibid., pp. 206–207.

4. Hannah Arendt, "Thinking and Moral Considerations," *Social Research* 38 (Autumn 1971): 420.

5. Gellner, *Legitimation of Belief*, p. 207.

6. Arendt, "Thinking and Moral Considerations," p. 420.

7. Manfred Stanley, "Beyond Progress: Three Post-Political Futures," in *Images of the Future*, ed. Robert Bundy (Buffalo: Prometheus Books, 1976), pp. 115–116.

8. If one defines *religion* as "ultimate concern," then of course anything can be religious; what would make it such would be the way a person relates to it. But if one defines the world ontologically rather

than psychologically, objectively rather than subjectively; if one attends less to the manifold directions in which people *can* deploy their religiousness than to the kinds of things that typically *have* drawn their religious concern, a different picture emerges. Churches are then assumed to be religious in ways that marketplaces are not; and certain ontologies, due to their transcendent registers, let us say for now, again seem obviously more religious than others. This distinction does not do justice to the force and subtleties in Wilfred Smith's proposal that our philosophical heritage as a whole be viewed as religious; I merely repeat that that is not the way I am viewing it here. While owing much to Professor Smith's suggestion, my enterprise is more conventional. I wish to look at the way the strands in our philosophical heritage that lie close to common-sense notions of religion get woven into the mantle of the Western religious tradition as a whole.

9. J. J. Smart has noted that positivistic arguments that long since have been rejected as invalid in ethics and aesthetics continue to be invoked against religious assertions.

10. In Asia one normally credits one's teachers, so let me again acknowledge my debt to Swami Satprakashananda of the Vedānta Society of St. Louis, now in his nineties, for a decade of near-weekly tutorials.

11. India assumes that every spiritual aspirant will do some meditating, and one can scarcely live without doing some work as well. Whether the yogi turns work to spiritual account by discriminating between the work and the fruits that accrue from it or by offering the work as a "living sacrifice unto the Lord" depends on whether the yogi's temperament is basically jnanic or bhaktic.

12. To see what Western religion would have looked like had it paralleled India's development, we need to picture the Greeks as conquering the Semites in the way their Aryan cousins who pushed on into India conquered the Dravidians. Greek *gnosis* would then have constituted the Upanishadic capstone that would have wrestled with Judaism, Christianity, and Islam in the way the Vedic, Brahmanic, Smarta (followers of the *smritis*) tradition wrestled with India's local, indigenous, sectarian theisms; but in the end it would have been integrated with them. The Athens/Jerusalem tension is not unheard of in India; in my introduction to Frithjof Schuon's *Transcendent Unity of Religions* and my review of that book in the December 1976 *Journal of the American Academy of Religion*, I posit that it is rooted in a fundamental difference in spiritual personality types that is cross-cultural. But in India the two types are gathered in a single tradition; *jñāna* and *bhakti* get woven as warp and woof into a single fabric. This cannot (as yet?) be

said of philosophy and religion in the West. "In the West . . . Athens [and] Jerusalem . . . have never set well together. . . . There is something indelibly plural in the very notion of the Western tradition" (Robert N. Bellah, in "Commentary and Proposed Agenda: The Normative Framework for Pluralism in America," *Soundings* 61:3 [Fall 1978]: 363).

13. Kathleen J. Raine, *Farewell Happy Fields* (New York: George Braziller, 1977), p. 73.

14. *Jñāna* is usually defined as knowledge, but as mind is the faculty that can break through our subjectivity and carry us beyond ourselves, the notion of pure or disinterested knowledge is strictly embedded in the jnanic concept. One comes to it very quickly.

15. Peter R. L. Brown, *Augustine of Hippo: A Biography* (Berkeley: University of California Press, 1967), p. 40.

16. I remind the reader that in using the word *philosophy* in this list of characteristics it is not the whole of Western philosophy that I have in mind. I am speaking of that quadrant of it that is circled in my diagram.

17. Josef Pieper, *Leisure: The Basis of Culture*, trans. Alexander Dru (New York: Pantheon Books, 1952), p. 77.

18. F. M. Cornford, *From Religion to Philosophy* (New York: Harper Torchbook ed., 1957), p. vi.

19. Ibid., p. 214.

20. Heinrich Zimmer, *Philosophies of India*, ed. Joseph Campbell, Bollingen Series 36 (Princeton: Princeton University Press, 1951), p. 403.

2

The Transcending Process and the Relocation of the Sacred

PETER SLATER

IF JESUS TODAY WERE teaching us to pray, he might conceivably begin, "Our Mother, who lives in our hearts." If Gautama the Buddha was about to be born, on the other hand, we would probably not refer to his embryo as a White Elephant. Somehow in religion we have to do justice to continuing patterns of faith in the traditions expressed in ever-changing conceptual schemes. With reference to ideas of *transcendence* and *the sacred*, therefore, we have to discriminate between the intentionality prompting our use of such terms and the cultural coloring with which we invest them at any one time. If we would be true to the traditions, we have not only to delineate their history. We must also evoke their present spirit of "ultimate concern" without trivializing their contents. This is no easy task.

In this essay I propose first to indicate what I consider the proper starting-point for discussions of faith. Then I shall review one classical Christian version of the saving experience in order to remind ourselves of the conception of transcendence with which it left us. At the same time I shall look at parallel developments in Buddhist history in order to develop my thesis that it is the transcending process, not any entity or state of being considered in isolation, which is absolute in the traditions. In the remainder of the paper I shall consider how my emphasis fits with developments in modern theology, having regard especially for the dynamics of sacrifice and a contemporary sense of what is sacred.

40

Where are we to begin our deliberations on such topics? I agree with those who say that we must begin with experience.[1] But which experience or pattern of experience provides the key? We must not fall into the atomistic trap of the British empiricists. Nor should we fall into the archaistic fallacy of seeking contemporary equivalents to ancient epiphanies. The intersection of Commonwealth Avenue and Beacon Street, for example, is not the sort of place at which we might encounter sacred trees, even if some are still standing there. If René Girard is right, and violence is the fulcrum of the sacred, the intersection might be where we cross the boundary between life and death in a religiously significant way. But then the focal point would be the car as cult object, not the place as such.[2] In any case, I submit, the relevant kind of experience will in some sense be *saving* experience. It will be the experience of one who was shattered and is now whole, was lost but is found, was bound but is now free, was alienated but is now reconciled, was utterly gloomy but is now ecstatically joyous. It will be the experience of one who has transcended, or is transcending, whatever conditions are hellish and is entering on the path to Nirvana. In William James's sense, it is the experience of the twice-born.

By beginning here, we turn our question into one concerning personal being and becoming. We might then embrace a more recent psychologist, Abraham Maslow, and describe transcendence by reference to what he called the "peak experiences" of self-actualizing people.[3] Although vague, his notion is attractive to any who regard maturity as a precondition or concomitant of saving experience. The transcending process may begin with deficiency motivations. But it cannot end in any extrinsic use of religious conceptions or institutions for the private comfort of deprived egos. The full process brings us beyond the strivings of ordinary Eros to expressions of a self-with-others which is self-assured. The erotic and/or agapeistic acts of this "self" have a different kind of purpose from that characteristic of unrequited lovers. In traditional terminology, the normative experiences in religion are those of the saints or, if sainthood be a matter of degree, of those furthest along the way to enlightenment or the beatific vision. In the language of self-realization, Maslow points us to the experiences of this spiritual elite.

Yet Maslow's conception is defective on several counts. It does not embrace the institutional and ontological ramifications of religious experience—even though all of his examples (maestros at the piano, mothers cooking their specialties) are of people in institutional settings. They are what they are because of a network of relationships. True, in all traditions there is a mystical strand which sets "peakers" apart from the crowd. But the intentionality of their way is often described as union with the All, that is, a kind of cosmic identification which is the opposite of unqualified individualism. The solitary shaman does not exist simply for his or her own benefit. In Buddhism, the *śravaka* or *pratyeka-buddha* is not the ideal in any of the traditions.[4] The fruits of a seer's seeing, or what a prophet hears, are passed on to disciples who teach others their way. One who relates neither to God or Brahman, on the one hand, nor to fellow sufferers, on the other, may fairly be said in religion not to have achieved the necessary perfections prior to taking the final step. As a psychologist, Maslow may be excused from exploring these ramifications. But if we would build from his insights in religious studies, we must inquire into the nature of that whole which defines such wholesome experiences. Thus we may begin with individual being and becoming. But we cannot end there.

Some sense of a wider whole may be found, for example, in that classic account of saving experience, Augustine's *Confessions*. By contrast with contemporary authors, he immediately broadens the referent of personal becoming by merging individual experience through language with the experience of others. For him, sensations are refracted through a kind of collective memory of early childhood. What illuminates the individual conscience is not some construct of the individual's imagination but the *arché* of Truth. And Truth, we recall, is one of the philosophical names of Christ, or God-with-us.[5] The path of introspection leads us to the same divinity that Thomas later adduces by gazing outward.[6] Because Augustine's conception of his conversion hinges on the turning of the individual will, we tend to forget that he wrote as a bishop, edifying his people, and to read him only as an exponent of existential choice. But the last word of the *Confessions*, like the first, is of opening ourselves to the Eternal Thou.

Augustine's own emphasis is not so much on free choice as on the power to act on a right choice. In the tussle between good and evil, he tells us, the experience of the divided self first attracted him to Manichean dualism. He believed that he would be wholly good when he finally put off the flesh. But his experience of wholeness came only when he learned to put on the Christ. What is put on or off, he discovered, is not something physical. In later idioms, it is a habit or mind-set. What enables us to make a right choice, and to keep on making right choices, is not self-effort but grace. What must be incarnated, acted on, by humankind is not the cool rationalism of the Manichees but the hot dedication of the Desert Fathers. The humility of the Christ, not his physical disguise, is what the devil cannot grasp and therefore cannot overcome. The transformation from being at war with the world, including oneself, to being utterly at peace depends upon habituating oneself in the Christian way of sacramental living. What is required is a shift of focus from self to God and an acceptance of the *rule* of faith. For Augustine the Christian, the Scriptures replace the Latin poets as the pattern of perfection. The character communicated by this pattern is the love and wisdom of the Christ. Its discipline is what draws the prodigal home from the empty distractions of life in the external world.[7]

A similar conception of the way to peace can be found among Augustine's contemporaries in the Buddhist world. Their saving experience begins with the resolve to become a bodhisattva.[8] What powers this resolve is not the individual ego but the Buddha nature active within us. Only over long periods of single-minded devotion does the pattern of wisdom and compassion become so imprinted that one breaks through to a level of understanding which is secure from the power of delusion. The ideal life, as for Augustine, is a monastic life sustained by neighboring townspeople. Among monks and nuns, those are most respected who live by the discipline of their order.

To our ears there is an air of spurious humility in Augustine's insistence on his own impotence before God, or in Shinran's insistence on his own foolishness in relation to the Buddha. Ours is such an egalitarian ideology that we have difficulty in tuning into either the heights of divine glory or the depths of the servant mentality. But if Victor Turner and others are right, it is precisely the abasement of the chief among us that symbolizes the kind of power inherent in the saving process.[9] Augustine the bishop is simply following Jesus the Christ in both asserting his leadership with full authority and accepting his personal nothingness, given that only God really exists.[10] *The experience of transcendence comes from the interplay between poles, not the contrasts in status ascribed to either end of a relationship taken in isolation.*

For medieval saints in all traditions the way to transcendence was ordered living. In Augustine's thinking, goodness was synonymous with order.[11] He could even regard predestination to hell as confirmation of God's goodness because hell is the proper destiny for hopelessly disordered souls.[12] His classic statement is found in Book 19 of the *City of God*:

> The peace, then, of the body lies in the ordered equilibrium of all its parts; the peace of the irrational soul, in the balanced adjustment of its appetites; the peace of the reasoning soul, in the harmonious correspondence of conduct and conviction; the peace of the body and soul taken together, in the well-ordered life and health of the living whole. Peace between a mortal man and his Maker consists in ordered obedience, guided by faith, under God's eternal law; peace between man and man consists in regulated fellowship. The peace of a home lies in the ordered harmony of authority and obedience between citizens. The peace of the heavenly City lies in a perfectly ordered and harmonious communion of those who find their joy in God and in one another in God. Peace, in its final sense, is the calm that comes of order [*pax omnium rerum tranquillitas ordinis*]. Order is an arrangement of like and unlike things whereby each of them is disposed in its proper place.[13]

To Augustine, writing after the Roman imperium had succumbed to wave after wave of barbarians, it seemed self-evident that peace means calm and calm comes from order. How to restore some semblance of order became the central religious problem. Its theoretical solution lay in a theory of atonement. Its pastoral solution lay in the cult. Saving experience came to mean religious experience in the context of theologically sophisticated and ecclesiastically sanctioned ritual. *Extra ecclesiam nulla salus.* After Augustine, *conversion* has meant conversion to an organized tradition of faith, not conversion to a philosophy of life.[14] The basic sentiment did not change at the Reformation, which substituted the ritual of Bible reading for the ritual of the Mass. (The Reformation is accurately described as a conflict among Augustinians.) The basic objective, whether for this life or the next, was to transform a school for sinners into a society of saints.

When we look only at theoretical positions, the parallel developments in Buddhist countries seem on the surface to be very different. In place of the Augustinian conception of a sublime magistrate imposing heavenly peace, we find in Nāgārjuna, to take an extreme example, a conception of ultimate emptiness which undermines any suggestion of a sacred cosmos.[15] But in both sets of culture the rules of monastic life, the ideals of celibacy and the like, are remarkably similar. The vertical thrust of Gothic arches as images of transcendence is not dissimilar to that of pagoda pinnacles in Bangkok or Pagan. In all medieval traditions there is a spectrum of opinion, ranging from the *via negativa* at one end to a full-fledged theism at the other. As each center of orthodox gravity shifts, the traditions harden on divergent interpretations of the saving experience. The resulting doctrines are therefore different. But if we focus on the transcending process, rather than on conceptions of supernatural order, we find that their testimony is not as divergent as is often supposed. It does not prove that all traditions at bottom point to the same indescribable Other. But neither does it indicate that rampant relativism reigns in religion. What it shows is that, wherever the sensible world is experienced in its fallenness, the saving experience must be expressed in otherworldly terms. Here what is religiously important is not the definitive description of some supernatural end. Concerning this, sages have agreed to differ. What is important is the vertical thrust of conceptions of transcendence in times when the promise of the future is bleaker than the memory of the past.

Where Augustine and other church fathers sidetracked our thinking concerning transcendence, I believe, is not in the vertical thrust that they gave to such thinking. For them at that time this was the right direction. But they, and especially their successors, tended to reify each pole in the interplay between natural and supernatural orders of being. Their obsession with goodness as order prevented them from perceiving, as Indian seers did, that transcendent bliss entails freedom from both good and evil in any conventional sense. Had Augustinians given harmony rather than order priority in their conceptions of goodness, they might not have enshrined a hierarchy of being in their doctrines of transcendence. They might have followed through on the incarnational strand of religious thinking which lies at the heart of Augustine's doctrine of atonement. In doing so, they would have allowed more room for what Gordon Kaufman, in his book *God the Problem*, calls the "interpersonal," as contrasted with the "teleological," model of transcendence.

What is striking in the history of both Christian and Buddhist traditions is the fact that, in time, the formally religious orders fell into disrepute. The ideal life came to be portrayed as that of lay householders.[16] The future, rather than the eternal order, began to capture the imaginations of religious philosophers. Among Christian theologians since Hegel, if not before, horizontal conceptions of transcendence came to dominate the thought of those who no longer accepted supernaturalism. Forgetting its basis in the polarity between nature and grace, they posited freedom in history as the ultimate goal. In an age of increasing bureaucratization we naturally stress goodness as freedom, whether in the bourgeois mode of existentialist authors or in the revolutionary mode of Marxist intellectuals. In our circumstances, we are right to do so. But we too would be wrong if we were to conclude from this shift in our conceptions that they alone are true for all time. What is constant, in my view, is not the particular thrust of the transcending process at any given time. That is time-bound and takes its direction from the circumstances of each age. What is constant is the fact of the transcending process as such, whether vertical or horizontal, since only through the constant dialectic of factors and agents do we experience that transition from alienation to reconciliation which marks the way to sainthood. As Augustine well illustrates, there is always in fact both a vertical and a horizontal aspect to the tran-

Being described by Otto. But the power evoking our response will be that of unimpeded technological development. The mystery expressed will be that of human relationships which are both demonic and divine. As we contemplate these images of modern culture we find that we too have our moments of wonder and awe, but not in the context of cloisters or pagodas pointing our eyes toward heaven. In the stories of our times, we find that what has been profaned is not the sanctuary of some tribal deity but the sanctity of individual human life. Not only the body, as the temple of the spirit, but the spirit itself has been denied all possibility of a dignified death. As we call the roll of current social issues — medicare and aging, population displacement due to urban renewal, abortion, unemployment, territoriality — we realize that our statistics obscure the facts. They cover over the desolation and desecration which powerful, sophisticated representatives of the common will direct onto the relatively innocent among us.

The ideas of covering over, of innocence and victimization, were central to the sacrificial cults of classical religion. One theory concerning such cults is that they served as lightning conductors to protect a shaky social fabric from the wrath of the gods. Perhaps statistics do the same for us. If Girard is right, blood sacrifices became obsolete with the development of judicial procedures for dealing with guilt on an individual basis. But the experiences of the death camps and the atomic bomb suggest an inversion of his conclusion that chance is the key to the cultus.[20] The surrogate victims of the twentieth century were not chosen at random. They suffered because of the insane logic of bureaucratic decision-making procedures.[21] Also, as our nightly newscasts on television attest, it may be premature to conclude that corporate violence has been brought under the control of law. The daily fare of our common culture is a litany of violence, not because violence is new or newsworthy, but because we too demand surrogate victims in our obsession with death. But is this experience of negation the sole source of religious aspirations for transcendence?

To wring some kind of saving experience out of the death camps has been the aim of such contemporary writers as Elie Wiesel and Emil Fackenheim. They tend, like Girard, to emphasize the negative side of our experience. But their quest is for the human face of God amid the suffering of the forsaken. Instead of seeing this quest as a sign of hopeless nostalgia for an obsolete creed, we should acknowledge its positive source. This, according to both Christian and Buddhist traditions, is the compassionate character which inspires true faith. What transcends suffering, in both the Jesus story and the Buddha story, is not some *deus ex machina* which wards off impending doom. It is, as Augustine emphasized, that love which is the inverse of pride. Mechanical transfer of destructive energy is not the crux of either story. The steam-pressure model of human behavior, favored still by many behavioral scientists, does not take adequate account of the depth of human misery. It presupposes that physical destruction is the worst that can happen to us. But the saving experience articulated by both the Buddha and the Christ is one which saves us, not from death but from the *sting* of death. The experience is of human solidarity, of identification with the sufferer in the moment of suffering, of evil shared and thereby confronted. The transcendence in question is of a power which incorporates the negativities of existence in a humanizing way.

Here again we must ask what is the nature of the whole affirmed by our saving experiences. And now we must answer that it is a world in which we establish a community of personal selves. This world includes both an element of order and that freedom which leaves room for the growth of individual persons in relationships with others. What generalized violence destroys, as Girard observes, is not simply the social order but the singularity of each individual existence. Dehumanizing events are those which deny selfhood to the individual. In tribal cultures the self in question may be that of the group rather than that of individuals as such. In medieval traditions the corporate identity of the saints is transposed to a heavenly key. What contemporary theologies of liberation attempt is an affirmation of both individual worth and the solidarity of the group in the present. If we follow Tillich concerning the polarity of autonomy and heteronomy that this entails, we shall conclude that contemporary aspirations may be realized insofar as they are theonomous.[22] But the *theos* in question must epitomize both the universal will — the standards of justice and truth — on which the social fabric is built and that personal regard for individual differences on which true love is founded. The transcendence of this *theos* is not to be ascribed to physical location elsewhere. Nor is it to be ascribed solely to the supposed metaphysical priority of the Form of the Good in relation to instances of it. It is the singularity of the divine in relation to the human which is *the* mark of the transcendent.

We cannot unpack in a few sentences what is covered here by the term *singularity*.[23] Western thinking on this topic must today be enriched by acquaintance with Indian philosophies of *nondualism*. The familiar slide is into monism and pantheism. But such is not our intention. By singularity is evoked a sense of identity not reducible to that of some universalizable particular. By nondualism is meant the recognition that the identity in question is of a relating structure and process which is the key to the power of love or compassion. This is what gives each instance its due, bringing it to the appropriate level of involvement in a deeper, wider whole, the life of the world.

In each generation, the transcending process is shaped by the situation to be transcended.[24] In the dynamics of sacrifice, for example, the need in ancient times was, as Girard contends, often defined by the destructive consequences of blood feuds among tribes. But the process was not simply determined functionally, by the need for a scapegoat. Besides, there were many kinds of sacrifice, not all expiatory. There were sacrifices of praise and thanksgiving, as well as sacrifices of atonement and committal. What is common is not the deflection of violence as such but the redirection of all aspects of power. This *may* be mechanistically conceived. But its symbolic impact comes from its promise of a different order of affairs relative to those which create our need. The occasion for a sacrifice may well be present deprivation. But its celebration is of orders of creation, preservation, and new creation, according to which such occasions of need do not arise. We do not explain a cult by reference to subconscious drives alone. Sacrifice is not only sublimation. It gives cultural shape to natural urges by setting these in a new context, that of God or the gods. Their ways are not simply our ways projected onto dream divinities. Divine law is set over against human custom, drawing it to a different plane of accomplishment. The agenda of renewal is shaped by a life which negates the conditions of deprivation in the name of something superior.

Consider in this context the life and death of Martin Luther King, Jr. Should we conclude that his only religious significance was as an escape mechanism for racial tensions in the sixties? We can say that he put his life in jeopardy because he saw the need for leadership in Birmingham and elsewhere. But can we say that his subsequent career was nothing but a function of that need and an expression of his own inner conflicts? Can we do justice to the impact of his "mountaintop" speech in the terms provided by some mechanistic theory of psychology? Or must we not insist that the moral tone of his vision is an essential element in his story?

If we take King as a recent example, we shall have to insist that the transcending process in our time is not simply from the level of I-It to I-Thou relationships. The key word in the titles of two of his books is not I or Thou but We.[25] He opposed the chaotic violence of his generation with a vision of brotherhood and sisterhood transcending racial lines. Of what was his dream a projection? With what did he construct his conceptual frame? From earlier biblical, Gandhian, and American images, to be sure, but also with assurance of a future other than the past. It is this juxtaposition of new community and thinly veiled chaos which gives power to his message. It is this dedication to a new agenda for society that prevents him from being deflected from his path, despite the shadow of assassination. The contents of his vision may be unclear. But its symbolic force is inescapable. By his deeds and words he focused this force. But he did not create it out of nothing. It may be diffused, but not dissipated, by his death. The sacrifice here is not just a giving up of one life in order that others may survive. It is a giving over of present life, in spite of the threat of violent death, to the realization of a new agenda, to the imperative of "freedom now!" Through the combination of his life and thought, King gave new urgency to the movement for equality. What he gave was moral force translated into political action, not simply physical presence. This force was not his alone, nor did it cease to exist when he was shot. It was, in theological terms, the power of God.

The singularity of the divine in King's saving experience is not that of an absolute Self in relation to an inner, individual self. What is singular is that strength of character, that spirit, which carries into the present the reality of the future first widely realized in his vision of it. The details of this vision were subject to amendment. But its creative effect in the minds of King's generation set it apart from the conventional wisdom of the times. Here was no perversion of the dignity of human being but a reaffirmation of it on a new plane. In his sermons we see both continuity and discontinuity with those of his predecessors. The elements of fascination and dread here are present in the prospect of a future which both shatters the past and brings wholeness to its survivors. But its experiential base is in prophetic consciousness, not priestly ecstasy alone. Something more than the status quo is at stake. It is a reverence for life which transforms the brutality of death.

Failure to do justice to the power underlying prophetic consciousness is the major weakness of all theories of religion which completely assimilate religion with celebrations of the sacred. Emphasis on the holy or the sacred, as distinct from profane worldliness, has been an important counter to some kinds of reductionist thinking. But we have also to avoid reducing the material to the spiritual order in our experience and supposing that the latter alone is religious. What prophetic consciousness affirms is a new material order on a firmer spiritual foundation, a new earth called into being by a new heaven. Transcendence here means not an emptying of all temporal processes into eternity, but a shattering of present patterns by the imperatives of changing times. No single picture of divine-human relationships is adequate to this experience. Our images both reveal and conceal what is emerging. The interplay of text and context in the articulation of true vision is never wholly fixed. Thus if Catholic and Protestant construe institutional religion differently, for example, they are not to be compared to blind persons defining an elephant wholly in terms of its trunk or its tail. They are more like people describing a lion as a cub and in its prime. The sense of timing in the process is crucial. Some images may be classical in the accumulation of a tradition. But, in Gadamer's sense, they must be re-presented to each new generation. Hence we have commentaries upon commentaries in the traditions.

In conclusion, what is absolute for every generation is the

transcending process at the heart of its saving experience. This is singular in the sense that each generation's experience is not simply a repetition of its predecessors' or a replica of some eternal pattern. Its thrust is both vertical and horizontal relative to the conditions of existence under which each new life begins. It is salvific in that it brings each individual to a realization of wholeness, in relation both to other selves and to the wider world. The movement is not unilinear. Nor is it to be schematized as a straightforward progression from thesis through antithesis to synthesis. What we have to consider rather is a spiral of ever more comprehensive concerns, in which both order and freedom, material and spiritual values, are translated from prophetic vision into political action. The power expressed in this process is never wholly immanent. There is rather a double movement, in which the transcendent spirit is newly incarnate and the contemporary word reaches out for a new agenda of existence. The spirit is nondual in the sense that no single picture, no dichotomy of thought or being, adequately defines its reality. Only through the intersecting and overlapping of our symbols and stories do we evoke its presence. The result for religion is not a mystically derived syncretism or the absolutizing of any one tradition. It is the recognition that each expression of faith is a response to both inner character and external pressure. Such a response is not simply a function of basic human needs. It is rather a celebration of that reverence for life which motivates all true religion.

Reverence for life, finally, must be the touchstone for our talk of the sacred. Not order as such, not violence or destruction, but the positive affirmation of life in spite of death, of love over apathy, is what fills us with wonder and moves us to worship. In our time, the locus of the sacred and the occasion for sacrifice are the emerging community of personal selves in a shared universe. The focus has shifted from places to people, from people as individuals to partners in the transcending process. The occasions for sacrifice are not the random targets of mob violence or collective military power. They are the lives, not simply given up, but given over to the imperatives of a higher order of being and becoming than that which defines the present conditions of our existence. The lives so sacrificed are not just those of Mahatma Gandhi,

Martin Luther King, Jr., or Malcolm X. They are the lives of every parent and child, of every community worker, of every poet, teacher, preacher, and musician, who acts from strength as well as common need, from maturity and not only out of desperation, to enhance the existence of the whole. In saying all this I do not claim any great originality for these views. Indeed, I am inclined to suppose that this truth is common to the intuitions of us all. Its articulation may even sound trite. But its realization is set against the horizon of ghetto and suburban living, of refugee camps, of the disorder which passes for the natural order of things in the recitations of our daily news. To this end our words are only a beginning. There must follow not only the eloquence of our actions but also the silent wisdom which can discern the *mysterium tremendum* in the expression of a little child. That, at least, is the tradition in which I was brought up and the vision which, I believe, is still powerful for our times.

NOTES

1. Gordon D. Kaufman, *An Essay on Theological Method* (Missoula, Mont.: Scholars Press, 1975), chap. 1. I use *experience* broadly in ways akin to *consciousness* or *awareness*. On this see Bernard J. F. Lonergan, *Method in Theology* (London: Darton, Longman, & Todd, 1971), pp. 6–10.

2. René Girard, *Violence and the Sacred*, trans. Patrick Gregory (Baltimore: Johns Hopkins University Press, 1977), p. 4. On automobiles see Nancy Corson Carter, "1970 Images of the Machine and the Garden: Kosinski, Crews, and Pirsig," *Soundings* 61:1 (Spring 1978): 105–122.

3. Robert N. Bellah, "Transcendence in Contemporary Piety," in *The Religious Situation 1969*, ed. Donald N. Cutler (Boston: Beacon Press, 1969), pp. 896–909; and Lucy Bregman, "Maslow as Theorist of Religion: Reflections on His Popularity and Plausibility," *Soundings* 59: 2 (Summer 1976): 139–163.

4. See the forthcoming papers on the concept of the bodhisattva, ed. Leslie Kawamura, from the 1978 Calgary Conference on Buddhism.

5. Augustine *Confessiones* 2.6, 7.10.

6. Paul Tillich, "Two Types of Philosophy of Religion," in *Theol-*

ogy of Culture, ed. Robert C. Kimball (New York: Oxford University Press, 1959), pp. 10–29.

7. Peter R. L. Brown, *Augustine of Hippo: A Biography* (Berkeley and Los Angeles: University of California Press, 1967), pts. 2–3.

8. Har Dayal, *The Bodhisattva Doctrine in Buddhist Sanskrit Literature* (London: Kegan, Paul, Trench & Trubner, 1932).

9. Victor W. Turner, *The Ritual Process: Structure and Anti-Structure* (Ithaca, N.Y.: Cornell University Press, 1969, paperback 1977), pp. 96–97.

10. Augustine *Confessiones* 7.11, 7.18.

11. Augustine, "De natura boni contra Manichaeos," trans. H. H. S. Burleigh in *Library of Christian Classics*, vol. 6, *Augustine: Earlier Writings* (Philadelphia: Westminster Press, 1953), chap. 3. On the contraction of the sphere of order to personal existence, as opposed to cosmic disorder, note the comments by Eric Voegelin, *Order and History*, vol. 4, *The Ecumenic Age* (Baton Rouge: Louisiana State University Press, 1974), pp. 22–23, 172.

12. Augustine *De civitate Dei* 21.12.

13. Ibid., 19.13.

14. On the differences see A. D. Nock, *Conversion* (London: Oxford University Press, 1933).

15. See the selections in Frederick J. Streng, *Emptiness: A Study in Religious Meaning* (Nashville: Abingdon Press, 1967).

16. In Buddhism on the exaltation of the lay householder note the portrayal of Vimalakīrti in Robert A. F. Thurman, trans., *The Holy Teaching of Vimalakīrti* (University Park, Pa.: Pennsylvania State University Press, 1976).

17. Peter L. Berger and Richard John Neuhaus, eds., *Against the World for the World* (New York: Seabury Press, 1976).

18. Robert N. Bellah, *Beyond Belief* (New York: Harper & Row, 1970), chap. 2.

19. I have argued this point more fully in *The Dynamics of Religion: Meaning and Change in Religious Traditions* (San Francisco: Harper & Row, 1978).

20. Girard, *Violence and the Sacred*, pp. 311–313.

21. R. D. Laing, *The Politics of Experience* (New York: Ballantine Books, 1967), 1:147–150. Cf. Robert C. Batchelder, *The Irreversible Decision 1939–1950* (New York: Macmillan Pub. Co., 1961).

22. Paul Tillich, *Systematic Theology*, 3 vols. (Chicago: University of Chicago Press, 1951–1963), 1:147–150.

23. The allusion is to Kierkegaard and Hegel.

24. I have discussed this further in "The Kerygma and the Cuckoo's Nest," *Scottish Journal of Theology* 31:3 (Fall 1978), 301–318.

25. Martin Luther King, Jr., *Why We Can't Wait* (New York: Harper & Row, 1964); *Where Do We Go From Here? Chaos or Community* (New York: Harper & Row, 1967).

3

The Civilizational Perspective in Comparative Studies of Transcendence

EDITH WYSCHOGRAD

I PROPOSE TO ASSESS the role of the civilizational perspective in comparative philosophical accounts of transcendence by suggesting a view of transcendence that bypasses some obvious difficulties that have plagued traditional accounts and, with this view in mind, to offer an appraisal of significant methodological models that have been applied in comparative study. Thus my paper addresses two issues: the first is the question of how transcendence can be grasped as a meaningful theme; the second, the question of cross-cultural study itself. I shall argue that, apart from a civilizational perspective, the inquiry into transcendence remains an empty speculative exercise which fails to acknowledge the wider sphere of metaphysical commitments from which its terms have been derived, since such inquiry is rooted in contexts extending beyond those it immediately discloses. The difficulty is compounded in comparative studies of transcendence, since not only the civilizational perspective of the inquiry but also that of its several objects must be rendered visible.

A civilization comprises identities of language, higher-level technologies, canons of decision-making, juridical rules; in short, the taken-for-granted structures, instrumental and spiritual, of a common world view.[1] The perspective of a civilization is shaped by its perceptions of self, time, and transcendence. Such an understanding of the relation between civilizations and transcendence may seem to beg the question: the civilizational perspective is alleged to be shaped by its comprehensions of transcendence, while at the same time no access can be gained to the theme of transcendence without bringing the civilizational perspective into view. But such circularity is only apparent since both are reciprocally constitutive. The transcendent is constituted through a *post hoc* act of civilizational understanding, while, conversely, this civilizational act is as it is in view of a civilization's grasp of transcendence. From the standpoint of the inquiry into transcendence, the civilizational perspective may be regarded as a weak a priori whose role is best described functionally as that of an instrument. To the term *instrument* I ascribe the meaning it has for I. A. Richards in his essay "Towards a Theory of Translating" (1952):

> Whatever is compared is compared in respect or in respects. These respects are the instruments of the exploration. And it is with them as it is with the instruments of investigation in physics but more so: The properties of the instruments enter into the account of the investigation.[2]

Any cross-cultural comprehension of transcendence is compromised wherever the civilizational perspective is ignored.[3]

Transcendence: the mystery of origin

Is there some special meaning complex designated by the term *transcendence*? If there is, does its use not present us with peculiar and irresolvable difficulties? If inquiry begins with a prior disclosure of its object, how can transcendence become the aim of such disclosure since as soon as it is disclosed it loses its character as transcending and becomes the object of a cognitive act?

This collapse of transcendence as an object is the consequence of a system of metaphors through which transcendence has traditionally been designated and to which spatial exteriority is central. Whatever transcends, whether conceived as unlimited in the absolute sense or as unsurpassable by any other being, acquires its meaning by virtue of its elusiveness. For if the object has been attained, a limit has been transgressed. What is exterior has been incorporated into a totality and what transcends now lies elsewhere.

When the problem of transcendence is conceived in this framework, the ensuing difficulties have traditionally been resolved in one of two ways. On the one hand, an appeal is made to "apical distance."[4] This position undermines the logic of identity and diversity governing ordinary experience, since these categories become meaningless the further removed one is from the objects to which they can be said to apply. On the other hand, the apprehension of transcendence may be seen as more or less accurately reflecting ontological features with which transcendence may be bound up. In the first case we adopt an otherworldly angle of vision so remote from the world of ordinary experience that the notion of separateness is no longer significant, as, for example, in the Advaita Vedānta view in which self and world-ground merge as soon as enlightenment is attained. In the second case the metaphysical terrain is parceled out so that both its processive aspects and its permanent features remain irreducible but seem to be equitably accommodated by developing laws for their apportionment. Thus, for example, Whitehead argues for the primordial and consequent natures of God, consigning one to the abstractness of ideality, the other to the concreteness and particularization of process. Within the consequent nature itself the same distinction is made when genuine novelty is spun out with the birth of each actual entity while still allowing comprehension of the laws of their spin. But, with this view, it is impossible to imagine the grasp of a Whole into which fresh elements intrude, defying cognitive apprehension.

Another understanding of transcendence is the familiar "negative way" of Neo-Platonic metaphysics and of the Indian Advaita and Visistadvaita Vedānta traditions. Denying qualities to the Absolute by maintaining that no quality can positively be attributed to it, the *via negativa* preserves the mystery of transcendence. At the same time, it safeguards the Absolute's unlimited character, since assigning any attribute to the Absolute entails the exclusion of some other attribute; the Absolute is necessarily limited as soon as it becomes determinate. The *neti neti* ('not this, not this') formula of the *Upanishads*, for example, places the Absolute beyond determinate predication in order for the Absolute not to be confined by the thought which thinks it. But the *via negativa*, no less than the position which is willing to apply superlatives to the Absolute, understands the Absolute as a referring term while placing the object at such a degree of metaphysical remoteness that the logic of predication seems not to apply.

These puzzles which arise within the framework of the logic of transcendence are actually second-order problems which conceal a tacit agenda — the attempt to locate a point of fixity or, as structuralist Jacques Derrida alleges, to discover "the proper word and the unique name" which would yield in one and the same cognitive act the meaning of transcendence as an ontological and linguistic origin. So long as transcendence is equated with a fixed point of origin — whether it is thought of as the One, the Unmoved Mover, the Infinite, the Absolute, the Inner Controller, the Golden Person, the Primordial Nature of God, Providence, the Logos, or even the Being of beings — the myth of the stable origin remains. When ontological primacy is granted to an aboriginal and fixed-meaning complex, the alternatives available within this framework yield accounts of transcendence which either break with ordinary canons of coherence or nullify the canons themselves.

The position I propose (and can sketch in broad strokes only) rejects the view that *transcendence* is a referring term — that is, the notion that "something" transcends or that this "something" can be interpreted as having causal efficacy. Bearing the post-Nietzschean de-construction of metaphysics in mind, I interpret the point of fixity revealed in the languages which transcendence "speaks" as constituted after the fact; transcendence becomes manifest only through this *post hoc* constitution. I shall, in accordance with the usage developed in the work of Martin Heidegger, Emmanuel Levinas, and Jacques Derrida, call this mode of manifesting a "trace."[5] With Derrida and Levinas I see the trace not as an effect of which transcendence is the cause; such an interpretation lies well within the sphere of natural theology. But, on the contrary, I interpret the trace as marking the disappearance of the origin through a reciprocal, back-and-forth oscillation which permits the emergence of both trace and origin. This movement is dialectical but not in a single direction. In *Of Grammatology* (1967) Derrida writes:

> The trace is not only the disappearance of the origin . . . it means the origin did not even disappear, that it was never constituted except reciprocally by a non-origin, the trace, which then becomes the origin of the origin.[6]

All access to the eruption of traces is foreclosed since what constitutes traces as such is the "effacement of origin." Were this not the case the trace would exist as something like a calligraphic mark, something empirical, the consequence of Being's move, as it were, and thus explicable well within the framework of a metaphysics of substance. But, for Derrida, the trace always refers beyond itself, not as "mapping an elsewhere," not as a presence,

> but . . . rather [as] the simulacrum of a presence that dislocates, displaces, and refers beyond itself. The trace has, properly speaking, no place, for effacement belongs to the very structure of the trace.[7]

The trace acquires its meaning from its unique relation to time. It refers to an immemorial past which can never become present, thus precluding the conformity of transcendence with the logic of presence. Transcendence can never come to light by becoming the content of a "now" and thereby forfeiting its otherness. The notion of a past separated by an untraversed interval from the present has been made familiar through the language of psychoanalysis. In the classical Freudian view, the conscious is the sphere in which objects emerge in their plenary presence, but at the same time the conscious contains residues of an aboriginal past. This past can never become present because its memory would only evoke an event which never occurred, such as sexual relations with one's mother or the killing of one's father.[8] Similarly, in the dialectic of trace and origin the moment of reciprocal constitution is a non-event in the same sense; as such it can never become the object of thought. Situated outside any system of cognition, it nevertheless opens a clearing in which thought can occur. The trace disappears in its appearing. In an essay "The Trace of the Other" (1963), Levinas writes, "[It] is not a sign like any other.

. . . It means beyond all intention of signifying anything."⁹ As for any effort to find a first or primal trace, Derrida argues, even if it could be found it is pragmatically futile, since "its concept would in no way enrich the scientific, positive, and immanent description of the system itself."[10]

The last is a matter of considerable importance for the comparative study of transcendence. For if the concept of a primal trace would in no way enrich positive inquiry, does this reading of trace, origin, and transcendence compel the shaping of new policies in cross-cultural inquiry? What difference does this concept make in the practical comparison of texts? Derrida writes in *Of Grammatology* (1967):

> I believe there is a short of and a beyond of transcendental criticism. To see to it that the beyond does not return to the within is to recognize in the contortion, the necessity of a pathway. That pathway must leave a track in the text.[11]

For Derrida, "the metaphysical text is *understood*; it remains to be read" in the sense that the tacit acceptance of metaphysical commitments must be made explicit. What is more, if I am right in assuming the inextricability of metaphysical assumptions and culture, these traces cut a swath not only in the history of metaphysics but also in the instrumental aspects of a civilization, its cultural pedagogies and practices as well as its technologies. These, together with its metaphysical commitments, must be read as reciprocally determining in regard to this history.

How is the cross-cultural study of transcendence affected concretely by this approach? How does interpretation based on these new criteria, a critical reading, differ from a precritical interpretation of texts? First, critical inquiry is suspicious; it refuses to accept the prima facie meaning of a text but attempts instead to educe what is not always in evidence. Critical observation persists in its sensitivity to difference, to minute breaks in the rules which govern the use of a concept, an institution, a rite. Such inquiry is also cognizant of itself as an instrument and remains reflectively aware of its procedures. It acknowledges traces as histories of a sort. Traces point to irrecoverable anterior histories; as such, they are always meta-traces, traces of traces rendering visible the many-faceted character of a seemingly indivisible intellectual space.

I shall explore five models which govern contemporary cross-cultural inquiry: the East-West bifurcation model, the problems model, the theological foil approach, the comparison of formal languages model, and the model of etymological or linguistic determinism.[12] I shall also propose a new structural paradigm which incorporates some of the features of the preceding types but proposes a new frame of reference.

The division into East and West

Perhaps the most common method for the cross-cultural study of philosophical themes presumes a spiritual entity which can be subdivided into two discernible types, Oriental and Western. In the study of transcendence, Eastern and Western views of this theme become the *relata* and are brought into relation by comparing them in terms of such matters as the nature of God, knowledge, and the soul. This method derives its typologies by abstracting and combining conceptions of transcendence disclosed in the philosophical and religious traditions of smaller cultural units. Thus a new cultural nexus is created, that of the East or the West, combining those features which are thought to be both predominant in and common to all the smaller cultural units included in the larger group. The common elements are added together, as it were, and believed to constitute an ideal type. This type is then located, that is, attributed to peoples of contiguous territories which form a geographical and demographic whole. East and West are constituted as polar opposites in which one, generally the former, is viewed as philosophically more naïve and less developed than the other. If no invidious distinctions are drawn between East and West, they are seen in terms of supplementarity. The former attitude is in evidence in nineteenth-century cross-cultural comparisons, preeminently in the work of Hegel; the latter, in that of F. S. C. Northrup.

In a section of *The Philosophy of History*, "The Oriental World" (drawn from lectures of the 1820s), and in *The Philosophy of Right* (1821), Hegel assumes that, for the East, the individual is subordinated to the universal. This subordination is contrasted with the Greek point of view which is able to "differentiate itself to individual mentality" and to "emerge into the daylight of knowing."[13] Hegel's analysis distinguishes four significant cultural regions, but each, despite its differences from the others, is faulted on the same grounds — the failure of the individual consciousness of freedom to develop. For China, "the sphere of subjectivity does not . . . attain to maturity . . . since moral laws are treated as legislative enactments"; for India individuals cannot reach determinate self-expression because of the caste system; for Persia Spirit understands itself as Light, which, for Hegel, represents something merely natural and therefore does not permit the emergence of a free self.[14] Since all deny individuality, Hegel sees the Orient as a whole bearing this characteristic. Thus in *The Philosophy of History* (from the lectures of the 1820s) he writes:

> The Constitution [of the Orient] generally is a Theocracy, and the Kingdom of God is to the same extent also a secular Kingdom as the secular Kingdom is also divine. What we call God has not yet in the East been realized in consciousness, for our idea of God involves an elevation of the soul to the supersensual. While *we* obey, because what we are required to do is confirmed by an *internal* sanction, there the Law is regarded as inherently and absolutely valid without a sense of the want of this subjective confirmation.[15]

One obvious difficulty in Hegel's model common to all versions of the East-West paradigm is its excessive inclusiveness based upon faulty generalization. Nuances within a given historical period and changes from one historical period to another are lost, since these can be discovered only by the discrimination of difference within discursive and institutional forms. Furthermore, when the Orient is taken as an already constituted sociocultural whole the question is begged, since it is just the existence of this sociocultural entity that is at stake.

A related difficulty, intrinsic to the East-West model, which also affects other paradigms is the assumption that such terms as *God*, *freedom*, etc., constitute licit categories for cross-cultural inquiry. But these terms play a key role in shaping Western self-conceptualization based upon the history of Greek ontology. I. A. Richards (1952) writes with respect to problems of translation:

> It is worth remarking with regard to Chinese-English translation that the great traditional metaphors of Western thought play so large a part in shaping our conceptions. . . . These great originative structures have acted in the West in innumerable minds which have no notion of how important such metaphors can be.[16]

Where terminological reciprocity is absent, a nominalist critique is in order; Hegel and others in effect use Western metaphors as Platonic forms which are then seen to have exemplifications in the East and/or the West. Thus, for example, the term *God* has, for Hegel, the status of an eternal archetype instanced in an inferior way in the Oriental context through the theocratic state. But, in fact, such ideal entities are constituted rather than located, since we have only particular sociocultural entities with their individual logics, cultural rationales, and institutions. Derrida suggests that metaphysical terms be thought of as "under erasure": while we are inevitably obliged to use metaphysically freighted language, this necessity is acknowledged within the inquiry itself.[17]

The East-West paradigm as used by F. S. C. Northrup recognizes the primacy given to Western self-conceptualization in previous analyses of Eastern thought and attempts to remedy the situation in his still influential *Meeting of East and West* (1946). The Orient is taken by Northrup as a solidary sociocultural entity:

> To specify [the philosophical and religious differences entering into the constitution of the East] is, at the same time, to indicate the equally evident interconnections and identities which tie them all together to constitute a single civilization of the East.[18]

The key respect in terms of which East and West are compared is that of presentational immediacy; the experience of things as fully present is contrasted with the experience of some experimentally controlled portion of reality. The former is seen as Eastern, the latter Western. In the East all symbolic expression refers to an aesthetic continuum in which the Oriental thinker is immersed, rather than to bits and pieces of experience. Thus an effort must be made to immerse oneself in such texts as the *Tao te Ching*, for in so doing one can find clues to apprehending the universe in this new modality. Altered Western attitudes will enable all to enjoy the "immediately apprehended factors of experience" since the capacity for such experience is common to humankind. Northrup's final interest is conciliatory: Eastern and Western points of view are supplementary, the former involving us in what is primary and ultimate in experience through the intuiting and contemplating of things in their aesthetic immediacy, the latter engaging us in the cognitive apprehension of things. Neither is to be regarded as the mere appearance of the other; instead the two stances should be seen as epistemically complementary.

Like the Hegelian model, this view suffers from the difficulty of faulty generalization. What is more, the polarities suggested by Northrup, "intuitive" and "logical," "synthetic" and "analytic," lose their descriptive power by virtue of the significant exceptions to them. For example, to speak of Eastern thought as intuitive ignores the systematic logical and epistemological investigations of Buddhist logicians such as Dignaga and Dhammakirti, and of the Chinese School of Names, while to think of Western thought as cognitive ignores such exceptions as Henri Bergson and the Western mystical tradition.

A more significant objection lies in the notion of supplementarity itself which cannot be dismissed as a mere strategy for remedying a defective conceptual structure. It lies beyond the scope of this paper to consider in detail the analysis of the meaning of *supplementarity* in the work of Derrida. Suffice it to say that, for Derrida, a supplement is added within a conceptual structure in order to make up for an original deficiency on the supposition that the original, in this case cognition itself, may be understood as a fixed though still deficient point of departure.[19] But if no such point of fixity exists, we cannot, as in Northrup's interpretation, add intuitive awareness, the Eastern view, to rational cognition, the Western mode of apprehension, to make up a new whole, some perfect archetype of knowing. If we do so, we lose sight of the only conceptual structures which open cognition for inquiry; namely, those civilizational perspectives through which the play of conceptual difference can be brought into view.

The most recent effort to overcome the dominance of Western theoretical conceptualization, that of Joseph Needham's massive *Science and Civilization in China* (in progress), attempts to find in the "demonstrable continuity and universality of science" an irreducible set of constructs, a presuppositionless language divested of cultural residues.[20] While Needham does not interpret the East as a solidary unit, the West *is* so determined on a de facto basis by virtue of its intimate connection with the rise and growth of science. The East then becomes its obverse as that complex of civilizations which failed to give rise to science despite the development of a wide variety of technological achievements. For Needham science is a neutral *tertium quid*, a universal language, since it provides the conceptual equivalent neither for Western metaphysics nor for Chinese thought but is seen as compatible with both. Moreover, Needham views science as an ultimate value which together with its applications forms a unity into which the comparable contributions of different civilizations can be poured. This process is interpreted as the consequence of a social evolution which is ongoing in human society and is moving humankind toward greater unity along with greater complexity of organization. Thus Needham in *Science and Civilization in China* (1974) writes:

> It is vital today that the world should recognize that seventeenth-century Europe did not give rise to essentially "European" or "Western" science but to universally valid world science, that is to say, "modern" science as opposed to ancient and medieval sciences. . . . When once the basic technique of discovery had itself been discovered, once the full method of scientific investigation of Nature had been understood, the sciences assumed the absolute universality of mathematics, and in their modern form are at home under any meridian, the common light and inheritance of every race and people.[21]

While it may be the case, as Needham alleges, that without science "plagues are not checked and aircraft will not fly," the decision to pursue the cure of disease and the flight of aircraft *because* they represent progress arises in a Western eschatological context and a Western tradition of natural laws. While evolutionary doctrines can be found in Chinese and Indian thinkers (as, for example, in the case of the *Tai Phing*, as Needham shows in his essay "Time in China" in *The Grand Titration* [1969]),[22] Needham concedes that the notion of a cumulative and open-ended body of knowledge is absent. The values which make the pursuit of science seem worthwhile are embedded in a Western civilizational context. Although common techniques can be found in China and the West, until the entry of Western science into China these do not constitute the end product of a mathematical interpretation of nature. Even on Needham's reading, science is not isolable from the civilization which gave rise to it; it would seem, therefore, that science cannot serve as a lingua franca of world civilizations. While Needham's pioneer studies of Chinese technology succeed in raising the estimate of Chinese technological sophistication, his work serves to heighten the contrast between China and the West as sociopolitical entities precisely at sensitive points of cross-cultural impact. By emphasizing science Needham's work falls victim to some of the difficulties of the East-West bifurcation model.

The problems method

Still another model for the comparative study of transcendence presumes that a specific problem considered within the confines of a given thinker or system can be examined from a cross-cultural standpoint. This model takes for granted the existence of core questions which constitute the shared concerns of philosophical traditions. Philosophy *as such* is believed to consist of certain problems of an epistemological or metaphysical sort. The logic of transcendence belongs to this group of perennial questions and constitutes a particularly vexing object for cross-cultural comparison.

The problems model is widely used in the current practice of comparative philosophy. I cite at random one such effort. At a symposium of the Society for Asian and Comparative Philosophy (1974), and in the proceedings subsequently published in *Philoso-*

phy East and West (1975), the concept of the world was examined from the standpoint of an American philosopher of science, Milton Munitz.[23] Using his contemporary perspective as a point of departure, the notion of *world* for Advaita Vedānta, Confucianism, and late Buddhism was explored and assessed in terms of contemporary viability. The analysis of the problem of the world sharpened the distinctiveness of the various philosophical traditions. Thus, for example, the Western answer presumed a coherent conceptual framework for the understanding of time and space from Hume to Kant as the background for a contemporary reading of the problem of the world, while the Advaita Vedānta was seen as establishing its position in terms of its relationship to an anterior history which included the *Upanishads*, the Samkhya school, and, in Śaṅkara, later Buddhism.

The significance of the problems approach lies in the manageability of the *relata*: increased magnification gives greater resolution of detail. If the comparison is undertaken with a sensitivity to the various uses of terms in the traditions compared, the elements of the comparison can be seen to bear a family resemblance to one another while allowing for the emergence of marked elements of uniqueness. Thus, in considering what the world is for the philosophy of Śaṅkara, such axial assumptions of Indian thought as *karma*, transmigration, and *maya* play a prominent role. When such comparative efforts are divested of civilizational context, they can degenerate into barren technical exercises in which criteria of validity predominate.

The theological foil approach

The theological foil perspective is related to the problems method except that, in the former, comparative material is used as a contrast for Western positions in order to provide a backdrop for some Western view as well as to give a sense of completeness. In this connection, Charles Hartshorne's introduction to a volume of essays on process philosophy (1965), which compares Whiteheadian perspectives to the "no-souls, no-substance" doctrine of Buddhism, might be cited.[24] The Eastern perspective used to present an unfamiliar standpoint as the reverse image of a Western view is found in W. T. Stace's *Man Against Darkness* (1967): Western conceptions of the soul's immortality are contrasted with the transmigration and "no-self" doctrines of Buddhism.[25]

An older tradition of comparison, the "moral edification" type, merits inclusion in any system of classification as a version of the theological foil model. Although it is, by now, discredited, its use still persists residually in recent work. This standpoint presumes that a knowledge of Indian or Chinese thought shows it to be in tacit agreement with the moral outlook of the West. In the otherwise still interesting work of older Indologists such as Paul Deussen, elements of this approach are clearly discernible. Thus, in *The Philosophy of the Upanishads* (1898), Deussen reflects:

> Suppose that there exists a certain planet in the solar system, say Mars or Venus, inhabited by human beings or other beings with their culture flourishing and with an established philosophy. Suppose we came to know their philosophy through one of the beings living there, who had entered into the sphere of our terrestrial gravitation after being shot out in a missile. In that case we might take an enormous interest in the results of their philosophy, and we might carefully examine their philosophy and ours. If there should be some difference, we would determine which side is true, and if it should be found that there is no difference between the two, then this would imply that the truth of the outcome of the philosophical contemplation of both sides had been substantiated. . . . We have a similar situation in Indian philosophy.[26]

More recently, Radhakrishnan's otherwise informative *History of Indian Philosophy* (1923)[27] falls victim to similar difficulties. In compiling a history of Indian thought, his interpretations are governed by late-nineteenth-century British post-Hegelian idealism. A reverse bias may be observed in recent American theology. I cite at random the work of John Cobb. In an article significantly titled "Buddhist Emptiness and the Christian God" (1977), Cobb argues for two ultimates each serving a different function: "the ultimate principle of rightness" governs moral norms and "is properly designated as God," while the other, the "metaphysical ultimate," can best be "understood precisely in its dissolution into dependent coproduction or Emptiness."[28] Thus, the Western Christian understanding of the metaphysical ultimate serves as the background for the now preferred Buddhist reading.

The comparison of modes of inference

The fourth model, the analysis of the formal structures of thought, can provide a fruitful field for comparative study. It might seem that in this area the civilizational perspective would be least conspicuous since the principles of inference should hold across cultural lines. But if we mean by logic more than the analysis of common or universal features of thought expressible in some metalanguage, we discover that both inductive and deductive modes of inference are inseparable from the sociocultural complex in which they occur and to which they give expression. The "object languages" in which arguments are formulated depend upon a larger complex including a culture's view of transcendence. In his study of the relationship between language and thought, *Ways of Thinking of Eastern Peoples* (1964), Nakamura writes:

> The features of the ways of thinking which are unconsciously embodied in language may possibly become explicit in logic and may moreover be displayed in a systematized, organized state. In this sense, logic is one of the most important keys for the study of the features of the ways of thinking of a people.[29]

While Nakamura's position is far from free of difficulty (a matter to which I shall turn shortly), I believe he has correctly assessed the contextual character of logic. Stcherbatsky's classic, *Buddhist Logic* (1930),[30] further exemplifies this principle by making plain the relationship between formal structures of thought and underlying epistemological concerns in the work of Buddhist logicians. Similarly, in reflecting on the *pramaṇas* ('modes of knowing') in Advaita Vedānta, Eliot Deutsch comments in *Advaita Vedānta: A Philosophical Reconstruction* (1969):

> The theory of inference in Indian philosophy generally differs from classical Western logic in many interesting ways,

but especially in this, that it involves a kind of scientific method of induction as part and parcel of it and hence is never purely formal in character. . . . Inference for Advaita is thus an empirical *pramaṇa*: its task . . . is to draw out the implications of sense experience.[31]

The notion that the structures of inference are culturally neutral is belied by the evidence, since marked differences reflecting axial assumptions of a civilization can be found in the inferential structures themselves.

The paradigm of linguistic determinism

Still another model consists in predicating a correlation between the linguistic structures of a given language and the conceptualization possibilities of the corresponding culture, that is, between the language and the ways of thinking of a given people. This model assumes that what can be expressed within the confines of a given language determines the parameters for the expression of conceptual problems. By analyzing a natural language in terms of the way in which judgments and inferences are expressed, the thought modes of a people can be uncovered and the limits of philosophical speculation on a specific problem established deductively. Thus, for example, one might compare the views of transcendence in Plato and Śaṅkara by investigating the linguistic roots of such terms as *Brahman* and *te on*. While specifically disavowing that comparative philosophy is the enterprise in which he is engaged, Nakamura's *Ways of Thinking of Eastern Peoples* (1964) is an instance of the philosophical character of purely linguistic inquiry of this sort. Consider Nakamura's discussion of a Sanskrit root *bhu* and its relation to the view of "becoming" in Indian thought:

In classical Indian languages, there was no word which corresponded to the word "to become." Although the verb formed from the root *bhu* connotes the meaning of "to become," this word also connotes the meaning of "to exist" at the same time. Why did the ancient Indians fail to distinguish the word meaning "to become" from the word meaning "to exist" in their daily conversation? It was because "to become" was one form or aspect of "to exist" for them.[32]

One obvious difficulty of this method lies in its assumption that we can know the limits of a language. But how are we to determine these limits? In what language is the observer to stand? In some other natural language? What of its rules and structures? In a formal language? Are *its* rules to be stated in still another formal language or in some natural language? What are the growth possibilities of any language if it is still to be counted as the same language? And, if language limits what can be thought to what can be thought within its confines, what of philosophy? Nakamura suggests the possibility of lexical novelty arising through individual creative effort, but out of what resources is such effort to come?

At a deeper level one must point to the vicious circle in which linguistic determinism finds itself. The terms of its interpretations are themselves reflective of an anterior conceptual scheme which enables us to oppose thought to language in the first place. We are forced to ask: By virtue of what are we able to draw the distinction between language and thought? If some lexical or grammatical element opens the space for the development of this distinction, what is this element? How is it constituted? Derrida, in an essay, "The Supplement of the Copula: Philosophy *Before* Linguistics" (1967), considers this difficulty:

> It would be wrong to believe in the immediate and ahistorical accessibility of a philosophical argument, just as it would be wrong to believe that we could without a preliminary and very complex elaboration, submit a metaphysical text to some "scientific" deciphering grid — be it linguistic, psychoanalytical or other. One of the first precautions must concern the origin and metaphysical bearings of the concepts which often constitute such a "scientific" grid. Philosophy is not only *before* linguistics in the way that one can be *faced* with a new science, outlook or object; it is also *before* linguistics, it precedes linguistics providing it with all of its concepts, for better or worse.[33]

Suggestions and conclusions

It must be borne in mind that the models I have suggested as operative in comparative philosophy represent a range of possibilities in a discipline which has not yet had a chance to establish rules and policies governing the character of the comparisons it generates. At this early stage, this is probably an advantage as long as we recognize the limitations of each method. One paradigm of fairly recent origin seems to me to offer interesting possibilities. This is the structural method used in the analyses of such phenomena as "madness," "the hospital," and "sexuality" in the work of Michel Foucault.[34] In an essay appended to his *Archeology of Knowledge* (1969), Foucault suggests that, to disclose the meaning of such complex entities, we must uncover the "groups of objects, methods, their corpus of propositions considered to be true, the interplay of rules and definitions, of techniques and tools" which define them.[35] The objective for Foucault is to discover discursive policies, the rules of what can and cannot be said within the confines of a given system. Thus, when "madness" is the subject of investigation the discursive policies constituting truth and falsity within a civilization and reflecting its deepest metaphysical and axiological commitments must be brought into view. Canons of rationality exclude from discourse not what is false but what cannot be said, what is "mad." The latter, "madness," acts as a constraint, a limiting concept, upon all discourse. The civilizational perspective is intrinsic to this method. For Foucault (1969) what is taken to be true and what is excluded from any given system depend upon

> whole strata of practices such as pedagogy — naturally — the book system. . . . But [it is] probably even more profoundly accompanied by the manner in which knowledge is employed by a society, the way in which it is exploited, divided and in some ways attributed.[36]

The problem of using this method for the comparative study of transcendence lies in the complex reciprocities that determine the items to be manipulated — the conceptual suppositions and institutional practices which express transcendence in a given civilization and the rules governing the act of comparing, themselves as much end products of these suppositions as instruments of investigation. As I. A. Richards points out in the context of the problems of translators, one could multiply the items to be taken into account ad infinitum by attempting to uncover the rules governing the original rules of the comparison. But such a regress is self-defeating and unnecessary; it suffices to comprehend that the instruments of the comparison belong to the comparison itself. I would concur with I. A. Richards's (1952) summary of the problem:

> I suppose that a first condition of the endeavor [speaking of the translation enterprise] is a recognition of its inherent willfulness. It is purposive; it seeks. If asked what it seeks its only answer should be: "itself." It seeks to comprehend what comprehending may be. What is sought is the search.[37]

Thus every structural comparative endeavor seeks to explicate not only the meaning of the terms compared but also the rules governing the comparison — why just *these* items and no others are to be brought into relation. In the unique case of transcendence, it is only through a recovery of its peculiar path in the material and spiritual expressions of civilization that we may discern its having passed.

NOTES

1. I am indebted to Benjamin Nelson for this conception of civilization. See his "Civilizational Complexes and Intercivilizational Encounters," *Sociological Analysis* 34:2 (Summer 1973): 81ff.

2. I. A. Richards, "Towards a Theory of Translating," *Studies in Chinese Thought*, ed. Arthur F. Wright (Chicago: University of Chicago Press, 1953), p. 248. Where discrepancies between dates in the body of the paper and in the notes are found, the former indicates the first appearance of a text; the latter, publication date of the source from which quoted material is derived.

3. Arthur F. Wright refers to Masson-Oursel as the propounder of a theory of comparative philosophy. See Wright, *Studies in Chinese Thought*, p. 2. Similarly Hajime Nakamura traces the history of the term to Paul Masson-Oursel's *La Philosophie comparée* (Paris: F. Alcan,

1923) and cites the work of George Misch and Charles A. Moore in this connection. See Hajime Nakamura, *Ways of Thinking of Eastern Peoples* (Honolulu: East-West Center Press, 1964), p. 13.

4. This is the position of J. N. Findlay in *The Transcendence of the Cave* (London: George Allen & Unwin, 1967).

5. See Martin Heidegger, *Holzwege* (Frankfurt am Main: Vittorio Klostermann, 1957), p. 3, for his conception of forest trails. Emmanuel Levinas borrows the conception to describe ethical transcendence in *En decouvrant l'existence avec Husserl et Heidegger* (Paris: Vrin, 1967), pp. 199ff. Jacques Derrida uses the term to suggest a preparation for venturing beyond our own *logos* in *Speech and Phenomena*, trans. David B. Allison (Evanston: Northwestern University Press, 1973), p. 156.

6. Jacques Derrida, *Of Grammatology*, trans. Gayatri Chakravorty Spivak (Baltimore: Johns Hopkins University Press, 1976), p. 61.

7. Derrida, *Speech and Phenomena*, p. 156.

8. Ibid., pp. 149ff.

9. Levinas, *En decouvrant l'existence*, p. 199.

10. Derrida, *Of Grammatology*, p. 60.

11. Ibid., p. 61.

12. Arthur F. Wright proposes such categories as history of philosophy, history of values, history of situations of intellectual choice, history of a group of thinkers, and history of symbolism as possible schematic categories for the analysis of Chinese thought. These schema can be seen as applicable to the enterprise of comparative philosophy. In addition he proposes the use of Chinese data to test a comparative scheme classing cultures in terms of thought forms and using Chinese thought forms as paradigms for comparative study. See Wright, "Introduction," in *Studies in Chinese Thought*.

13. G. W. F. Hegel, *The Philosophy of Right*, trans. T. M. Knox (Oxford: Clarendon Press, 1942), p. 218.

14. G. W. F. Hegel, *The Philosophy of History*, trans. J. Sibree (London: George Bell & Sons, 1890), pp. 118–120.

15. Ibid., p. 117. For a critical evaluation of Hegel's deprecation of Chinese and Indian culture see Helmuth von Glasenapp, *Das Indienbild deutscher Denker* (Stuttgart: K. F. Koehler, 1960), pp. 39–60. Von Glasenapp points to the uncritical amalgam of Brahmanism (the Vedic tradition) and Saṅkara's metaphysical monism in Hegel's interpretation of Hinduism. Reinhold Leuze, *Die ausserchristlichen Religionen bei Hegel* (Gottigen: Vanderhoeck & Ruprecht, 1975) reveals Hegel's wavering view of the relationship between Buddhism and Hinduism. In the

lectures of 1823 Hegel treats Buddhism as subsequent to Hinduism but in 1824 reverses this order. His final view in the lectures of 1831 is not known, since no record of this lecture is extant. Since Buddhism in his day was little understood, Hegel was able to borrow the notion of nirvana in order to criticize the German Romantics through criticizing Indian "otherworldliness." Moreover his view of nirvana was limited to Mahāyāna sources. For a summary of this literature and a picture of Hegel's use of the concept of Oriental despotism see Clark Butler, *G. W. F. Hegel* (Boston: Twayne, 1977), chaps. 3 and 4. For further evaluation of Hegel's orientalism see Kurt F. Leidecker, "Hegel and the Orientals," in *Hegel's Philosophy*, ed. Warren E. Steinkraus (New York: Holt, Rinehart & Winston, 1971), pp. 156–167.

16. I. A. Richards, "Towards a Theory of Translating," p. 258.

17. Derrida, *Of Grammatology*, p. 61. This conception is derived from Heidegger. See the latter's *The Question of Being*, trans. William Kluback and Jean T. Wilde (New York: Twayne Pubs., 1958), pp. 80ff.

18. F. S. C. Northrup, *The Meeting of East and West* (New York: Macmillan Pub. Co., 1946), p. 312. For a more recent use of the model in which East and West are interpreted as complementary, see Erich Jantsch, *Design for Evolution* (New York: George Braziller, 1975).

19. Derrida, *Of Grammatology*, pp. 244ff.

20. Joseph Needham, *Science and Civilization in China* (Cambridge: At the University Press, 1974), vol. 4, pt. 3, p. liii.

21. Ibid., vol. 3, pp. 448ff.

22. Joseph Needham, "Time in China," in *The Grand Titration: Science and Society in East and West* (London, 1969), argues for both a compartmentalized and continuous time continuum, the latter conception prevailing in relation to the art of clockmaking. The *Tai Phing* ('Great Peace'), originally a Taoist conception, takes on the character of a millenarian movement. See pp. 260ff.

23. A meeting of the Society for Asian and Comparative Philosophy in Atlanta in 1973 considered Milton Munitz's concept of the world as its focus. Participants also included Robert McDermott, moderator, Kenneth Inada, Bernard Cua, and Edith Wyschograd. The papers and proceedings of the meetings are published in *Philosophy East and West* 25:3 (July 1975).

24. Charles Hartshorne, "Introduction: The Development of Process Philosophy," in *Philosophers of Process*, ed. Douglas Browning (New York: Random House, 1965), pp. xvff.

25. W. T. Stace, *Man Against Darkness* (Pittsburgh: University of Pittsburgh Press, 1967), pp. 53ff.

26. Paul Deussen, "Vorrede," in Badarayana, *Die Sutras des Vedānta*, trans. Paul Deussen (Leipzig: F. A. Brockhaus, 1920), p. 6, as cited in Nakamura, *Thinking of Eastern Peoples*, p. 30.

27. Sarvepali Radhakrishnan, *Indian Philosophy*, 2 vols. (London: George Allen & Unwin, 1923).

28. John Cobb, "Buddhist Emptiness and the Christian God," *Journal of the American Academy of Religion* 45:1 (March 1977): 197.

29. Nakamura, *Thinking of Eastern Peoples*, p. 9.

30. Theodore Stcherbatsky, *Buddhist Logic* (Leningrad: Academy of Sciences, 1930).

31. Eliot Deutsch, *Advaita Vedānta: A Philosophical Reconstruction* (Honolulu: East-West Center Press, 1969), p. 9.

32. Nakamura, *Thinking of Eastern Peoples*, p. 76.

33. Jacques Derrida, "The Supplement of Copula: Philosophy *Before* Linguistics," trans. James Creech and Josue Harari, *Georgia Review* 30:3 (Fall 1976): 543.

34. Michel Foucault, *Madness and Civilization*, trans. Richard Howard (New York: Random House, 1965); see also his *Birth of the Clinic: An Archeology of Medical Perception*, trans. A. M. Sheridan Smith (New York: Random House, 1973).

35. Michel Foucault, *The Archeology of Knowledge*, trans. A. M. Sheridan Smith (New York: Random House, 1972), p. 222.

36. Ibid., p. 219.

37. Richards, "Towards a Theory of Translating," p. 248.

PART II

Brahmanism, Buddhism, and the Gnostic Way

4

Transcendent Brahman or
Transcendent Void:
Which Is Ultimately Real?

J. G. ARAPURA

THE WORD *transcendent* expresses a problem underlying all thinking about reality. But today it is difficult to speak meaningfully of
the transcendent because in modern thought it has largely been
eclipsed. The modern world no longer views it as the supreme
sphere of operation for philosophy.

I will make a brief analysis of the origin of the concepts of
transcendence and the transcendent, somewhat along the lines of
what is today called phenomenology. Then I will examine two
approaches to ultimate reality as transcendent Brahman and
transcendent Void (*śūnyatā*).

The eclipse of the transcendent in modern thought

Modern thought's inhibition about the transcendent has, no
doubt, stemmed from several causes. In philosophy itself one
source is the work of Immanuel Kant, who, in dealing with the
problem underlying thought about reality, left a double-barreled
legacy with regard to the question of the transcendent. He rejected the claimed capacity of pure reason to obtain knowledge of
the real as such. His hope was to pave the way for that which is
ultimately real, namely, the eternal, to be held as the unconditional reference for moral and spiritual life. On the other hand,

insofar as what we can theoretically know was felt to be limited to mere appearances,[1] critical philosophy and the future metaphysics for which it sought to lay the foundation were to serve the goals that were in harmony with the positive sciences.

Kant had no doubt that this method alone would "sever the roots of materialism, fatalism, atheism, free-thinking, fanaticism, and superstition."[2] He argued that appearance and reality must be held apart through critical reason because speculative reason, on account of its "pretensions to transcendent insights," transgressed their mutual boundary, thus actually getting in the way of the development of critical reason with regard to God, freedom, and immortality.[3]

These are the ways in which Kant "denied knowledge in order to make room for faith."[4] But this seminal thought of Kant contributed to developments he himself could not have anticipated. As he had rejected "transcendent insights," the only threads on which the problem of reality hung were faith and its companions, namely, reverence and the imperative of moral perfection. In later developments thought shifted its ground and became largely a territory of certain immanentist structures of ends and means, closing humankind within restrictive boundaries. The transcendent was no longer the problem of reality, because no difference remained between appearance and reality so as to justify any such focus. Even within these immanentist structures, however, there has still remained some scope for recognizing and dealing with a few genuine problems in at least a piecemeal fashion, whether existential, moral, cognitive, or ontological. Even in the profoundest expressions of immanentism the transcendent has surfaced occasionally, although mainly as the deepest dimension to which these essentially immanently conceived problems can be pushed. Notions like the being of beings and the essence of time are clear examples of these.

The concepts of transcendence and the transcendent,
and the structural orientation of consciousness

The term *transcend* (*trans*-scend) means to pass beyond, to go across, to cross over, to overcome. Its Sanskrit equivalent is *tarati* 'he, she, it passes beyond', from which is formed the noun *taraṇam*. Pursuing the word in its original context is instructive. For this purpose let us adopt a variation of the method called "critical phenomenology," which Paul Tillich hinted at but did not seem to have developed. We can agree with Tillich that it "is the method best fitted to supply normative descriptions of spiritual (and also Spiritual) meanings."[5] Tillich's preference for it over against "pure" phenomenology is also acceptable because unlike the latter it unites what he calls "an intuitive-descriptive element with an existential-critical element."

The realm in which we apply this method is consciousness, but we will use the word *consciousness* in the double sense which its Sanskrit equivalent (*cit*) warrants, that is to say, as understood in the everyday, empirical parlance as well as extraordinarily in a mystical sense.[6]

Accordingly, when we stipulate in advance that transcendence is the essential structural orientation of consciousness, the analysis will have to be both vertical and horizontal, although — at least in the primary literatures from which we seek to draw — the two are utterly inseparable.

Consciousness (*cit*) leads to thinking and thoughtfulness (*cintā*). This is where at least the phenomenal origin of the idea of transcendence lies. Through critical phenomenology it can be found in consciousness just as truly today as it can be discovered in the earliest of our religio-philosophical literatures.

In consciousness' movement toward reality, self-centeredly no doubt, although existentially too, it comes up against a barrier which it finds it cannot cross. It wants to come to terms with life as given, with death itself, and with the mystery of the whole; and it wants to make sense of existence. It soon finds that it cannot do these things because there is a barrier set between itself and whatever it is that is *ultimately* real. What it seeks to grasp is engulfed in an abyss. This encounter is the presupposition of transcendence (*taraṇam*). Perhaps the encounter with the barrier merely awakens the idea of transcendence from its somnolence. But they clearly function together as they are but two sides of what is one and the same.

Where ordinary consciousness cannot speak for itself, great

texts of our primary literature take over the speaking. The great
texts can do so because they *are* the language of discovered "mystery" (Sanskrit *guhyam* 'hidden in a cave', or *rahasyam* 'secret').
These texts awaken in us the sense of the great mystery that consciousness hides in itself, veiled over by everyday activities. It is
thus revealed to us that transcendence is the essential structural
orientation of consciousness.

Ordinarily, empirical consciousness carries the idea of transcendence lightly, not giving much thought to it. But as expressed
through the primary texts of our literatures we see consciousness
engaged in heaving itself across the abyss. In that act the abyss,
too, is more fully manifest than ordinarily. In trying to cross over,
we learn better what it is we have to cross over, and our consciousness is stretched in the process. There the *tremendum* (Sanskrit *bhayam*, *mahat bhayam* 'dread, great dread') of the abyss is
unfolded to consciousness. What is it *to* which consciousness
heaves itself over the abyss? That is the far shore or "the beyond,"
which we call the transcendent. The far shore is, certainly from
consciousness' own side, to be primarily understood as a ground
or a dimension, or, as the Indian tradition calls it, the "highest dimension" (*paramam padam*).[7] So then, the transcendent is to be
understood as the dimension to which consciousness is structurally oriented, and in understanding this with clarity the uniting
of the intuitive-descriptive and existential-critical elements is absolutely indispensable. The understanding is indistinguishable
from that which is understood; in the words of the *Maitri Upaniṣad*, "Water cannot be distinguished in water, fire in fire, space in
space."[8]

One view is that the transcendent is the Void itself. Properly
grasped, it can be the object of ultimate spiritual concern and
hence the saving truth, as powerfully demonstrated by Buddhism. The Buddhists see all things, including consciousness itself, as being of the nature of flux (*saṁtāna*). There is no place
other than the whirling flux from whence to survey consciousness.

Others, however, chiefly the Vedantists, view the nature of
the transcendent as substantial. According to the Vedānta, consciousness' orientation to the transcendent itself reveals the transcendent as an eternal and unchanging entity. Consciousness is

oriented as it is because its essence is the self (*ātman*) that struggles to be free from the bondage of phenomena. Therefore, in the
very orientation of consciousness the self serves as its own bridge
leading to the far shore or the ground beyond the abyss. In fact,
the far shore, consciousness, the bridge (i.e., the self), and the
abyss all get welded into one homogeneous and self-identical reality. *The Chāndogya Upaniṣad* had a striking simile to express this
truth. It says, "Now this self (*ātman*) is the bridge (*setuḥ*), which
is also the barrier (*vidhitir*) that keeps these worlds apart. Over
that bridge day and night do not cross (*na taratah*), nor old age,
nor sorrow, nor good and evil deed. All evils turn back from it for
the world of Brahman is free from evil."[9] Commentators clearly
show that the terms *day and night, death, sorrow,* and *evil* stand
for temporality, flux, and phenomenality (*saṁsāra*). According
to the Vedānta, the idea of transcendence is earlier and is not
predicated on consciousness at all. The transcendent is held to be
the ground which accounts for the particular behavior of consciousness which is not self-accounting nor explicable in terms of
the abyss it encounters.

In Buddhism, on the contrary, transcendence has no ground
other than what it seeks to cross over, on which is predicated the
notion of what is crossed over *to*, although as a religious system it
does have an infinite spiritual interest in the latter. In the view of
the Vedānta it is this interest that makes Buddhism self-
contradictory ontologically. However, a system which is ontologically self-contradictory need by no means be so spiritually. But
for this self-contradiction, the antinomies of reason which Buddhism also faced in its own way would have remained purely at
the formal level. They did not, but became existential "irresolvables" (*avyātkṛtavastūni*). Thus, for instance, the contradiction
in the nature of time was seen as the existential contradiction arising from the attempt to resolve the problem of eternity in time,
unsteady and constructed of fleeting moments as it is—not having, as in the Vedānta, an ontology of eternity in which to solve
the problem of time. The same is true of immortality. The same is
true of the soul.

But such a fate does not mean that thought must turn away
from its forward course or abandon the route of consciousness'

orientation to the transcendent. Buddhism as an existential system has stretched thought to the dimensions of an impossible task, namely, to make the abyss itself (niḥsvabhāva) serve the cause of transcendence. Where it is understood clearly and deeply, as it is by the Buddhist thinkers, that the urge to transcend does not come from a deliberate human choice, it is self-evident that the impossible alone must be attempted. This course no doubt marks the greatest courage, comparable to what Tillich calls "the courage to be."

Transcendent Brahman

In considering the transcendent the Vedānta rejects the literal meaning of the verb to transcend. Therefore the philology of the word transcendent is held as irrelevant to grasping the transcendent; the emphasis here is that what is grasped is already at hand and is a definite and concrete ground. This problem is treated in Śaṅkara's celebrated Commentary on the Brahma Sūtra,[10] in which the bridge simile of the Chāndogya Upaniṣad is cited. The question is raised as to what is to be understood by the transcendent (here the word used is para). Śaṅkara pits a revolutionized meaning over against the conventional, philological one. The hypothetical objectors to whom he replies had assumed that in view of the accepted meaning of the word transcend (tarati-śabda prayogāt), there can be no bridge that connects with the transcendent, but it must always lie unattainably far beyond in the literal sense.[11] Śaṅkara shows that, even in ordinary usage, in some cases to transcend means not 'to go beyond indefinitely', but 'to reach'.[12] To reach means 'to grasp entirely' just as when we speak of a student having completely learned grammar (yathā vyākaraṇam tīrṇa iti prāpta ityucyate). Here transcendence does not mean going even further beyond (na atikrāntaḥ). The confusion due to literalist philology is now ended. To transcend (tarati) is the same as 'to reach', 'to attain' (āpnoti or prāpnoti). The term āpnoti, with or without the prefix pra, is a verb used with a very strong sense, conveying the meaning of total identity of the attainer and the attained (or the grasper and the grasped). The gulf between them is obliterated.

This understanding revolutionizes the definition of the transcendent as that to which consciousness is structurally oriented. The transcendent comes first and its pull accounts for consciousness' orientation, which is no longer predicated on the barrier it encounters nor on the way consciousness inherently and by itself is.

The beyond does not remain forever elusive and indefinite but is grasped as the ground close at hand, that upon which we stand. Standing upon it we can ponder the great gulf separating it from the consciousness that still seeks to overcome it. From the ground thus grasped the gulf too can be grasped and reduced to zero distance. The gulf so measured is called *māyā*, from the root *mā* 'to measure', a concept wrongly interpreted as illusion. How is the measuring done? It is done by using the only scale — namely, the self (*ātman*) — which is adequate to span a seemingly infinite distance. The absconding of the self from itself through ignorance (*avidyā*) is the mother phenomenon of all infinite distances. Yet this is a metaphor, and upon this metaphor are based all notions of temporal and spatial infinity and all antinomies of reason.

The transcendent is the ground which is also close at hand. The transcendent furnishes the certainty which allows us to speak about it, and we may only speak of it if it is already known. A proper understanding of the holy always includes a reference to knowledge.

If, on the contrary, we were to declare some other kind of knowledge of that which is beyond, following in Kant's words "the common fate of human reason to complete its speculative structures as speedily as may be and only afterwards to inquire whether the foundations are reliable,"[13] then we would be guilty of gross dogmatism. This is the error of those who adopt the literal meaning of the word *tarati* 'transcendent'. According to them, the beyond must always remain far off, and yet they declare that transcendent insights are relevant to it. This kind of thinking has given speculation a bad name. Śaṅkara criticizes it as groundless speculation (*aprasiddhakalpanā*), and he pronounces it "to be not reasonable" (*na etat nyāyyam*).[14] However, one must not condemn speculation as such, for, as was discovered after the first flush of critical thought, without it philosophy itself is not possible.

The ground beyond, already close at hand, is that in which everything takes place — the seeking, the rise of a sense of the abyss, and the urge to transcend. It is what is called Brahman. Here we are given the real meaning of the transcendent as that which comprehends and encompasses what otherwise remains uncomprehended and unencompassed. But because it is already at hand, the words *reach* and *attain* are used metaphorically in the same manner in which the idea of the self absconding from itself is used. But the metaphor must be taken seriously, as, structurally, it coincides with consciousness itself and has the same orientation to the transcendent. Metaphor is the speech proper to consciousness understood the way we have outlined it.

Brahman and the questions of being and knowledge

Transcendent Brahman clearly offers a new foundation for considering philosophy's two most vexing questions, namely, those posed by the verbs *is* and *is not* and by the verb *to know*. It will not be henceforth legitimate to pursue the meanings of these verbs to some so-called ontological foundations of their own. Brahman has already taken us beyond whatever meanings we may independently arrive at for the verbs *to be* and *not to be*. We ourselves have no logic by which to come to a point where we can decisively say what ultimate reality is. The *logos* operative here comes wholly from Brahman, and that presents us with a radical situation expressed in this way: if it is the case that ultimate reality may be either being or nonbeing, then it is only being. The conditional part is formulated according to our logic, but the consequent is according to the *logos* that resides in transcendent Brahman. Otherwise we will have only a meaningless tautology such as, "If it is either being or nonbeing, then it is either being or nonbeing." But that is not the case. Now substitute *God* for *Brahman* and we get the same proposition. Thus, if God can be said to exist or not exist then God can only be said to exist. This is the ontological ground for the existential leap of faith which, therefore, is not ungrounded. This principle of the annulment of the alternative to being belongs only to the transcendent; by no means can it be generalized in the form, "If *something* is either being or nonbeing, then it is only being."

The choice of being over against nonbeing was expressed by the *Chāndogya Upaniṣad*, when it posed this question long ago and then declared: "How could Being come from nonbeing? But, my dear, this was Being itself in the beginning, one only without a second."[15] In our ordinary thinking, being is met by its other, namely, nonbeing. Where do we find being that is not so met by its opposite? It is obtained in Brahman, which is only being, hence said to be one without a second. Interpreting this Upaniṣad statement, Śaṅkara declares that Brahman is being alone (*satkevala*) and it responds only to the notional word *being* (*sachabda-buddhi-mātra gamyan eva*).[16]

However, we do not know being (in the sense of Brahman) through analogies of beings. In that respect it always remains hidden. But it comes to us in the self-revelation of Brahman through the *logos* (*vak*, *śabda*) that belongs to Brahman. There is an analogy between the self-revelation of Brahman and the way things present (reveal) themselves to us. The determining notion is self-luminosity. Brahman is immediate to us through its own self-shining, analogous to the self-preservation of things by the light of their own presence. This idea is fundamental in the Vedānta. Cit-sukha, a late medieval writer, has a classic formulation for this: "Although not known, it [Brahman] is the only entity that is fit to be called immediate [to us] as in the case of a pot sitting out there."[17] We may call this the "analogy of revelation" (*analogia revelationis*), which may very well be what underlies the "analogy of being" (*analogia entis*). The examples of seen things (*dṛṣṭānta*) as analogies of revelation, Śaṅkara observes, are necessary, for without them the highest secrets "are not known even to the gods" (*devairapi durjneyatvam*).[18] The source of analogical knowledge is, however, *logos*, not our conceptions.

On the ground of revelation the question whether we can know the ultimately real is already answered. Brahman is what we know but do not know that we know. Therefore, the real questions are, How is it that we do not know that which is immediate to us? Is it because the self-shining light obscures and conceals like darkness?

Here one must consider the function of thinking. Do these questions—although the only real ones—necessarily mark out the domain of thinking to the end that answers must be found for them? Or, rather, are they merely for the purpose of rousing thinking so that it may reach a destiny not at all determined by them? For the Vedānta it is clearly the latter. That is the reason why it views knowledge, in the sense of gnosis (*jñāna*), to be the true end to which thinking is directed. The directing of thinking to gnosis is the function of the *logos*, and it is exactly the same as the revealing. Thus the Vedānta does not believe that thinking itself can ever be the subject matter of thinking except as a secondary activity.

Thinking as a secondary activity pertains to the proposition: "The world is what we do not know but *think* that we know." The world (Sanskrit *jagat* — etymologically, 'that which is of the nature of movement') is, metaphysically speaking, a constant and unsteady shifting between two false poles of "is" and "is not." Because the world ordinarily serves as the ground of thinking, especially in respect to the question of being, it calls for critical investigation. The thinking based on it, therefore, is similarly to be investigated, but in itself it is not directed to gnosis.

Transcendent Void and the questions of being, nonbeing, and knowledge

Having briefly set forth the view of the transcendent in terms of the Vedantic doctrine of Brahman, let us take a look at the Buddhist doctrine of the Void (*śūnyatā*) in the same manner. The Void represents an ultimately concerned effort to grasp the meaning of the transcendent as underlying all thought about reality. In this connection I repeat an earlier statement: Buddhism has convincingly demonstrated that, far from turning back to consciousness' empirical ground with a sense of defeat, thought can actually be stretched to the dimensions of an impossible task, namely, to make the abyss itself (*niḥsvabhāva*) serve the cause of transcendence, thus to hold it under its power and spell.

Whatever is said about the abyss of indeterminateness can also be said about the transcendent, and what is over and above that can never be said, thought, or imagined — nay, *must not* be said, thought, or imagined, lest one fall into the trap of views (*dṛṣṭi*), all of which are mutually falsifiable and hence falsifiable all together. This accounts for the celebrated silence of Buddha on the question of the transcendent when urged to describe it other than in terms of the indeterminate abyss of our experience. It is entirely possible that the silence was a symbolic recognition of the fact that there is more to the transcendent than the abyss absolutized as the Void. But the express teachings of the Buddha and his followers urge us to turn our thought to the Void and not to what may be beyond it. All existential and salvific knowledge comes from meditating on the Void. And what one does not and cannot know one must not speak about, as it obviously does not contribute to salvation (nirvana). Therefore, the Void itself must be taken as the transcendent by the test that it is that which contributes to salvation. Nāgārjuna, the greatest of the Buddhist thinkers, declares, "There is no non-Void entity (aśūnyo-dharmaḥ)."[19] Other great Buddhist writers like Ārya Deva and Prajnākaramati concur. The latter adds that knowledge of the Void is the only thing that profits the soul, leaving no need for considering a self-existent reality beyond it.[20] At the same time it would be a mistake to conclude that the Buddhist thinkers denied the existence of something beyond the Void. They neither denied nor affirmed it. They merely inculcated the salvific self-sufficiency of the Void with regard to the existential question, What is ultimately real?

If the absolutized abyss or the Void itself serves as the transcendent, there arises no question of any bridge such as the self spanning it, because it is itself self-comprehending and all-encompassing. Actually, when Buddhism says that there is no ātman this is what it really means. The questioning self — the soul to be saved — somehow remains, primarily as the focal point of all the irresolvables. As their bearer its salvation is a legitimate concern.

It is clear that in a system such as this there is no place for the logos in conjunction with transcendent Brahman. Therefore, it is thrown into thought without the logos. Thought, whatever it is, must not be confused with speculation. And critical reason, although an important accessory to thought, is not itself thought. We have to understand this in the context of the common tradition of which Buddhism and the Vedānta are the two most important branches: accordingly, thought means meditation (dhyāna).

Meditation has the character of thought in its pure form for two reasons, negative and positive, respectively. Negatively, its character is independent of anything else, either formal or material, and of any kind of data support or logistical support. Positively, we may use Heidegger's definition of Socrates as the purest thinker of the West: he put himself in the draft or current of "what addresses itself to thought."[21] What is it that addresses itself to thought in Buddhism and the Vedānta? The answer can already be anticipated. For Buddhism it is the reality of the Void; for the Vedānta it is the *logos* that has its source in Brahman, taking up residence in thought to direct it to gnosis.

Buddhism deals accordingly with being and nonbeing and with knowledge in terms of the Void. So then, "if the transcendent is either being or nonbeing," what is the consequent? Certainly not "then it is being"; rather, "then it is both being and nonbeing" (regarded as an absurd conclusion); or "then it is neither being nor nonbeing" (also regarded as an absurd conclusion). In this way the full frame of the four-cornered dialectic is expressed as "is," "is not," "both is and is not," and "neither is nor is not." These are the four possible views (*dṛṣṭi*). The dialectic develops in this manner because there is no possible negation of the alternative to being. This negation is possible only with the *logos* that resides in the transcendent as understood by the Vedānta. The Buddhist dialectic therefore develops freely, and even absurdly in a calculated way. The very absurdity of it is intended to challenge logic, and without *logos*, logic has no ground to stand on. That this frame is a complete expression of the foundation of the conditional "if the transcendent is either being or nonbeing," is stated by Nāgārjuna's greatest commentator, Candrakīrti, who writes, "The four-cornered frame is based on the two views [of being and nonbeing]."[22] The classic formulation is given by Nāgārjuna in the following stanza, in an almost algebraic fashion:

> All is suchness, not-suchness, both suchness and nonsuchness
> Neither not-suchness nor suchness, that is the teaching of the Buddha.[23]

The same four-cornered frame can be approached in another manner, that is, as an exhaustive list of the four ways in which we view the transcendent: like, unlike, both partially like and partially unlike, and neither like nor unlike what we know as being. The transcendent totally defies the categories of similarity and dissimilarity. We can draw instances from the history of metaphysics, both Eastern and Western, to exemplify all these four angles or point-limits (*koṭi*) of views. The view based on analogy (like what we know), the view based on the irrational principle or the *via negativa* (unlike what we know), the view based on the dialectics of becoming (both like and unlike what we know), and the view based on the final limit situation, or a possible radical dialectic (neither like nor unlike what we know), have all been well represented in metaphysics. Buddhism argues that the voiding of the whole frame *in toto* through criticism goes hand in hand with meditation on the Void.

In Buddhism, the four-cornered frame is simply the clinical bed in which the irresolvable questions are laid for examination and through diagnosis confirmed as irresolvable. These questions come from consciousness by virtue of its structural orientation to the transcendent, implicit in which is the encounter with the abyss. Therefore, they come as existential signals. They are not just theoretical viewpoints. The abiding questions of metaphysics, namely, those about ultimate reality and eternity, become the subjects of infinite brooding. But inescapable contradictions remain: the problem of ultimate reality in terms of the flux and that of eternity in terms of time. Therefore, everything is absorbed into the Void. The Void is the transcendent; the Void is what is ultimately real, certainly for salvific purposes. Finally, although here there is a refusal of the *logos*, there is still an infinitely powerful spiritual adventure, not to say an adventure of thought, that takes one to the farthest limits possible without the *logos*. In this respect it does not lack authenticity. And it is fully the equal of the Vedānta in representing in its completeness a powerful spirituality and a challenging approach to reality.

Concluding remarks

We are committed to ask the question, Which is ultimately real, transcendent Brahman or transcendent Void? The answer to this question has already been developing, although only implicitly, all along the way. The answer, however, can now be made explicit by employing this decisive criterion: whichever of them has fully accounted for the problems most crucial to the other, and yet has surpassed the other, is qualified to be considered the more adequate expression of ultimate reality. With this criterion we can see that transcendent Brahman, by completely comprehending the abyss, has removed the possibility of its being absolutized as the transcendent Void and hence has surpassed the Buddhist view. On the other hand, Buddhist philosophers maintain that the Void is the dispersing (though not the grasping) of that, namely, being, of which they consider Brahman to be the absolutization. And so according to them such absolutization has to be inauthentic. The problem here is that the Buddhist tradition sought to disperse what it ought to have grasped.

Their reason for doing this lies in the way Buddhists approach being and with it all similar matters like eternity and the soul. They see nothing that is not of the nature of the Void. When they approach being in order to grasp it they see the equal claim also of its other, namely, nonbeing, which counters it. Thus they are led on to the four point-limits, which only serve to disperse being and ultimately to disperse themselves through their own relentless self-application.

Transcendent Brahman is the complete comprehension of the abyss, which means also that it is the grasp of being. But the grasp of being is not accomplished within the abyss, for already the abyss itself has been comprehended. The grasp of being is nothing other than the negation of the alternative to being, and such negation is the nature of transcendent Brahman. The possibility of reaching a knowledge of being comes only via the *logos*, which has its source in Brahman.

It is the clearest implication of transcendent Brahman that this knowledge (gnosis) is what is already there. Our efforts to know the transcendent, which is what metaphysics — or, in a larger sense, philosophy as a whole — is, merely clarify this supreme truth to ourselves, or, more appropriately, remove the veil of darkness that obscures it from our view. The same *logos* which reveals to us that gnosis is of the nature of ultimate reality also directs our thinking to this gnosis. This is the ground of absolute certainty; all other certainties are but a flash of it. And it frees metaphysics, making it a joyful task.

Transcendent Brahman is ultimate reality not only in the sense of knowledge but also in the salvific sense, and the two are by no means separate. The difference from Buddhism in this respect is worthy of note. It is seldom realized that in Buddhist philosophy there is difficulty in working out a clear internal coherence between the Void as ultimate reality and a salvific absolute, nirvana, which is spoken of sometimes in terms identical with the Void and sometimes in different terms. This salvific absolute of nirvana is often described in positive terms as the perfectly blissful reality beyond all anxiety, beyond the flux. It is called the goal.

The Buddha himself is reported to have said, "There is, O monks, a not-born, a not-become, a not-created, a not-formed. If there were not this not-born, not-become, not-created, not-formed, there would be no escape, no way out of this phenomenal bondage."[24] Metaphysically, however, is this salvific absolute the same as the Void or not the same? Surely, in affirming the reality of nirvana there is acknowledgment of gnosis, a fact adumbrated in Buddhist mysticism as *prajñā-pāramitā* 'transcendent knowledge'. But metaphysics as such is not released to be a joyful task.

This lack of coherence is brought about by a distance between a gnosis mode of thinking and a questioning mode of thinking. In the Vedānta's approach, on the contrary, gnosis does not move in one path and questioning in another, nor is it the case that the questions (existential and other) arise first and knowledge afterward. Gnosis is such that questions do not get an independent vogue; rather they are grasped as already answered questions, as needing no further existential engagement other than review and re-enactment. However, the review and re-enactment of already answered questions by no means inhibits thought. Thought is instead *released* to go to the ultimate depths; thus it can join the questioning mode utterly and without restraint. In the absolute security of the transcendent, one has already triumphed over the terrors of the irresolvables.

In all the above respects the debate between the Vedānta

and Buddhism is seen as a truly representative debate which goes to the very heart of our metaphysical enterprise; its implications are not limited to the tradition in which it historically took place. And on either side of the debate the transcendent remains the supreme sphere for the operation of philosophy and speaks with unconditional authority to an age in which the transcendent has suffered eclipse.

NOTES

1. Immanual Kant, *Critique of Pure Reason*, trans. Norman Kemp Smith (New York: St. Martin's Press, 1965), p. 29.

2. Ibid., p. 32.

3. Ibid., p. 29.

4. Ibid.

5. Paul Tillich, *Systematic Theology*, 3 vols. (Chicago: University of Chicago Press, 1951–1963), 1:106–108.

6. Ibid., pp. 108ff.

7. *Maitrī Upaniṣad*, 6:34; *Dhammapada*, 385.

8. āpam āpo 'gnir agnau vā vyomni vyoma na lakṣayet, *Maitrī Upaniṣad*, 3.34.10.

9. *Chāndogya Upaniṣad*, 8.4.1.

10. Śaṅkara, *Commentary on the Brahma-Sūtra*, 3.2.31–37.

11. setum tīrtvā iti ca taratiśabda prayogāt. Yathā laukikam setum tīrtvā jāngalam asetum prāpnoti, evan ātmānam setum tīrtvā anātmānam asetum prāpnoti iti gamyate, ibid., 3.2.31.

12. tarate atikrama asambhavāt prāpnoti ityartha eva vartate, ibid., 3.2.32.

13. Kant, *Critique of Pure Reason*, p. 47.

14. Śaṅkara, *Commentary on Brahma-Sūtra*, 3.2.32.

15. *Chāndogya Upaniṣad*, 6.2.2.

16. Śaṅkara, *Commentary on the Chāndogya Upaniṣad*, 6.2.1,2.

17. avedyatve sati aparokṣavyavāhara yogyatvam . . . yannaivam tannaivam yathā ghaṭa, Citsukha, *Tattvapradīpikā*, chap. 1.

18. Śaṅkara, *Commentary on the Kena Upaniṣad*, 4.4.

19. aśūnyo hi dharmaḥ kaścinna vidyate, Nāgārjuna, *Mādhyamika-kārikā*, 24.19.

20. hetupratyaya-sāmagrīm pratitya jātasya parāyattātmalābhasya pratibimbasyeva kutaḥ svabhāvatā. T.R.V. Murti, "Bodhicarya

Avatāra Pañcika of Prajñākaramati," in *The Central Philosophy of Buddhism* (London: George Allen & Unwin, 1960), p. 229 n.

21. Martin Heidegger, *What is Called Thinking?*, trans. J. Glenn Gray (New York: Harper & Row, 1954), p. 17.

22. dṛṣṭidvayopādānam upalakṣanārtham catasras tu eta dṛṣṭavyaḥ, Candrakīrti, *Prasannapadā (Commentary on Mādhyamika-kārikā)*, 27.2.

23. sarvam tathyam na vā tathyam tathyam ca atattyam eva ca naiva atathyam naiva tathyam etat buddhānuśāsanam, *Mādhyamika-kārikā*, 18.8.

24. *Udāna*, 8.1.

5

Transcendence and the Sacred in the Mahāyāna Middle Way

ROBERT A. F. THURMAN

MAITREYA'S CELEBRATED *Ornament of the Scriptures of the Universal Vehicle* opens its "Enlightenment" chapter with a description of what is both transcendent and sacred in Buddhism.

> After countless hundreds of ordeals, after countless harvests of virtues, and after countless breakings of barriers over immeasurable periods of time, Omniscience is attained, unhindered by the slightest block; like a casket of jewels thrown open, it is celebrated as Buddhahood. (*MSA* 9.1–2)

The supreme evolutionary goal of all living beings, the experience of omniscient and omnicompetent being is here celebrated as Buddhahood. This, far from being a lifeless, barren emptiness transcending all relationship with the mundane, is pregnant with value, with a wealth of radiance and splendor. It is perfect beatitude for its winner and great blessings for all living beings, as is powerfully conveyed in the metaphor of a casket of jewels thrown open.

Enlightenment is not an annihilation, a weary turning away from the world of pain and death and meaninglessness to a cold and anaesthetic yet safe absolute, whether called nirvana or Buddhahood. It is not only life, it is Boundless Life (Amitayus), as is called the Buddha of the Western Paradise. It is perfect compassion as well as perfect wisdom, perfect fulfillment of altruism as well as perfect fulfillment of individualism. It is the tender sensi-

100

tivity symbolized by the lotus petal united with the hard, brilliant wisdom symbolized by the diamond.

To understand the Universal Vehicle's capacity to reconcile this dichotomy without losing the vitality of either pole, one must master the subtleties of the doctrine of nonduality. To return to Maitreya's text:

> Although all phenomena are Buddhahood, no phenomenon whatsoever exists. Although it consists of virtuous qualities, they do not define it. It is like a jewel-mine, source of the jewel of the Dharma. It is like a rain-cloud, source of the harvest of beauty. (*MSA* 9.3–4)

Vasubandhu's commentary explains that "all things are Buddhahood because thusness of Reality is free from differentiation, and is manifest through purification." And yet in Buddhahood no thing exists at all with respect to the conceptually constructed reality. "Buddhahood consists of virtuous qualities, since all virtues and transcendence are transformed by its presence. Yet they do not encompass or define it, for none of these is established intrinsically in the perfect reality" (*MSAV* 9 ad 3–4).

We begin to get a sense of the difficulty, subtlety, and intellectual challenge of Middle Way thinking. And we should not be satisfied with an easy dismissal of these coupled thought-inversions as mere paradoxes. Ah yes, these people are saying that language is delusory, leading the intellect in a vicious circle. These paradoxes are intended to entrap the mind and inspire us to cast it away, to dwell in the ineffable silence! That is, I think, how the usual mysticism interpretation runs, missing the point entirely in its simplistic assumption that philosophical rigor is a Western invention or prerogative. The fact is that the great Indian philosophers, Nāgārjuna and Asaṅga and their followers, were extraordinary in range and depth of genius and should be recognized as champions in the arena of world-circle philosophy.

All things are Buddhahood because nonduality admits of no differentiation, certainly not between the enlightened and the unenlightened. Note that it is said it *is free from differentiation* and not that it is a oneness. This is a mistake mystics and scholars often make, taking nonduality to be monism, when it is clearly said by all nondualists that nonduality is *neither* unity *nor* multiplicity (*anekārtham anānārtham*). One has meaning only in relation to many.

Further, the ultimate reality of things, their Buddhahood or Thusness, is manifest through purification, in the fact that generations of saints, sages, and great yogis have demonstrated that it is possible to transcend passions, selfishness, delusion, and so forth. This purification in the world of defilement and affliction is taken by Vasubandhu as a manifestation of the ultimate Buddhahood.

The first sentence of the passage moves the mind into a strong critical awareness of the immanence of Buddhahood, which might bring it to a point risking complacency. Ah, all these things are impregnated with Buddhahood. There is nothing for me to do, nothing to cultivate, nothing to restrain. All is perfect, as it is . . . and so on. This kind of monistic perversion of nonduality leads nowhere, so Vasubandhu strips it away with his *in Buddhahood no thing exists with respect to its conceptually constructed reality*. That is to say, our everyday, concept-governed mode of perception and reification causes us to see a world of things that does not exist in any ultimate sense. This is not to say that things do not exist at all utterly. That would be nihilism. Things rather do not exist in the way that we habitually conceive that they do. We therefore must seek to penetrate their ultimate reality, to attain enlightenment.

So we cannot sit back with this our constructed world, neatly parceled out in our conditioned perceptions, consider it impregnated with Buddhahood, and stand complacently pat. No, we have things to do, an evolutionary destiny to fulfill through conscious striving. How do we conceive the goal? Vasubandhu continued: *Buddhahood consists of virtuous qualities, since all virtues and transcendences are transformed by its presence*.

Thus we cultivate virtue in our lives, in deed, word and thought. We must refrain from killing, stealing, sexual perversion, lying, slander, abuse, chatter, greed, malice, and delusions, to mention the obligatory moral restraints. We must cultivate the virtues of generosity, morality, tolerance, energy, meditation, and wisdom, all of them to a transcendent degree. In so doing, we participate in that Buddhahood consisting of all virtuous quali-

ties, we enjoy it in its "suchness," and we manifest it in its purifi-
catory activity.

But virtue is tricky in that it grows only insofar as it is cast
away, especially in its transcendent reaches. Thus generosity is
the foremost transcendent virtue on the bodhisattva path. It provides all things to all beings and brings all wealth to the giver.
And yet, the more intense it becomes, the less can its virtuousness
be appropriated by the generous one. For even generosity must itself be constantly given away, and the fortune that it brings must
be re-given to all living beings. Fortunately, these transcendences
are transformed by the presence of Buddhahood, thus constantly
self-emptied, constantly self-transcending.

The habitual mind tends to want to fasten itself in an ultimate state of virtue, purification, holiness, enlightenment, liberation, nirvana, or what you will. Since such fixation would destroy the energy of compassion, Vasubandhu adds a final thought:
*Yet the virtuous qualities do not define Buddhahood, since no vir-
tues or transcendences are established intrinsically in the perfect
reality.* Thus, transcendences self-transcend. Buddhahood itself,
along with all things from which it is not different, is revealed as
always something more than whatever it might be conceived to
be. The wisdom intuiting this operates as the openness to enlightenment and life as tolerable without being grasped by any conceptual construction. And this openness is the fountainhead of the
sensitivity and tact which are, respectively, the function and
competence of universal compassion.

Following Maitreya's four sentences, then, we have opened
our four avenues of thought, skirting the metaphysical extremes
of nihilism and absolutism, and the moral extremes of monistic
complacency and dualistic legalism, and have kept to the vital
Middle Way. The two aspects of Buddhahood we have been oscil-
lating between are vividly conveyed in the two extreme metaphors of the hard, bright, sterile beauty of diamonds and the dull,
obscure, fecund vitality of raindrops. This ubiquitous yet ever-
elusive Buddhahood is imagined both as a jewel mine, from
which are quarried the precious gems of Teaching that make enlightenment accessible to all living beings, and as a rain cloud
that nourishes abundant harvests of virtues in the lives of beings

sustained even in their ordinariness, yet strengthened to rise above it.

The diamond of the transcendent sustains these living beings in all their ordinariness, and the raindrops of the sacred strengthen them to rise above it.

II

Holding these two metaphors suspended in the imagination, let us pause for some conceptual clarification. I will first examine *transcendence* and *sacred* in their lives in Western English, before going on to consider their reincarnations in the English of the translation of Mahāyāna Scriptures.

The *Oxford English Dictionary* provides a number of meanings of transcendence that are surprisingly ordinary, such as excellence, extraordinariness, superiority, and so forth. More important for us is the theological meaning, as applied to Deity. In this context *transcendent* means "exalted above, distant from the universe," and is precisely the opposite of "immanent." This meaning is picked up by Kant in his use of *transcendental* for that which is apart from or beyond all experience, the opposite of the sensuous. Etymologically, from *trans-* 'beyond', and *scendere* 'to proceed', we obtain the sense of that which goes beyond, i.e., the Deity beyond the world, or the transcendental beyond sensibility, yet we note that the idea of the transcendent as not a possible object of experience, beyond comprehension, is the main thrust of both main Western usages. The term seems to have lost any sense of *movement beyond*, and rather to represent a static pole of utter extraworldliness. There seems to be no mode of contact between it and the world, even though the *directional* idea of *movement beyond* the world is central to the term.

For the sacred, the *Oxford English Dictionary* is quite restrained, mentioning only that it refers to what is favorite of the Deity, hence inviolable, or else dedicated to some religious purpose, and hence venerable. So let us consider, as a framework, Rudolf Otto's fivefold characterization of the sacred. Considering the holy to represent aesthetically the *mysterium tremendum*, he unpacks this into five qualities of the holy or sacred, the "numinous" as he calls it. The five are (1) awe-fulness, in the sense of absolute unapproachability; (2) majesty, in the sense of overpowering, crushing presence; (3) energy, in the sense of imparting a dramatic and undeniable sense of urgency through even the slightest encounter; (4) radical otherness, generating stupefying astonishment; and (5) fascination, creating joy, rapture, calm, and exuberance. From these qualities, it becomes generally apparent that the term *sacred* expresses the aesthetic quality pertaining to what is presumed to move from the transcendent back to the mundane. An actually unapproachable absolute, that is, could not be perceived at all, as such perception itself would violate its absoluteness. Thus, the transcendent cannot generate mysteries and tremors of response, but only its presumed manifestations, experienced somehow spiritually if not sensually.

Directionally then, we see the sacred as related to the movement to immanence from transcendence. Thus, a religious situation where only the absolutely transcendent was sacred would be absolutely deprived of aesthetic content, as the locus of value would be totally apart from the world, hence beyond all relationship to any living being. At the opposite pole, where only the immediate world is sacred, all experience is equally valued, there is no possibility of growth or freedom, and *sacred* loses all meaning, from loss of contrast with profane. It is interesting that, as a value term, *sacred* can only be meaningful in a system that fits somewhere between radical monism and radical dualism, both of which rob it of its value, the former by overextending it to everything, and the latter by removing it utterly from all possible worlds.

Buddhism's particular solution to this problem comes in the doctrine of nondualism, which describes reality as just as much *not one* as it is *not many*. Directly related to it is the psychological nonduality of wisdom and compassion, *prajñā* and *karuṇā*, which we can also relate to the transcendent and the sacred. Thus, wisdom sees through all appearances of the superficial reality (*saṁvṛtisatya*), probing for ultimate reality, opening up through the tolerance of inconceivability to the transcendent reality (*paramārthasatya*), reaching the utter extraworldly quiescence of emptiness, signlessness, and wishlessness in the freedom of nirvana. Compassion, on the other hand, will not rest in any self-centered peace or wisdom, remains sensitive to other beings' sufferings, and reaches out through liberative techniques (*upāya*) to help other beings also to reach freedom. Wisdom fulfills one's own selfish aims, reaching final fruition in the Body of Truth (*dharmakāyā*), whereas compassion fulfills the aims of others, reaching final fruition in the Bodies of Beatitude (*Saṁbbhoga*) and Emanated Incarnation (*nirmāṇa*). Wisdom by itself is dead, leading to realms of nihilistic trances, and compassion by itself is trapped in the life cycle with suffering beings, having no way to alleviate their pains and make good its own motivating power which is to remove their suffering and give them happiness.

Now let us work on the Sanskrit words that can and have been rendered by transcendence and sacred. First is Sanskrit *lokottara*, literally 'beyond this world', which could also be rendered simply as 'transmundane'. Related to this meaning is the idea of Sanskrit *niryāna*, 'escape' or 'renunciation', the determination to transcend the world and escape from its pains.

Next in line is Sanskrit *pāramitā*, literally a 'having gone beyond, reached the other shore,' which is perfectly rendered by transcendence. There are six transcendences, listed above as generosity, morality, tolerance, energy, meditation, and wisdom. What makes them transcendent (transcendent generosity as opposed to ordinary generosity, for example) is that they are virtuous actions performed with no apprehension of the "three spheres" (*trimaṇḍala*) which are agent, patient, the act itself. One thus goes beyond the conceptual appropriation of these virtues as virtues, hence transcending any sense of virtuousness of generosity itself as well as stinginess through generosity transcendent. A final word in this category is *niḥśreyasa*, literally 'summum bonum,' which is a classification of goal and doctrine paired with *abhyudaya*, literally 'high estate', the pair renderable as transcendence and ascendance. The above four uses all embrace the sense of transcendence as a movement beyond the world to something other, greater, and higher.

A second set of terms can then be shown to correspond to the more objectified meaning connoted by *transcendental*, something to which one moves beyond the world. This type of something is usually described in negational terms, since normal positive reference cannot so well refer to "that" beyond normal discriminative ken. Thus, when one treads the transmundane (*lokottara*) path, cultivates renunciation (*niryāna*), practices the transcendences (*pāramitā*) of generosity, etc., and attains the transcendent (*nihśreyasa*) supreme good, one achieves *mokṣa*, freedom, transcendence of bondage of the world, *nirodha*, cessation of suffering, nirvana or extinction of all sorrow, and so forth. All of these terms for the indescribable experience of the transcendent are technically equated with ultimate reality (*paramārthasatya*) and its numerous synonyms. It is perfect (*pariniṣpanna*) as opposed to relative (*paratantra*), uncreated (*asaṃskṛta*), selflessness (*nairātmyā*), wishlessness (*apraṃhita*), signlessness (*animittā*), and emptiness (*śūnyatā*). All of these terms, to forestall the tendency of objectification, describe Transcendent Reality by means of absolute negation (*prasajyaniṣedha*); that is, negation that merely negates its negatee, implying no positive fact in its place, as opposed to implicative negation (*paryudāsaniṣedha*) which affirms a second fact while negating its negatee. These two are sometimes conveyed as exclusion negation and choice negation, respectively.

Emptiness or *śūnyatā* has attracted considerable attention, and so we should go more fully into it, to emphasize that the Mahāyāna philosophers fully acknowledge the utter transcendentality of ultimate reality.

The most common expansion of emptiness is into sixteen varieties: internal emptiness, external emptiness, internal and external emptiness, emptiness emptiness, greatness emptiness, ultimate emptiness, created emptiness, uncreated emptiness, extreme-free emptiness, eternity emptiness, nonrefusal emptiness, intrinsic reality emptiness, universal emptiness, intrinsic identity emptiness, nonperception emptiness, and nothingness emptiness.

Internal emptiness refers to the lack of intrinsic reality in personal faculties, the five senses and the mentality. It is taught first to inculcate awareness of the perishable and causally relative nature of one's physical and mental self, devoid of any extraneous inner agency naïvely assumed to anchor their operations.

External emptiness refers to the lack of intrinsic reality in the objects of those faculties, form, and so on being empty of intrinsically real form, and so on. *Internal and external emptiness* refers to emptiness contemplated in subjects and objects simultaneously.

Emptiness emptiness refers to the lack of intrinsic reality in emptiness itself, in that it is only a relational absence of intrinsic reality in things and not itself intrinsically real. This is taught in order to eliminate the habit of an intellectual perception of a substantial emptiness. This emptiness is particularly important to refute the nihilistic misinterpretation of emptiness, as well as to cure the ascetic's very dangerous addiction to nihilistic meditational experience.

Greatness emptiness is lack of intrinsic reality in all directions and immensities, inculcating awareness of their relativity to particular perspectives. It is taught especially to cure the addiction to the substantiality of the meditative realm of immeasurability attained in the contemplations of love, compassion, joy, and equanimity.

Ultimate emptiness teaches the lack of intrinsic reality in the ultimate reality, otherwise called nirvana, Truth, and so on, inculcating an awareness that any reified ultimate is nothing more than a nonultimate concept of the opposite of everyday, relational nonultimacy. It is taught especially to cure addiction to any intellectual perception of a substantial nirvana. This is extremely interesting in revealing the transcendentality *qua* incomprehensibility of the ultimate reality, in that any conceivable, referentially accessible ultimate is empty of its own ultimacy in its intrinsic reality.

Created emptiness simply refers to the lack of intrinsic reality in causal things, they being empty because of their conditional relativity. This is the usual emptiness we think of through the example of the emptiness of a table, a chariot, etc., when we can find no intrinsically real chariot among all the parts and components whose functional assemblage we tend to designate as *chariot*. Note that far from annihilating things, this emptiness confirms their causal conditionality.

Uncreated emptiness refers to the emptiness of space, nirvana, the unborn, the undestroyed — all the negative abstractions we can conceive as the opposite of the relative created things of the world. It is especially useful to cure philosophers' addictions to abstractions, universals, and other mental constructs which they tend to reify and by which their intelligence becomes bewitched.

Extreme-free emptiness refers to the lack of intrinsic reality in the state beyond extremisms such as absolutism or nihilism, the emptiness of state of moderation, transconceptual states beyond binary paradoxes. While little is said about this emptiness, it may safely be considered a cure for the addiction to the intellectual perception of a substantial, transrational, intuitive, enlightenment state.

Eternity emptiness refers to the lack of intrinsic reality of time, and is critical of the reification of any timeless, dreamlike state of being in any beginningless and endless or eternal saṁsāra.

Nonrefusal emptiness refers to the fact that there is no intrinsic reality in any state of all-embracing nonrefusal of all phenomena, such as a monistic conception of the ultimate would predicate of the undifferentiated whole.

Intrinsic reality emptiness is just the usual emptiness, consisting of the selflessness of persons and things. Intrinsic reality (*svabhāva*) here means a reality in things that is unchanging, independent, and real, such as that assumed at the core of each thing by the naïve realist.

Universal emptiness is the emptiness of all things, physical and mental. *Intrinsic identity emptiness* refers to all things' lack of intrinsic identifiability (*svalakṣaṇa*), that fixed identity within them that anchors the referentiality of their names.

Nonperception emptiness refers to the emptiness of any state of nonperception. This is particularly noteworthy in our context here, since an essential component of the transcendent is its incomprehensibility to human experience, an acknowledgement of which might well be expressed as a noncomprehension, a nonperception. This emptiness then is a criticism of, or cure for, addiction to any intellectual perception of a reified, substantial state of nonperception, as some sort of mystical encounter with the unencounterable. Finally, the *nothingness emptiness* is taught in criticism of the reification of nothingness by indicating that nothing is only meaningful in relation to something, and is precisely nothing in itself.

The purpose of the expansion of the concept is to expand its

critical range, to apply it as a remedy to a wider variety of attitu-
dinal distortions, ideological absolutisms, reificational experiences, or views, as they are called in Mahāyāna thought. Hence,
there can be no compromise with the Kantian sense of transcendent as not experientially accessible, or as conceptually incomprehensible. The radical transcendentality of the ultimate is rig-
orously established, and all counterviews criticized in detail. It is
even called inconceivable, incomprehensible, objectless, and so
forth. And there is even a caution against reification of that
nonperception!

That having been established, there is a crucial difference
between this Mahāyāna Transcendent Reality and the Kantian
one, or even the pre-Kantian Western theological transcendent,
which as the *Oxford English Dictionary* says was fundamentally
other, totally apart from the world. This difference is clearly conveyed in the fact that the transcendent reality for Mahayanists is a
knowable object or fact (*jñeya*), just as much as is the mundane
reality. That is to say, without absolutistically reifying incomprehensibility, the incomprehensible, while it cannot be grasped, is
encounterable in a nongrasping way. This is accomplished by
Mahāyāna philosophers, starting with the Buddha, by their discovery of a higher faculty in human beings. This faculty they var-
iously called wisdom (*prajñā*), holy intuition (*āryajñāna*), and
genius (*dhī*), distinguishing it from consciousness (*vijñāna*), intelligence, (*vijñapti, buddhi*), intellect (*mati*), cognition (*saṁjñā*),
mentality (*manas*), and experience (*saṁvedana*), to name but a
few of the cognitive terms so abundant in Indian thought, especially in the fertile Buddhist psychologies.

All of the latter faculties operate on the mundane level and
are infected by the primordial misknowledge (*avidyā*) that naïvely
presumes intrinsic reality in things merely conditional, seeing
that hypostatized essence as purity, permanency, self, and happiness. And it is in terms of such mundane consciousness that the
transcendent, ultimate reality is inconceivable and incomprehensible. For, ultimate reality transcends the world given to conditioned perception, and cannot be brought into that world, hence
cannot be experienced in mundane experience.

However, one can cultivate a tolerance (*kṣānti*) of that inconceivability. One can become critical of the naïve notions that, transmitted linguistically and culturally, anchor the misknowledge of reality that restricts beings to a superficial existence in cyclic life, such notions as purity, happiness, substantiality, independence, peace, as well as I (self) and mine (property). Through cultivation of critical insight into the conventionality and superficiality of these constructs, one begins to strip away the conceptual and perceptual conditioning that molds one's experience, and begins to develop an intuitive awareness of unmediated reality, of ultimate reality of the profound depth of experience that lies beyond the superficial notional universe. This intuitive, critical awareness is the above *prajñā* — which literally means 'intense' (*pra-*) 'knowing' (*jñā*) — and this wisdom can experience, understand, encounter the transcendent reality. This wisdom is itself transcendent in a sense, but this we will save for later.

So the difference between the Mahāyāna critical philosophers and the critical philosophers of eighteenth-century Europe is that the Mahāyāna philosophers did not consider human potential limited to given mundane cognitive faculties. It is not irremediably imprisoned in the experience allowed by its aspect of *tremendum;* it is *adbhuta* 'awesome'; it is *anuttara* 'beyond which there is nothing'. It is *parama-artha* 'the supreme object'; it is *samyaktva* 'perfection'; it is *prakṛtinivṛta* 'naturally extinct'. Personified, it is the Body of Truth (*Dharmakāya*), seen here in realization as *Anuttarasamyaksaṃbuddha* 'Unexcelled, Perfectly Enlightened', *Devātideva* 'the God beyond the gods', *Anupama* 'uncomparable', expressed in early Buddhist art by the fact that a blank space was always left in scenes where the Śākyamuni Buddha should have been.

For the second aesthetic element, majesty is conveyed in the names *Bhagavān* 'Lord', *Jina* 'Victor', *Mārajit* 'Devil-Beater', and so forth, all invoking a Buddha's triumphal, terrific manifestation as overwhelming the forces of evil. This aspect of the deep reality in person is said to be *bhīrubhīṣaṇaṃ* 'terrifying to the timid', and the Buddha in this aspect is compared to a Lion (*Narasimha*), Bull (*Purushārshabu*), Great Elephant, or even deadly Serpent. It is also expressed in Buddhist art by the terrific forms called *iṣ-tāṃdevatā*, often confused by Westerners with demons, when they precisely represent the conquest of the demonic. Over-powering majesty is also presented to the imagination in the opening scenes of all Mahāyāna scriptures, wherein the Buddha invariably emits a ray of light from his tongue, forehead, heart, or *ushnisha* (crown-protuberance), that illuminates the entire assembly, often granting his audience some galaxy-spanning vision of countless other world-systems containing countless other beings and Buddhas teaching them and emitting rays of light. One scripture particularly rich in visionary material, the *Gandavyūha*, describes how at this initial moment all members of the assembled multitudes perceived their past lives back for innumerable aeons, and perceived their future lives as well, up to and including all their activities of being perfectly enlightened Buddhas, incarnating, growing up, renouncing the world, defeating Māna, attaining enlightenment, turning the wheel of Dharma, attaining *parinirvāṇa*. They thus visionarily saw how every moment of time was contained in that very moment, and yet each moment was itself intact.

Third, the element of urgency, or intense energy, is conveyed as *mahākaruṇā* 'great compassion', symbolized as *vajra* 'thunderbolt' as well as 'diamond'. Buddha is also said to be *Daśabala* 'One Who Has Ten Powers'.

The energetic activity of a Buddha through his Body of Emanated Incarnations (*nirmāṇakāya*) is conveyed by Maitreyanatha; "Through many hundreds of doors, He manifests somewhere the turning of the Wheel of Dharma, somewhere else birth and disappearance, somewhere else perfect enlightenment, and somewhere else final nirvana, (all simultaneously) and over and over again. He does not budge from That Place yet He brings about everything" (*MSA* 9.51).

Next we come to the two *mysterium* elements: utter otherness and fascination (perhaps better charisma). The wholly other aspect seems to return again to transcendence with its sense of being apart from the world, and here this is conveyed by the famous *gambhīrya* 'profundity', the ultimate conveyed aesthetically as a sense of unfathomable ineffability, nondual, as inaccessible to silence as to eloquence. Technically, we can fit here the important *tathātā* 'thusness, suchness', often conflated with *tattva* 'thatness' above, but actually quite different. *Thatness* points at the inex-pressible mean, approaching from the pole of immanence, where each thing in just its own *it-ness* is ultimate, is real. *Thusness*, composed by taking the word for bare relationship *tathā* (liter-ally, 'like that'), hence *such* or *thus*, giving it an abstract nominal ending to convey the indescribable bare *otherness* of each aspect of reality. Each thing is like something else, like ultimate reality, that is, like what cannot be said, just that it is such or thus. It thus indicates the differential nature of even bare perception, that even raw givenness is not without an automatic act of conceptual discrimination.

Personifying this ineffable quality of reality experienced as ultimately other in itself, there is the important Buddha named *Tathāgata*, literally *tathātā* '*thusness*', *and āgata* 'realized', hence, The One Who Realized Thusness. This name conveys powerfully the sacredness of any Buddha in that, whether coming or going in the service of living beings, he is unmoved from his realization of the transcendent Truth. Inconceivably, he remains utterly tran-scendent, while apparently involved in the world for the benefit and liberation of all beings. It is this unique quality that makes a Buddha fascinating or charismatic, as beings are attracted by his stability, ultimacy, peace, and calm, as he seems only there for them, with no tremor of being there for himself, as it were. An ex-traordinary verse from Maitreya's *Ornament*, illustrating a Bud-dha's ultimate inactivity in activity, and his compelling charisma, is worth quoting here: "The Dharma was not, in fact, taught by the Lord, as each must realize it individually (for himself). How-ever, the Compassionate One, like a boa-constrictor, attracts peo-ple with the venomous drool of His persuasive teachings, making them fall into the gaping mouth of His own peace, which is exten-sively pure, universal, and inexhaustible" (*MSA* 12.2).

In sum, we find that all the elements discerned by Otto are uncannily present, although the Mahayanists keep dualism balanced by nondualism, after having used it to correct naïve mo-nism. Hence, the terrible otherness, thusness, of transcendental-ity of Truth is tempered by the gentle thatness of immanentality of Compassion.

What finally partakes of and manifests this nondual sacredness of the mean between extremes is *ārya* 'holy' (being the trans-valuation of a social and racial value term into a spiritual value term, just as *brahma* was transvalued from 'divine,' in a priestly sense, into 'pure', in an ascetic sense). And what represents this sacredness to sentient beings — makes the inaccessible accessible, as it were — is *ratna* 'jewel', the three holies of all Buddhism being the three jewels of Buddha, the Enlightened One; Dharma, his teachings; and Sangha, the community practicing it.

SELECTED BIBLIOGRAPHY

Candrakīrti. *Madhyamakāvātara*. Tibetan translation edited by L. de la Vallee Poussin, *Biblio c Buddhica*. Petersburg, 1910. Cited as *MA*.

Maitreyanatha. *Ornament of the Scriptures of the Universal Vehicle*. Edghill translation edited by Robert Thurman. Amherst, Mass.: American Institute of Buddhist Studies, 1980. Cited as *MSA*.

Nāgārjuna. *Wisdom Fundamental Middle Way Stanzas*. Translated by K. Inada. Tokyo: Hokuseido, 1972. Cited as *MMK*.

Otto, Rudolf. *The Idea of the Holy*. Translated by John W. Harvey. London: Oxford University Press, 1975.

Thurman, Robert. *The Holy Teaching of Vimalakīrti*. University Park, Pa.: Pennsylvania State University Press, 1976. Cited as *VKN*.

Vasubandhu. *Commentary on Ornament of the Scriptures of the Universal Vehicle*. (See Maitreyanatha's *Ornament* above.) Cited as *MSAV*.

6

The Problem of Transcendence in Comparative Religion: The Quest for the Sacred in Kamakura (Japanese) Buddhism

ROBERT LEE

IN A STUDY OF *transcendence* and *the sacred* in Japanese Buddhism there arises immediately a severe theoretical problem. Western theories of religion based upon the twin concepts of transcendence and the sacred imply a dualism, such as the distinction between the transcendent and the mundane or the sacred and the profane. Japanese theories require a strict nondualism, such as in *hongakushisō*, literally a theory based upon primordial or original enlightenment, a monistic concept to be described later. While both types of theory may be faithful to the religious experiences of their respective constituencies, obviously neither theory without modification is useful for the comparative study of religion. Hence, the first task in this paper will be to reconsider the Western understanding of the phenomenon of the sacred and its correlative meaning of transcendence.

Secondly, the Japanese Buddhist experience needs to be understood in terms of its social and historical contexts. Too often Western scholars limit their understanding of the Buddhist experience to that of Indian (primitive) Buddhism or that of the popular Zen Buddhism espoused by D. T. Suzuki. In more general terms, as Eliade has so vividly demonstrated, in the history of re-

ligions the phenomenon of the sacred and the correlative understanding of transcendence can neither be limited to a particular
time and place nor confined to a particular object or symbol but,
nevertheless, are manifested and experienced in space, time, and
objects or symbols.[1] Because of this cultural and historical relativity of the manifestation of the sacred, there arise in the history of
religions a continual quest for the locus of the sacred and a perennial problem of the meaning of transcendence mediated in relative objects or symbols. In this paper, the study of the development of Kamakura Buddhism in thirteenth-century Japan is seen
as an illustration in the history of religions of a historical quest for
the sacred and for the meaning of transcendence — a process that
was begun in India, radically transformed in China, and reformed in Japan.

Finally, this paper will conclude with observations on differences and preferences in theories and interpretations which again
may reflect the continuing quest for personal meaning (transcendence) and self-identity (the sacred) in contemporary Japan.

I

The Western understanding of the twin concepts of transcendence and the sacred is dependent upon the theories developed by such theorists of religion as Rudolf Otto, Mircea Eliade,
and Emile Durkheim. Otto defines the experience of the sacred
by contrasting it with the experience of the profane or ordinary
everyday existence, especially by emphasizing its "wholly other"
(*ganz andere*) quality.[2] Eliade, following Otto, speaks of "the
abyss that divides the two modalities of experience — sacred and
profane,"[3] and states that one "becomes aware of the sacred because it manifests itself, shows itself, as something wholly different from the profane."[4] According to Durkheim:

> Since the idea of the sacred is always and everywhere sepa-
> rated from the idea of the profane in the thought of men,
> and since we picture a sort of logical chasm between the
> two, the mind irresistibly refuses to allow the two corre-

sponding things to be confounded, or even to be merely put
in contact with each other; for such a promiscuity, or even
too direct a contiguity, would contradict too violently the
dissociation of these ideas in the mind.[5]

From this understanding of the sacred with its emphasis
upon the logical chasm or the abyss between the sacred and the
profane, Western thinkers develop a paradigm for understanding
religious experience. For the devotee this sharp differentiation
between the sacred and the profane leads to a clear devaluation of
the profane or the realm of everyday human existence and correlatively to a high valuation of the sacred, now defined as the realm
of the transcendent, the "wholly other." Although everyday
human existence is likewise sharply differentiated from the sacred
or radical transcendence, the sacred or the experience of the
"wholly other" becomes available to persons in what Eliade terms
a "hierophany," a revelatory or salvific experience, in which the
sacred becomes immanent in but never identical to the profane.
As described by Eliade:

> The sacred tree, the sacred stone are not adored as stones or
> trees; they are worshipped precisely because they are
> *hierophanies*, because they show something that is no longer
> stone or tree but the *sacred*, the *ganz andere*.[6]

According to this paradigm the experience of the "wholly
other" or radical transcendence leads the devotee or believer to
experience an equally radical devaluation of everyday human existence in the world of family, tribe, or community. In a sense this
radical denial brings freedom, freedom from all ascribed social
identities. Indeed, for the first time, a personal or individuated
self arises independent of its social nexus. Further, according to
this paradigm, the experience of the sacred as hierophany is an in-
tegrating experience in which the devotee finds union or the right
relationship with the sacred, a revelatory or salvific experience in
which he or she now acquires a new personal identity that transcends everyday social identity.

To summarize: The experience of the sacred as a radical
transcendence is a process of sharp differentiation—the sacred

from the profane, God from human, the self from society — or, in other terms, a process of freedom and the individuation of the self. The experience of the sacred as immanence in a hierophany is a process of integration or reintegration, such as in the harmony of humankind and the universe, the redemption of individual and society, the salvation of the self who acquires a new identity often in the context of a new social order.

Although this paradigm, especially in the work of Eliade, is based upon a profusion of examples taken from a wide variety of primitive and archaic religions, not surprisingly it also accords well with the biblical and especially the Christian theological understanding of religious experience. God and humankind in the biblical tradition are sharply differentiated in terms of God as eternal creator and mortals as temporal creatures. The Christian doctrine of creation functions to guard against any attempt to identify God with creation (*creatio ex nihilo*). Although God alone is the ultimate source and sustainer of the world, he nevertheless transcends creation. Correlatively, the creatures then have an independent, although limited, existence alongside the creator. This differentiation between God and mortals is reinforced by the fall, which alienates human persons not only from God but also from their own world of nature and fellow humans. Some theologians have also argued that the fall is not all evil but is actually the development of the autonomous self, the individuated being. Further, following the paradigm, differentiation is followed by integration; radically transcendent deity becomes available to radically negated human existence. In Christian theology, God becomes incarnate in Christ to offer redemption and salvation to otherwise hopelessly negated human existence. In Christ humankind is integrated into the divine order and acquires a new identity and a new way of life, namely, to have dominion over the world.[7]

Such a paradigm describes the human being as an autonomous individual with a highly motivated will to dominate the social and natural order and indeed threatens those with a different primordial religious experience. Such Western categories as transcendence and the sacred are too dualistic in contrast to the nondualistic nature of Japanese religion. Japanese apologists such as

Masao Abe and D. T. Suzuki in their critique of Western dualism prefer to define reality in terms of the slogan of "not-two," that is, one-in-two and two-in-one.[8] These cryptic formulas may be better understood by examining a doctrinal expression of these slogans in the theory of primordial enlightenment or *hongakushisō*.

The Japanese term *hongaku* is difficult to translate since its usage can extend from the personal to the cosmological, and the theory itself has a historical development that extends from India to China and finally to Japan. The literal English translation of the term is usually 'original' or 'primordial enlightenment', *original* in the sense of innate, intrinsic, or essential. Thus the expression can mean that the Buddha nature is innate in every individual being or that the Buddha nature is pervasive in all of reality. Consequently, on the personal level every individual being is immediately pure and impure or enlightened and defiled, and on the social and cosmic levels all reality is simultaneously permanent and provisional. What is affirmed in both instances is both the differentiation and the unity of reality; hence, one-in-two and two-in-one; reality is therefore nondual.

The above description of nondualism, of course, cannot be limited to Japanese Buddhism, since such theories were already present in Indian Buddhist thought. To understand the distinctiveness of the Japanese doctrine of *hongaku*, we need to review briefly the development of the meaning of enlightenment in the history of Buddhist thought.

II

Instead of a story of creation-and-fall to depict the condition of human existence, primitive Buddhism posits three marks or characteristics of existence to describe causally conditioned phenomena or *saṁsāra:* namely, that (1) all things in this world are impermanent, that is, all things are arising and passing away (*anicca*); (2) all things are unsatisfying or cause suffering (*dukkha*); and (3) all things are nonsubstantial or, more specifically, there is no immutable entity called the self (*anattā*). Implied in the above marks of existence is that human existence is causally conditioned. Men and women through sense faculties receive impressions which produce pleasurable or painful feelings. Ego-consciousness then arises and generates cravings or desires which lead to grasping. What persons crave is eternal happiness, but the things from which they desire such happiness are themselves impermanent and hence lead to suffering or dissatisfaction. Furthermore, primitive Buddhism rejects the idea of a permanent self, such as the *ātman* in the Upanishadic tradition, because such conceptions are another form of craving and grasping for eternity. Such craving could only lead to selfishness and egoism and in the end to dissatisfaction. In short, human beings are hapless victims of obsessions.

The answer of primitive Buddhism to the plight of human existence is enlightenment or nirvana, a state to be contrasted with *saṁsāra*. The human problem is ignorance of the true conditions of human existence, for example, the intrusion of ego-consciousness. Through mental concentration we can learn to control our minds so that when external objects impinge upon the senses we can prevent the intrusion of the ego-consciousness that would generate cravings and attachment to things in this world. This elimination of ego-consciousness, following a causal pattern, produces revulsion with regard to things earlier grasped as being substantial. Revulsion produces detachment, and detachment produces freedom. Such a person is enlightened, feeling secure and at peace in the midst of a confusing and destructive world.[9]

Because primitive Buddhism focused primarily upon the religious experience of enlightenment, it left the speculative understanding of this experience undefined. For example, what was the relation between nirvana and *saṁsāra*? The two were clearly differentiated, and within that context nirvana could be said to transcend *saṁsāra*. In experiential terms, the devotee did aspire to move from the state of *saṁsāra* to that of nirvana. Nevertheless, whether reality was one or two, or neither one nor two, was left ambiguous, perhaps deliberately.

Early Mahāyāna Buddhists in India sought to eliminate any felt sense of dualism by clearly affirming that nirvana is *saṁsāra* and *saṁsāra* is nirvana. In their polemical debates to affirm the nondual nature of reality, they introduced the concept of emptiness (*śūnya*). *Saṁsāra* and nirvana are one because both are characterized as empty. *Saṁsāra* is empty because it comes into existence as a result of causes and conditions, and hence has no independent existence of its own. Nirvana is also empty because it is devoid of all discriminations, particularities, and definitions (that is, it cannot be predicated). Therefore, it could be argued, nirvana and *saṁsāra* are the same reality, or more precisely, they represent a not-two or nondual reality, which at the same time is differentiated in terms of religious experience.[10]

In these debates the term *emptiness* functioned as a regulative idea, a negative metacritical principle, that is, as a nonreferring word, for "emptiness too is empty." At the same time the term implied a negative concept of transcendence and pointed to an undefinable and indescribable ultimate reality, a reality that transcended all linguistic expression but, nevertheless, could be experienced. Thus, the idea of emptiness came to depict reality as not only nondual but also nonconceptual and differentiated from or transcending worldly experience.[11] Consequently, the negative connotations of the symbol of emptiness led to the quest for the sacred or the enlightenment experience in India in the form of a strong negation of this-worldly existence.

In China such philosophical schools as the T'ien-t'ai and the Huā-yen transformed Indian Buddhism. Both schools used Indian Buddhist philosophical categories. The T'ien-t'ai was based upon the Lotus sūtra (*Saddharma-puṇḍarīki-sūtra*) and the Huā-yen upon the Garland sūtra (*Avataṁsaka-sūtra*). Both schools constructed a distinctively Chinese view of reality by transforming the Indian negative dialectic into a more positive harmonizing principle, typical of Chinese philosophy.[12]

For example, the T'ien-t'ai school established the doctrine of the threefold truth: empty, provisional, and the middle path. They argued that because all things have no independent reality of their own, they are empty. Nevertheless, emptiness does not mean nothingness. Even though a thing is empty, it has temporary or provisional existence as phenomenon. The synthesis of emptiness and provisional existence is the truth of the middle way, namely, that every reality is simultaneously empty and provisional. Here, the middle way does not mean a third, something between the two, but a unity or totality that both transcends and permeates the two. In other terms, the middle way emphasizes the totality and the mutual identification of the whole and its parts. Emptiness is in the provisional, and the provisional is in emptiness; there is no emptiness apart from the provisional. There is the total interpenetration of universal emptiness and the provisional or particular phenomenon. According to this theory, the cosmos and all the Buddhas are present in a single grain of sand.

Whereas the T'ien-t'ai school focused upon the relation of the universal and the particular, the Chinese Huā-yen school clarified the relationship between one particular phenomenon and another. The Huā-yen school taught that emptiness has two aspects: the static aspect as universal principle (*li*) and the dynamic aspect as particular form (*shih*). As before, the universal and the particular are interfused. Since the universal as principle has no form of its own, it is manifested only in particular phenomena. Correlatively, all phenomena are manifestations of principle. Further, because every event or thing in the phenomenal world represents the universal completely and perfectly, all phenomena are mutually identified with one another. Therefore, on the one hand, particular phenomena remain differentiated, that is, distinct from other phenomena and dissimilar from the universal; and, on the other hand, all phenomena are unified in perfect harmony as manifestations of the one immutable universal.

The consequence of doctrinal innovation in China led to a transformation of the function of the Indian dialectic of negation. In India the concept of emptiness functioned to devalue all mundane existence, to destroy all conceptual approaches to concrete existence, and to deny all linguistic access to the ultimate or absolute. In China the concept of emptiness became descriptive of the true mode of (phenomenal) existence. Instead of the negation of mundane things and experiences, the idea of emptiness functioned to sacralize phenomenal existence, that is, to affirm it absolutely.

This Chinese transformation of Indian Buddhism led to a shift in both the locus of the sacred and the meaning of transcendence. Instead of seeking the ultimate or the absolute in personal experiences that transcended mundane social existence, the Chinese discovered the sacred within everyday existence. Now the everyday life of the laity was part of the life of the Buddha. Correlatively, the Chinese ideas of transcendence no longer denied but now affirmed the sacredness of the mundane world, because the Buddha nature is found everywhere, even in the tiniest particle of sand. In Weberian terms the Chinese transformed the Indian preference for an abstract, otherworldly conception to a concrete, this-worldly conception of reality.

Although the ingredients for the Chinese Buddhist world view described above were available, or at least germinal, in Indian Mahāyāna Buddhist texts,[13] these ideas did not become popular or central until the Chinese historical developments of the fifth and sixth centuries. These ideas especially came together in a very popular and influential text, *The Awakening of Faith*, attributed to the Indian poet Aśvaghoṣa, but probably produced by some anonymous writer in the fifth or sixth century in China.[14] Along with teachings of the Huā-yen and T'ien-t'ai schools, this text provided a world view that revealed the absolute in the temporal and mundane order and integrated the particulars of this mundane order into the universal absolute. Because reality was seen as both nondual and an organic unity of its parts and the whole, the locus of reality now easily coincided with the whole social order. Hence, in the reunification of China by the rulers of the Sui Dynasty (581–604), such texts and teaching provided the ideological basis for unifying the different races and cultures in diverse areas into a vast empire.[15]

When this Chinese world view was transmitted to Japan, it developed into the *Tendai Hongaku Shisō*, the Tendai concept of primordial enlightenment. According to Tamura:

The *Tendai Hongaku Shisō* brought original enlightenment to its climax, and gave it the meaning of absolute enlightenment transcending the relativity of enlightenment and defilement or Buddhahood and manhood. It may be defined as absolute monism, for all things of the actual world came to be absolutely affirmed as identical with those of the enlightened world. For example, man is regarded as Buddha himself or an actual manifestation of Buddha, because there is neither correlation nor difference between Buddha and man. In the same way defilement is regarded as equivalent to enlightenment, the actual world to the eternal world, and the present moment to eternal time. . . . It can be said that the *Tendai Hongaku Shisō* broke through the limitations of ordinary thinking and reached the zenith of philosophical principle.[16]

If we can bypass for the moment this claim of a breakthrough of the limitations of ordinary thinking to the zenith of philosophical principle, we need to remember that pre-Kamakura Buddhism in Japan functioned primarily to safeguard the nation from the forces of evil and to insure the prosperity of the nation. It was not primarily a religion for personal salvation. Hence, the Chinese teachings that identified the phenomenal world, in this instance the nation of Japan, with the absolute, served well to legitimize, if not sacralize, the state. In this process the issue of personal enlightenment became subordinated to that of national salvation.

III

In Japanese history the rupture of this monistic identification of the nation with the absolute came with Hōnen (1133–1212), the first of the Kamakura reformers.[17] Hōnen, for the sake of personal salvation, not only repudiated the Tendai world view but actually broke from the state-sponsored Buddhism to establish a new sectarian Buddhism. He sharply differentiated the phenomenal world from the universal realm by juxtaposing *jōdo* (the Pure Land or realm of enlightenment) with *edō* (the land of defilement, his own world), and *busshin* (Buddha mind) with *bonshin* (earthly mind). He emphasized the distance between Buddha and humankind by maintaining that Amida (Buddha) was on the yonder shore (*higan*) and humankind was on the nearer shore (*shigan*) and that humankind and Amida could not be united in this life. Clearly, *Hōnen* fractured the Tendai monistic *hongaku* theory by transferring the union of humankind and Buddha chronologically to the next life and spatially to the yonder shore.

In short, Hōnen provided the Japanese a radical world-rejecting religion that became the basis for a religion of personal salvation.

Hōnen's radical reinterpretation of Tendai Buddhism was based upon two related insights: a prophetic understanding of his sociopolitical milieu as *mappō*, the degenerate age, and a personal understanding of the depravity of the human condition. Hōnen shared with his contemporaries the Buddhist notion of a degenerate age in which the teachings of the Buddha would no longer be viable for salvation. He had witnessed the feudal wars that had traversed the nation and had transformed the fortunes of monks, aristocrats, warriors, and peasants alike. Further, he was aware of the internal factionalism and corruption within the monastery at Mount Hiei from which he finally fled. At the same time he was personally aware of the meaninglessness of the traditional acts of piety for the purpose of accumulating merit for national salvation, especially when his own salvation was at stake. He finally drew the conclusion that in the age of *mappō* the traditional path of severe disciplines, called the holy way, to attain enlightenment, was no longer operative. He reasoned that if the difficult path of the holy way was impossible in the age of *mappō*, he would seek out the easy path, the way of the *nembutsu.*

The recitation of the *nembutsu* (the invocation of the name of Amida Buddha) meant that Hōnen had given up reliance on his own merits (*jiriki* or self-power) — useless anyway in the age of *mappō* — and turned to the mercies of Amida Buddha, to reliance on other, more effective power (*tariki*), specifically the power of Amida's original vow. According to the Pure Land tradition, Amida had vowed as a bodhisattva in the eighteenth or original vow that all living beings, except those who had committed atrocities or had slandered the teachings of the Buddha, could be born into the Pure Land if they only so desired with sincere faith by calling this desire to mind as few as ten times. In other words, the eighteenth vow assured that even a common person with evil passions would be released from his or her karmic sins by reciting the name of Amida and at death would be born immediately into the Pure Land. Therefore, in 1175 in a decisive act of faith Hōnen abandoned the Tendai Buddhism of Mount Hiei and selected the Pure Land teachings as the exclusive path to attain salvation, an act that later led to the founding of a new and independent (sectarian) Buddhism in Japan.

Hōnen remains an anomaly in Japanese history. Japanese historians feel a certain uneasiness about a Japanese otherworldly religion, especially when it can be compared favorably with Western religion, for example, the Protestant Reformation. They point to the abuses that arose from the undeveloped thought of Hōnen, and they are quick to assert (correctly) that the succeeding wave of reformers, Shinran (1173–1262), Nichiren (1222–1282), and Dōgen (1200–1253), all returned to a *hongaku* type of world view, even though each selected a different tenet of Tendai teaching as the exclusive path to salvation. All of this led to further fragmentation of the unity of the earlier established state religion of Mount Hiei. These three figures, rather than Hōnen, remain the heroes of contemporary Japanese in their search for personal meaning in the context of an overpowering, if not sacred, social order. To these figures[18] we need to turn to examine how the locus of the sacred (*hongaku*) and transcendence are relocated in order to provide personal meaning that is not absorbed into the social nexus.

Because Hōnen in his simple faith and teaching left severe ambiguities which often led to abuses in practice, Shinran, his disciple, worked these out doctrinally and in practice for the Japanese Pure Land tradition. As discussed earlier, Hōnen fractured the monistic world view of Tendai Buddhism by sharply differentiating the Pure Land and the defiled land. At the same time he sought to link these two realms by the causal power of Amida's vow from one side and the sincere aspiration of humankind in the invocation of Amida's name from the other side. For Hōnen the answer to that human plight was simple — recite the *nembutsu* with purity of motivation and unquestioning trust in the promise of Amida as revealed in his original vow. According to Hōnen:

> Birth into the Pure Land is certain when you think it so, but also uncertain when you think it so. . . . And so a man who would be born into the Pure Land must concentrate his energy upon believing that he will of a certainty be so born.[19]

In his experience Shinran, however, sensed an inconsistency — in the age of *mappō* how can an evil person ever have a sincere heart or sufficient faith, since he or she is incapable of conceiving of a good deed, much less doing one sincere act:

> I know absolutely nothing about good and evil! If I were able to know good so thoroughly that the Tathāgata would recognize it in his mind as good, then I could say I know good. Were I able to know evil so thoroughly that the Tathā-gata would recognize it as evil, then I could say I know evil. We are ordinary men possessed of evil passions and our world is the burning house of transiency; hence, all things are entirely empty and nonsense and not true. The *Nem-butsu* alone is true.[20]

Shinran therefore concluded that it was not the recitation of the *nembutsu* many times (*tanen*) that was the cause of birth in the Pure Land.

Like Hōnen, Shinran maintained the sharp differentiation between the pure and impure, but he shifted the problem to the mind or heart of the individual being. As quoted above, Shinran realized that the human heart is so filled with impurity that we are incapable of sincerity, faith, or desire for birth in the Pure Land. In contrast, he pointed to the pure and true mind of Amida Buddha who offered his true mind to all persons bound by the sorrows of this world:

> Therefore the Tathāgata, pitying all the beings fettered in pain and sorrow, practiced the ways of bodhisattva in the inconceivable, unknown, longpast . . . and not for one moment, not even for the smallest fraction of a moment, lacked purity and truthfulness. With the pure and true mind did the Tathāgata accomplish the all perfect, unhindered, inconceivable, inexpressible, unutterable, utmost virtue. His sincere mind the Tathāgata gave to all beings who are illusion-clad, evil-acting and vile-minded. This at once tells the Tathāgata's true mind that will help others. Therefore no doubt comes in between. The body of this true mind is his name that has utmost virtue.[21]

According to Shinran, Amida in the fulfillment of his original vow has already transferred his true mind to the mind of humankind, that is, he has planted the seed of truth that brings

forth sincerity, faith, and desire for birth in the Pure Land into
the human heart. In effect, Shinran collapsed the distance between Amida and humankind as taught by Hōnen by uniting the
Buddha mind and the earthly mind, and he promised salvation in
this existence instead of a future existence. Hence, for Shinran the
practice of the *nembutsu* was no longer a petition of a hopelessly
lost person but rather an expression of gratitude for the mercies of
Amida Buddha.

Shinran's remarkable reinterpretation of Hōnen's teaching
can best be understood in terms of his Tendai philosophical heritage, especially *hongakushisō*. In the Tendai identification of
phenomena with the absolute, there is the doctrine of the absolute mind which embraces the universe in its entirety; that is, all
things in the world depend on this mind for their existence. Furthermore, this absolute mind originally and forever contains two
natures, one pure and the other impure. Its pure nature is the basis for the attributes of the Buddha, while its impure nature is the
basis for the myriad of things in the phenomenal world. In its
substance the absolute mind is everywhere the same and undifferentiated, but in its function it is diverse and therefore differentiated. Based upon this doctrine, Shinran could teach that union
with the Buddha has already taken place in a single moment of
thought (*ichinen*), that "the great believing mind (*shinjin*) is at
once the Buddha nature," that "the Buddha nature is at once the
Tathāgata," that "all beings are endowed with the Buddha nature," and at the same time he could admit that his mind is
"floundering in a sea of passion."[22]

For Shinran, Amida Budda is identified with a saving power
that fills the universe and permeates the mind of every individual. Hence the heart (or mind) of each individual is simultaneously the respository of the Buddha mind and the earthly mind.
Instead of humanity's aspiring or arising to Buddhahood in a future life, Amida Buddha descends and merges in the human
heart. Here the Buddha exists naturally within each person or, in
Shinran's language, *jinen hō ni*:

> *Ji* means "of itself," or "by itself." As it is not due to the de-
> signing of man but to Nyorai's vow [that man is born in the
> Pure Land], it is said that man is naturally or spontaneously

(*nen*) led to the Pure Land. The devotee does not make any conscious self-designing efforts, for they are altogether ineffective to achieve the end. *Jinen* thus means that as one's rebirth into the Pure Land is wholly due to the working of Nyorai's vow-power, it is for the devotee just to believe in Nyorai and let his vow work itself out.

Hōni means "it is so because it is so"; and in the present case it means that it is in the nature of Amida's vow-power that we are born in the Pure Land. Therefore, the way in which the other-power works may be defined as "meaning of no-meaning," that is to say, it works in such a way as if not working [so natural, so spontaneous, so effortless, so absolutely free are its workings].

Amida's vow accomplishes everything and nothing is left for the devotee to design or plan for himself. Amida makes the devotee simply say "Namu-amida-butsu" in order to be saved by Amida, and the latter welcomes him to the Pure Land. As far as the devotee is concerned, he does not know what is good or bad for him, all is left to Amida. That is what I — Shinran — have learned.

Amida's vow is meant to make us all attain supreme Buddhahood. The Buddha is formless and because of his formlessness he is known as "all by himself" (*jinen*). If he had a form, he would not be called supreme Nyorai. In order to let us know how formless he is, he is called Amida. That is what I — Shinran — have learned.[23]

IV

To return to the theme of this essay, we can see that the key terms *transcendence* and *the sacred* cannot have the same meaning in Japanese nondualistic thinking as in Western thought. Although the sacred and the profane can be differentiated in Japanese thought, the idea that the sacred is in any sense *sui generis* or a wholly different order of reality cannot be supported by the Japanese materials. Likewise, although the concept of transcendence differentiates the universal from the phenomenal, the eternal from the temporal, the pure (holy) from the impure, the idea that transcendence can be conceived of as other, outside of, or more than its polar opposite also cannot be substantiated. For the Japanese, *hongakushisō* provides the most adequate explanation of the process of differentiation and integration in their religious tradition.

For the purposes of comparative religion we need to modify the traditional Western usage of the two terms *transcendence* and *the sacred* in order to understand the Japanese experience. As a beginning, let us bracket the classical metaphysical meanings of the two terms and, instead, see them in functional terms. Functionally, as I have used the terms in this study, *transcendence* refers to differentiation and *the sacred* to integration. Secondly, as can be seen in the historical study of Hōnen's and Shinran's thought, differentiation and integration are dynamic processes that focus upon the meaning of personal existence, that is, personal identity or salvation. Hence, both transcendence and the sacred need to be seen as dynamic processes.

Hans J. Mol, in his recent book *Identity and the Sacred*,[24] offers a revision of the conception of the sacred that is more useful for the study of modern religion and is especially appropriate to the study of Japanese religion. Rather than seeing the sacred and the profane as two static states as in primitive religion, he prefers to see a sacralizing process that provides us personal identity, meaning, or salvation. Correlatively, for Mol, there is a desacralizing or differentiating process, commonly described as secularization, in which we are stripped of our personal identities, meaning, or salvation. Sacralization, as the total process of differentiation and integration, describes a process in which modern persons on the one hand are being stripped of traditional identities and meaning and on the other hand are acquiring a new identity and personal meaning. In this process the locus and scope of the sacred are being continually relocated and redefined; however, functionally, the historical process of sacralization leads finally to reintegration of the elements that make up personal identity.

According to Mol the elements of sacralization are at least the following:

(1) objectification: the projection of order in a beyond where it is less vulnerable to contradictions, exceptions, and contingencies — in other words, a rarefied realm where major outlines of order can be maintained in the face of temporal but all-absorbing dislocations of that order;

(2) commitment: the emotional anchorage in the various, proliferating foci of identity;

(3) ritual: the repetitive actions, articulations, and movements which prevent losing sight of the object of sacralization;

(4) myth: the integration of the various strains in a coherent, shorthand symbolic account.[25]

If we may discount the dualistic tendencies in Mol's account above, we can summarize briefly Shinran's sacralization of personal identity in terms of Mol's four elements as follows: (1) Objectification: Shinran's objectification or projection of a transcendent order was certainly based upon his received tradition of the Tendai *hongakushisō*, especially the doctrine of the absolute mind in which all reality is embraced, both the pure and the impure, the universal and the particular. Although this absolute mind was usually seen in cosmic terms to legitimate the state in the earlier Tendai tradition, Shinran chose to relocate the sacred to the heart/mind of the individual, in particular in his own mind. Thus the Buddha mind and the earthly mind became one in the person of Shinran himself. In this way order could be maintained in spite of the social upheavals and personal failures that caused the loss of identity for many monks at Mount Hiei. (2) Commitment: Shinran's commitment was his deep faith in the compassion of Amida Buddha, whose mind was immanent in the human mind. This faith enabled him to live a life of acceptance, trust, gratitude, and compassion — that is, to live in this impure world but not of this world because his identity or salvation was in Amida Buddha. In short, Shinran lived *jinen hōni*. (3) Ritual: Shinran ritualized his experience by continuing the practice of the *nembutsu* of Hōnen. However, the ritualized recitation of the name of Amida no longer was a cry of help from a soul trapped in his karmic sins as in Hōnen's case, but was now a song of thanksgiving for salvation! (4) Myth: For Shinran the explanation of his faith or new identity was found in the myth of Amida Buddha, who resided in the Pure Land after the fulfillment of his original vow. As expressed by Shinran:

> When I consider the vow which Amida brought forth after five *kalpas'* contemplation, I find that it was solely for me, Shinran alone! So how gracious is the Original Vow of Amida who resolved to save me possessed of many karmic sins![26]

Just as the term *the sacred* is more descriptive today as the sacralizing process, the term *transcendence* becomes more meaningful when seen as a dynamic process, that is, as a transcending process. Transcendence is a differentiating process and describes the functional differentiation between religious symbols, the social order, and personal identity in the context of cultural and social change. For example, as in the quasi-typical stages of Bellah's religious evolution scheme,[27] in primitive and archaic societies religion, nature, and the social order are often fused in a sacralized order. In such an order, personal identity is absorbed into and limited by ascription in the sacred religio-political order. In the development of historic religion, radical transcendence in the form of world-rejection leads to the differentiation between a mundane social order and a sacred or ultimate order. In this context the individual self is freed from its ascribed social identity; therefore, the possibility of an autonomous, centered self arises in a new and personal identity based upon a transcendent source. According to Karl Jaspers, historically the so-called world religions that arose during the middle of the first millenium B.C. were all world-rejecting religions.[28] These religions and their offshoots have provided humankind with the symbolic resources for this transcending process that has led to the individuation of the self, a phenomenon so familiar to Western culture.

From this perspective of a transcending process, our interpretation of Kamakura Buddhism leads in a different direction from that of the perspective of the sacralization of identity. Although primitive Buddhism in India was a historic religion, the Buddhism that was first officially introduced into Japan in the sixth century functioned as an archaic religion that sacralized nature, throne, and society. Only in Kamakura Buddhism, especially in the teachings of Hōnen and Shinran, did Japanese religion clearly break through to historic religion. Hōnen ruptured the Tendai monistic identification of the absolute and the nation by radically devaluating Japan as *edō*, the defiled land, in contrast to *jōdo*, the Pure Land abode of Amida Buddha. However, his teaching of the radical transcendence of Amida, although freeing the individual from socially ascribed identities, left the meaning of human existence problematic in this world, since true meaning could be found only in the next life in another world. In wrestling with this problem Shinran returned to the Tendai monistic philosophy of *hongaku* and universalized the concept of Amida Buddha as not only the eternal ruler of the Pure Land but also as universal truth and power which permeated all beings. Thus Shinran made the radically transcendent Amida Buddha of Hōnen's teaching immediately immanent in every individual being in this world. This view provided his followers not only with the symbols for a self-identity independent of the social order, as in Hōnen's case, but also with a basis for a meaningful existence in this world and in this lifetime. In effect, Shinran, for the sake of Amida Buddha, relativized and thus desacralized both the sacred vocation of the Buddhist monastic orders and the quasi-sacred sociopolitical order to offer personal salvation and meaning to people of all classes and in all vocations.

The two analytical views of Kamakura Buddhism presented above overlap. Both deal with the complex differentiating and integrative processes of religion in dynamic terms. Hence, the two views could be united into one. Yet to collapse these two analyses into a single view would distort the contemporary religious situation in Japan. The two views not only represent the state of the field in Japanese scholarship, but they also represent alternative views or paradigms in the continuing Japanese search for meaning in modernity. Religion interpreted as the sacralization of identity clarifies the perspective of Japanese scholars who offer *hongakushisō* as the central doctrine for understanding the particularity of Japanese personal and cultural identity, commonly referred to as *Nihon seishin/reisei* (the Japanese spirit).[29] Religion interpreted as a transcending process represents the critical perspective of Japanese scholars who seek a personal identity that transcends the particularity of one's own sociocultural identity and, especially, resists absorption into a sociopolitical order that tends toward sacralization of society (dedifferentiation of nature, throne, society, and individual).[30]

The basis of this critique of the *hongaku* character of Japanese religion is historical, what Bellah describes as the problem of submerged transcendence in the history of Japanese religion. Submerged transcendence refers to the characteristics of a sacralizing process in which the primary locus of value is shifted from the individual to the group and the group in turn is embedded in the sacred, whether in nature or a divine history. Individual or personal existence, then, has meaning only to the degree or level of participation in a sacred sociopolitical hierarchy.[31]

In Japanese history Hōnen and Shinran broke through the sacralized sociopolitical order of Heian or pre-Kamakura society by a radical rejection of Heian society and a radical reinterpretation of Heian Tendai *hongakushisō*. However, in later years, Shinran's followers organized themselves into tightly knit feudal units. Shinran had urged his followers to make every act of life an act of thanksgiving to Amida Buddha, but in later years these acts of gratitude became acts of obligation now redirected to Shinran's lineal descendants, who were now identified as Amida's official representatives on earth. Instead of the radical religious faith that led to a highly individuated self, as in Shinran's case, the later Pure Land followers organized themselves in terms of a religious faith that led to the subordination of the personal self to the demands of group solidarity, that is, to a sacralized social order, now the Pure Land sects (*ikkō ikki*).

The example of submerged transcendence in the case of Shinran's followers is reduplicated historically in the followers of the other Kamakura reformers, Nichiren and Dōgen. It is this perennial problem of submerged transcendence in Japanese history that has led some Japanese intellectuals to question and to search for a more adequate paradigm than *hongakushisō* as the defining characteristic of Japanese identity.

This continuing search for personal meaning and cultural

identity in postwar Japan itself represents a continuing quest for the sacred and the meaning of transcendence, and as such becomes a central issue in the comparative study of religion.

NOTES

1. Mircea Eliade, *Cosmos and History: The Myth of the Eternal Return* (New York: Harper & Row, 1959), pp. 3ff.

2. Rudolf Otto, *The Idea of the Holy: An Inquiry into the Non-rational Factor in the Idea of the Divine and its Relation to the Rational* (London: Oxford University Press, 1958), pp. 24–30.

3. Mircea Eliade, *The Sacred and the Profane: The Nature of Religion* (New York: Harper & Row, 1961), p. 14.

4. Ibid., p. 11.

5. Emile Durkheim, *The Elementary Forms of the Religious Life* (New York: Free Press, 1965), p. 55.

6. Eliade, *The Sacred and the Profane*, p. 12.

7. The issue here is not that reality is dualistic but that God and humanity in Western religion are differentiated both qualitatively and functionally.

8. The terminology is that often used by Professor Abe at professional meetings.

9. This understanding of "primitive Buddhism" (an abstraction) follows that suggested by a contemporary Buddhist philosopher, David J. Kalupahana. Cf. his *Buddhist Philosophy: A Historical Analysis* (Honolulu: University Press of Hawaii, 1976), pt. 1.

10. The complex arguments of the different schools of early Buddhism need to be understood in terms of their polemical and soteriological concerns. For a recent essay in these terms, see David J. Kalupahana, "The Early Buddhist Notion of the Middle Path," *The Eastern Buddhist* 12:1 (May 1979): 30–48.

11. I have in mind the teaching of the Prajñāparamitā-sūtras and the development by Nāgārjuna (c. 250).

12. For the development of the Chinese T'ien-t'ai system, see Leon Nahum Hurvitz, "Chih-i: An Introduction to the Life and Ideas of a Chinese Monk," *Melanges Chinois et bouddhiques* 12 (1963): 538–597. For the Huā-yen school, see Francis H. Cook, *Huā-yen Buddhism: The Jewel Net of Indra* (University Park, Pa.: Pennsylvania State University Press, 1977).

13. For example at least part of the Avataṃsaka-sūtra, which is

the basis of the Huā-yen sect, was available in India in the first or second century. For discussion, see Hajime Nakamura, "Kegoncho no shisōshiteki igi," in *Kegon shisō* [Studies in the thought of the Avataṃsaka-sūtra], ed. K. Kawada and Hajime Nakamura (Kyoto, 1960), pp. 90–95. Nakamura also suggests that this text or at least ideas from this text influenced Plotinus. Cf. ibid., pp. 127–134.

14. See introduction, commentary, and translation by Yoshito S. Hakeda, *The Awakening of Faith* (New York: Columbia University Press, 1967).

15. For discussion, see Arthur F. Wright, "The Formation of Sui Ideology, 581-604," in *Chinese Thought and Institutions* (Chicago: University of Chicago Press, 1967), pp. 71–104.

16. Tamura Yoshirō, "The New Buddhism of Kamakura and Nichiren," *Acta Asiatica* 20 (1971): 45 ff. Cf. also Tamura's *Kamakura shin bukkyō shisho no kenkyū* (Tokyo, 1965).

17. For a life of Hōnen, see Harper Havelock Coates, *Hōnen, the Buddhist Saint: His Life and Teaching*, trans. Ryūgaku Ishizuka (Kyoto, 1925).

18. In this paper I shall use only Shinran as an example.

19. Coates, *Hōnen, the Buddhist Saint*, p. 400.

20. Attributed to Shinran in *The Tannishō: Notes Lamenting Differences*, trans. Ryosetsu Fujiwara (Kyoto: Ryukoku University, 1962), pp. 80 ff.

21. Shinran, *Kyōgyōshinshō or The Teaching, Practice, Faith and Attainment*, trans. Kōshō Yamamoto (Tokyo, 1958), p. 105 (translation altered).

22. Ibid., pp. 94–102.

23. Translation by Daisetz Suzuki in his *Mysticism: Christian and Buddhist* (New York: Harper & Row, 1971), pp. 171 ff.

24. Hans J. Mol, *Identity and the Sacred: A Sketch for a New Social-Scientific Theory of Religion* (New York: Free Press, 1976).

25. Ibid., p. 15.

26. Attributed to Shinran in *The Tannishō*, p. 79.

27. Robert N. Bellah, "Religious Evolution," *American Sociological Review* 29 (June 1964): 358–378.

28. Karl Jaspers, *The Origin and Goal of History* (New Haven: Yale University Press, 1953), chap. 1.

29. For example, see Daisetz Suzuki, *Nihonteki reisei* [Japanese spirituality] (Tokyo, 1962).

30. For example, see Ienaga Saburō, *Chūsei bukkyō shisō kenkyū* [A study of the history of medieval Buddhist thought] (Kyoto, 1955).

Also, Robert N. Bellah, "Ienaga Saburō and the Search for Meaning in Modern Japan," in *Changing Japanese Attitudes toward Modernization*, ed. Marius B. Jansen (Princeton: Princeton University Press, 1965), pp. 369–423.

31. Robert N. Bellah, "Value and Social Change in Modern Japan," *Asian Cultural Studies* 3 (October 1962): 32–42.

7

Deceiving the Deity: Self-Transcendence and the Numinous in Gnosticism

PHEME PERKINS

POPULAR ATTENTION HAS BEEN drawn to the Coptic Gnostic man-
uscripts found at Nag Hammadi by widely publicized claims that
Gnosticism represented a creative spirituality that was repressed
by an authoritarian, male-dominated Church.[1] Rather than concern ourselves with the various charges of ecclesiastical politics,
we turn instead to a fundamental issue that has not yet been
widely appreciated: What is the spiritual position advocated by
Gnosticism? How did Gnostic spirituality fit in with the spiritual
contours of the second and third centuries? Without a critical appraisal of Gnostic spirituality, one can hardly decide whether its
modern advocates are pointing to authentic aspirations of the human spirit or to what some reviewers have called "Club 54 religion,"[2] the "crazies of the second century."[3]

The transcendence of God and contact with the divine

Twentieth-century interest in mysticism and symbols of God
which transcend the culture-bound categories of much of our religious language is more readily drawn to mystical Gnostic writings than to common second-century A.D. attitudes toward the
divine. Most people thought that access to divine power was a
simple matter, that relationships with the gods followed the same
familiar patterns as those with one's human neighbors.[4] Gnostics,

on the other hand, demote such "worldly gods." Their writings are filled with expressions like "the non-being God" which seek to show that the truly divine completely transcends the relationships and language that people use to describe this world.[5] A person might well ask how such a God could have any contact with this world at all. Some of the second- and third-century opponents of Gnosticism protested that their understanding of a God completely beyond this world, which was dominated by demonic powers, destroyed the clear harmony and order of the cosmos, a harmony that was designed to lead the human spirit upward to contemplation of the divine. The Gnostics, for their part, could only hold such a view of divine transcendence by developing an understanding of revelation which provided access to the supra-cosmic divine world, which they called the Pleroma.[6]

Since the material world could hardly provide such lines of contact, the Gnostics anticipate more widespread religious developments of the third century by turning to the inner self as the locus of contact with the divine.[7] It became a common conviction that the human self was multiple, that the true self was as far above the composite layers of the soul as the soul was above the body.[8] People came to believe that they had a relationship with a personal divine protector, which bordered on identification. This development was often used to reinforce the social hierarchy: a great person had a great protector. Thus status in this world was defined by connection with the permanent hierarchy of the invisible One.[9] The Gnostic divine-in-self served the opposite function: it lifted one out of the rigid structures of hierarchical society. Gnostics found their opponents, both pagan and Christian, protesting this breakdown in hierarchy as well as the Gnostic view of the world as demonic creation.[10] The two views are closely related. The divine mediators were understood to be intracosmic deities. The Gnostic view of creation reduced these deities to hostile, demonic powers and claimed that one could only gain access to the divine by crossing barriers erected by them.

The Gnostic self and philosophical mysticism

The Gnostic turn toward an inner divine self might, at first glance, be equated with religious traditions of mysticism that base themselves on a turn inward toward the soul as the human link with the true order of being. One of the most common metaphors for salvation in Gnostic writings is that of the upward ascent of the soul.[11] Yet this ascent is rarely, if ever, described as a process of interior transformation. Therefore, scholars like Hans Jonas have refused to consider Gnosticism an example of mystical self-transcendence.[12] Others point to the difference between the various ecstatic phenomena in Gnostic writings, dreams, visions, and claims to more or less permanent identity with the divine, and the mysticism of their contemporary and critic, Plotinus, who describes a solitary, individual, interior vision of the divine.[13] Thus it is argued that, although Gnostics are concerned with the self and with the transcendence of the divine, they still lack the metaphysical awareness of self and the order of being required to complete the move from *mythos* to philosophical gnosis.[14]

Several of the Coptic treatises from Nag Hammadi have reopened the question of the relationship between Gnosticism and Plotinian mysticism. They have modified the dualism of Gnostic myth in the direction of a monistic system in which evil never acts as an independent force, and they contain striking terminological parallels to Plotinus. Two of them seem to be the writings mentioned by Porphyry as having been read by Gnostics in Plotinus's circles.[15] But even these more speculative systems do not abandon the narrative account of the ascent of the soul through heavenly regions. Hence they retain a "mythic" character. Hans Jonas has argued that a dogmatic metaphysic must precede genuine mysticism, since the mystic is not seeking private experiences of the divine but a vision of reality which the system develops.[16] The Gnostic account of reality never attains such philosophical articulation. It remains embedded in narrative accounts of the origins of the cosmos. Nevertheless, many have read these new writings to be referring to a Gnostic mystical experience similar to that advocated by Plotinus. The following investigation will suggest that neither they nor Jonas have adequately understood the basis of the Gnostic experience of transcendence.

Narrative, vision, and the modes of knowing

One approach to the difference between the two positions is

to ask about the relationship between self-understanding and the metaphors used for knowing. Cognition as vision has been the cornerstone of Western metaphysics.[17] Along with that metaphor goes an understanding of the self as solitary, individual, inner reality. Eric Havelock has shown that a decisive turn toward the cognitive as what is "seen" — the word or concept as 'shape', *eidos* — took place with Plato. Though it is the foundation of the analytic discourse of philosophy, that shift did not penetrate all levels of society to the same degree at the same time.[18] Many people continued to think and speak in the older oral patterns which cast all information in the syntax of narrative. There abstract nouns appear as the subjects of active verbs. They are not linked to equally abstract predicates by the copula *is*. Such syntax employs dualistic opposition between characters and constantly speaks of obstacles to be overcome even if the subject is a "scientific" one like medicine.[19] We find many of these features in the Gnostic treatises. To a person accustomed to abstract, analytic syntax they seem mythological and imprecise. However, Gnostics do not live simply in the old oral world of Homer. In their world, the analytic, abstract speech of Platonic metaphysics dominates "intellectual" circles and may come into conflict with the more conventional narrative modes of knowing and explanation that are still widely employed.[20] The value placed on the abstract language of philosophy seems to have led to its being adopted into Gnostic accounts of the order of things, which are still predominantly narrative.

The Gnostics are clearly fascinated by the abstract language and terms of philosophical analysis. But they rarely handle those terms as part of a sustained analytic argument. Instead, the terms become actors in a story — strange actors, devoid of the particulars of personality. Thus, though the Gnostics claim the self as the locus of contact with the divine and accept the common view that philosophy confers immortality,[21] they have not conceptualized the self in such a way as to make it the object of analysis. Hence a description of the interaction of contemplation, thought, and knowledge in the transfiguration of the self such as one finds in Plotinus would be impossible. Some Gnostics shared in the debates over the order/disorder of the cosmos provoked by Stoic determinism, but even the most theoretical of them could not give an account of the order of the cosmos without telling the story of the origins.[22]

The Gnostic project also seems to require a peculiarly Stoic innovation in the understanding of mind and will. The proper application of thought is not simply reasoned reflection on the world but controlling impressions, "what is in our power." Since consciousness is a sovereign entity absorbed in its impressions rather than in the *logos* of the outer world, reality does not touch the individual. A Stoic could "think himself or herself out of it." This self-absorption initiated the discovery of willing as a power directing thought and imagination.[23] Such a Stoic doctrine of self meant that the power of reality and passion, *pathē*, over one's life, might be reversed by imperatives directed to the soul as the seat of impressions. Gnostics are equally obsessed with the power of *pathē*. They also seem to presume that the mind can reverse reality, but they do not develop a doctrine of the inner life. Instead, they tell a story in which the *pathē*, usually associated with the demons who rule this world, lose their power over those whose gnosis shows that they are superior to the archons. When cast as a narrative, this discovery of a self which says no to the powers seems to involve an almost magical transformation of reality. Hence Gnostics have often been seen as representatives of a decline in rationalism. It is more likely that their stories represent the impact of the new rational syntheses on those who have not yet advanced beyond finding symbols of order in narrative.

Deception as divine presence

Such a commitment to narrative would lead us to expect the kind of dualism and personification of the lower powers as obstacles to self-realization that characterize Gnostic stories of the soul. The startling feature of Gnostic accounts is the relationship of out-and-out deception between the higher world and the lower one of intracosmic gods, now demons, obstacles on the way of ascent. Jonas comments, "There is an element of cunning and outsmarting even in the strategy of salvation."[24] One can argue that deception is the mode of divine presence in this world. Whenever the cosmic gods find out that there is something greater than themselves, they are thrown into turmoil, they become angry or envious, and they attack the one who bears that higher reality. Deception appears in all phases of the story. The revealer must adopt the disguise of the body in order to sneak into the world to bring humanity the knowledge of divine reality. Sophia, the Logos, or the Holy Spirit regularly directs the cosmic process toward the liberation of the Gnostics by deceiving its rulers. Some Christian Gnostics even argued that the sacraments conferred one's true identity secretly so that the powers would not know about it. The powers might even be duped into serving the elect.

Gnostic creation stories focus on the theme of the secret inner identity which makes the Gnostic superior to the creator god and his powers. Through an elaborate process of revealing an image in the heavens and deceiving the creator into giving humankind some of the light power that he derived (or stole) from the divine world, humankind is created in the image of the heavenly human being — or even of the true God. This identity, the source of immortality, reveals that the glory claimed by the creator is sham. He and his powers are to be condemned and destroyed by a humanity which knows its real origin. Here is part of that story from a section of Gnostic Genesis interpretation.

> He [the creator] blew into his [Adam's] face the spirit which is his Mother's [the fallen Wisdom's] power. He did not know this for he lives in ignorance. The Mother's power went out of Ialdabaoth into the psychic soul which they [the archons] had fashioned according to the image of the One-who-exists-from-the-beginning. His body moved, gained strength, and was luminous. At that moment, the rest of the powers were jealous, since he had come into being through all of them, and they had given their power to the man. His understanding was greater than that of those who created him and that of the first archon. When they realized that he was luminous and thought better than they did and was free from wickedness, they took him and threw him into the lowest part of all matter.
>
> But the Blessed, the Mother-Father, the beneficent and merciful One, had mercy on the power of the Mother, which

had been brought out of the first archon, lest they again gain power over the psychic and perceptible body. Through his beneficent spirit and his great mercy, he sent a helper to Adam, a luminous Power of Thought (*epinoia*), the one who comes from the one called Life. And she aids the whole creature (*ktisis*); laboring with him; restoring him to his fullness (*pleroma*) and teaching him about the descent of his seed and about the way of ascent, the way he came down. The luminous power of thought was hidden in Adam so that the archons would not know her, but that the Power of Thought might correct the Mother's deficiency.[25]

Occasionally deception may appear in the upper world. One account has Silence cajole Greatness into emanating[26] — a mythological solution to a metaphysical dilemma in monistic systems!

Gnostic deception depends upon a distrust of what is seen. The deceitfulness of the image and the illusory character of what is presented to sight make the secret possession of a higher power of Gnostic insight possible. For the Gnostics, the primary metaphor of saving knowledge is a call to awakening or the voice of the Mother, which speaks out against the divine claims of her demiurge son.[27] Another treatise presents salvation as a threefold speaking of the trimorphic God manifest in Voice, Sound, and Word.[28] This metaphor may derive from the perception that voice or sound can indicate the presence of what is not seen.[29] When we turn to Gnostic accounts of the ascent of the soul, we find that hearing takes priority over vision. Thus, while the silence in Plotinus is the silence of visionary absorption, the Gnostic silence is stillness in the midst of sound.

Plotinus: contemplation against the narrative

Before turning to these Gnostic writings, it is worth considering Plotinus's arguments against the Gnostics, since they set the standard for the philosophical rejection of Gnosticism. Many of his objections demand that the Gnostic speak the language of metaphysics. His anti-Gnostic work concludes a long exposition of the principles which bind the intelligible world and the visible one together and which make the inner ascent to the vision of the One possible: contemplation as the foundation of all activity (3.8), the beauty which binds the whole together as the motivation for the return in contemplation (5.8), and the mind as the true medium of contemplation and relationship to the One (5.5). As the individual ascends, he or she discovers the self as part of the largest whole, the cosmos, and is carried out of self by the Good, by the eternal, cosmic movement of return.[30]

When Plotinus comes to criticize the Gnostics (2.9), his tone changes from dispassionate analysis to rhetorical polemic. The Gnostics are castigated for their immorality (9.15) — a common charge against philosophical opponents, but not one justified by Gnostic writings. However, the asceticism for which he condemns them (9.17) is clearly represented in one of our writings, *Zostrianos*. Underlying Plotinus's various objections, one finds a fundamental opposition between conclusions reached on the basis of philosophical analysis and those predicated on narratives of the unfolding and return of the cosmos. Plotinus is not unaware of this difference. He charges the Gnostics with the failure to use philosophical language, reasoned argument, and genuine exegesis of Plato (9.6, 9.10). Their arguments, he says, could only appeal to the "uneducated" (9.13.10). Gnostics fail to understand the basic principles of intelligible reality because they treat it by analogy with material reality and do not exclude from it attributes that only apply to the latter. For example, their doctrine of the demiurge with its passions depends upon an improper analogy between the human soul and the world soul (9.7). Similarly, Gnostics multiply beings in the Pleroma to correspond with the plurality of the material world because they do not understand that the intelligible world is to be explained on the basis of the fewest principles (9.6). Improper distinctions between the spiritual and the material also lead them to think that they must literally strip off the body to reach the Divine. Gnostics do not realize that the wise person ascends from the sense-perceptible to the intelligible world interiorly (9.17). Therefore, no educated person could ever accept the "tragedy of terror" put forth by such people (9.13).

At the same time, this sarcastic remark about the Gnostic

"tragedy of terror" shows that the narrative character of their discourse underlies many of the philosophical mistakes that Plotinus detects. For example, their view that the lower world results from the fall of a divine being and that the consequences of that fall will be reversed when its light returns to the Pleroma could hardly be maintained by a person who holds, as Plotinus does, that temporal unfolding does not apply to the realm of being. The cosmos is an eternally ordered hierarchy in which time emerges only with the multiplicity of the world soul. Therefore, the "flaw" to which the Gnostics point would have to be a permanent imperfection in the intelligible world; it could not be reversed by a new creation (9.3–5). Similarly, their talk about the arrogance of the demiurge and the imperfection of his creation would require that he created by contemplating an imperfect image in the intelligible world – a more manifest absurdity than the imperfection in the material world itself (9.10–14). As we shall see, in its more speculative forms Gnostic cosmology is not nearly as insensitive to these points as Plotinus suggests. But to accept his viewpoint, they would finally have to abandon their commitment to narrative syntax and its temporality.

Even worse, they would have to abandon claims to transcend what appears to be the established hierarchy of the cosmos through contact with the divine. Plotinus says as much. He associates Gnostic rejection of the demiurge and his powers with an impious claim to be higher than the intracosmic gods. He insists that the truly wise person is content with his or her place in the cosmos (9.9).[31] Though shot through with the irony and disdain of the educated upper class, Plotinus's remarks point out that for the Gnostics the "educated" discourse of the philosopher was not common fare. And such a person may have been more anxious to escape the bonds of a rigidly hierarchical society towering above, however symbolically, than to fit harmoniously into his or her place.

Tripartite Tractate: cosmology and ascent

Terminology links *Tripartite Tractate* with Neo-Platonism.[32] The first part describes the devolution of the intelligible world and the powers ruling this one; a brief account of the creation of humankind follows; the concluding section rejects all other philosophical and religious opinions for the salvation brought by the Gnostic revealer. Ascent to one's real place in the Pleroma only occurs at the culmination of the cosmic process when the material and psychic world ends as all the light returns to its source. Though this is one of the most difficult treatises in the corpus, the interaction of motifs taken from philosophy and the syntax of Gnostic narrative emerges clearly enough.

Described with lists of negative attributes, the highest God is ultimately unknowable, but the names have a function: they serve as praise of God (CG I.54.2–11, 65.35–66.5). They perform the same function in texts on the ascent of the soul. Plotinus might agree with *Tripartite Tractate* that the true activity of the intelligible realm is the desire to know the One,[33] but he would never accept a picture of aeons restlessly searching for a Father of whom they are ignorant. In *Tripartite Tractate* they have no *nous* through which to contemplate the One. In fact, the author holds the Father responsible for their ignorance[34] and then gives several reasons why keeping them ignorant for a time was neither malicious nor envious: (1) sudden revelation of his greatness would have caused them to perish (64.28–39); (2) love and longing for the Father constitute the unity and eternal activity of the aeons (71.8–19); (3) knowledge of the Father from the beginning would have led the aeons to exalt themselves and think that they alone were responsible for attaining it (a shot against Platonist mystics? [62.12–26]). Ignorance of the Father increases as one descends. Logos, the youngest aeon and closest to Plotinus's Soul,[35] attempts to grasp the incomprehensible One. As a result he is split in two. The lower half falls into forgetfulness (76.13–77.25) and the lower powers derive from this descent. The Logos must be called to awaken, that is, redeemed (82.1–9, 125.25–34).

Tripartite Tractate incorporates a Platonic concept of beauty into its account of the lower world. There are two orders of beauty and images, an intermediate realm formed by the contemplation of the awakened Logos, and a material one, a realm of mere shadows, which is to perish (90.14–92.4; 95.17–28, 100. 19–35).[36] Since the Logos is working secretly through the demiurge to administer this world, its beauty and order ultimately depend on the images of the intermediate world (100.37–101.5, 102. 11–104.3).

The creation of humankind is interpreted by a doctrine of substance close to what sometimes appears in Plotinus.[37] Human ignorance derives from the multiplicity of human form (105.29–106.31). Human spiritual substance is a unity having a single image but is weak because it is determined by many forms. Human psychic substance has a double determination. It is capable of knowing and confessing the exalted One and should not be understood as inclined to evil. But human material nature is of a different substance from the spiritual and psychic. It not only exists in many forms but is subject to many kinds of inclination. Human attention is divided between the two substances; that is, the inclination of the soul toward the passions results from its association with material substance, as Plotinus himself argues against the Gnostics (2.9.2).[38] But Plotinus would not accept the creation story this doctrine is interpreting. He objects to the Gnostics' claim that humankind is superior to the demiurge, whose jealousy they say stems from his lack of spiritual nature. *Tripartite Tractate* interprets the punishment of death as total ignorance, not only of the Father but of the aeons as well (107.30–108.2). In the account of Gnostic salvation, the three parts of humankind are considered analogous to three types of person, not to three natures as opponents often hold. The doctrine is close to some of Plotinus's statements on attention: the soul is assimilated to what it is preoccupied with.[39] The three types are distinguished by their response to Gnostic revelation (118.14–28).

The author rejects all previous philosophies as conflicting and inaccurate doctrines of the order of the universe — Platonists included (109.24–110.22). He accuses them of being deceived by images and arrogantly claiming to have attained truth! Redemption as a cosmic ascent made possible by the Gnostic savior applies not only to humanity but to the lower aeons (including the savior), which have also been affected by the forgetfulness of the Logos (124.13–125.11). At the cosmic *apokatastasis* the material and the psychic (?) realms are destroyed, and all that is saved is drawn up into the Pleroma (136.15–24). Plotinus accused the Gnostics of claiming to be next after God. In *Tripartite Tractate*, the Pleroma is the resting place of the elect, since the Church, like the Son, exists from the beginning (57.33ff.). However, return there is only possible at the end of the cosmic process and through Gnostic redemption. No individual or class of individuals could claim it for a present reality. *Tripartite Tractate* considers Platonic claims to knowledge of God as the kind of false knowledge that the very incomprehensibility of the Father kept even the aeons from attaining lest they think it due to their own abilities.

The gnostic ascent: Allogenes, Marsanes, Three Steles of Seth, Zostrianos

One might assume that *Tripartite Tractate* refuses to internalize the ascent to God because of its commitment to a Christian Gnostic salvation history. But even writings linked to Plotinus's Gnostic opponents, which are not explicitly Christian and are not concerned with a cosmic salvation history, express reservations about an internalized ascent tradition. *Allogenes, Marsanes,* and *Zostrianos* are accounts of a Gnostic seer's ascent through the heavenly and divine realms. *Three Steles of Seth* gives prayers for each of the three highest levels, said to have been engraved on stele by Seth, the ancestor of the Gnostics. We find allusions to ascent and withdrawal that have led some to assume that these Gnostics shared a mystic piety similar to that of Plotinus. In *Marsanes* we read: "We all withdrew (*anachorein*). We became silent. When we came to know him, that is, the Three-powered one, we bowed down; we . . . praised him" (CG 10.9.21–27). An obscure passage in *Zostrianos* suggests that, as in Plotinus, withdrawal might be repeated. "If he wishes, he can separate from all these again and withdraw to himself alone. For this one becomes divine. He has withdrawn to God" (CG 8.44.17–22). The conclusion to *Three Steles of Seth* refers to a pattern of blessings — silence — blessings (on descending [CG 8.127.3–21]). In Plotinus, silence is the condition of contemplation and self-withdrawal. Here, it stands between the two recitals of blessings. Similarly, in *Marsanes*, silence is immediately followed by praises to the three-powered One. Thus, silence is being associated with the sound of praises rather than with solitary, enraptured vision.

The middle section of *Marsanes* is entirely devoted to the

sounds, names, and syllables that correspond to various types and shapes of soul and make it possible to ascend through the spheres of the planets and zodiac. Plotinus charges the Gnostics with falsely thinking that magic can influence the stars and aid the ascent; he finds this idea impossible since the planets are of unchanging nature (2.9.14). For *Marsanes*, of course, the sounds are effective because they harmonize with those various natures! But in Plotinus's universe of visual forms, sounds and natures have nothing to do with each other. The Gnostics can only appear to be magicians, unable to distinguish between the intelligible universe discovered through intellect and the external, visual one.

All three accounts stress the transcendence and unknowability of the highest God.[40] Often, as in *Marsanes*, one only ascends to the level of the Three-powered, who stands below the highest, unknowable Father.[41] *Marsanes* has the three-powered, invisible One and the Spirit without substance at the eleventh and twelfth levels of the thirteen levels of reality (CG 10.4.25–5.26). The seer asks for information about the kingdom of the Three-powered and what derives from him (6.7–29). Thus, the height of ascent is praise of the Three-powered, not some form of union with the unknown, silent One. *Three Steles of Seth* requires a similar interpretation.[42] There, the list of negative attributes terminates with the exchange:

> Lay a command on us that we may see you; that we may be saved. Your knowledge is salvation for all of us. Command! If you command, we are saved. Truly we have been saved. We have seen you by mind [*nous*]. You are all these, for you save them all. (CG 8.125.11–18)

Before one makes the mistake of assimilating this passage to Plotinus, one should remember that the revelation opens with the words, "Many times have I joined with the powers in giving glory and through them have become worthy of immeasurable majesties" (118.20–23). Thus, though one may see through the mind, the focus of the Gnostic ascent tradition is still on joining the praise of the powers. Silence only comes in the midst of this praise. The highest (silent?) form of that praise seems to be the list of negative attributes recited before the acclamation. There are no indications that the Gnostics developed a psychology to explain such experiences as union with/through the *nous*. Salvation comes through the "command" of the highest God. Despite its emphasis on praise, *Three Steles of Seth* tells us that human praises are not really adequate (126.18–32). The first person plural in which these accounts are cast suggests community recital, not solitary contemplation. The community may have been understood to be joining the heavenly aeons. Their praise realizes the highest possibilities of human nature.

Other criticisms of the Platonic position appear in *Allogenes* and *Zostrianos. Allogenes*' remark that the Gnostics "do not know if the One has angels, or gods, or anything within himself" (CG II.67.25–36) shows the author to be familiar with a Neo-Platonic interpretation otherwise only known through Proclus, namely, that on analogy with soul and *nous*, there are *henades* within the One[43] — a view not held by Plotinus himself. The opening of *Allogenes* consists of doctrines and revelations received while the seer is still in the body. He is able to realize his own divinity during this process (57.7–12). When he asks to see the three-powered One, the seer is told that he must prepare for one hundred years. After that preparation, he is taken out of the body on an ascent during which he "saw all those about whom I had heard" (58.26–37). Upon reaching the One, who can only be known by being ignorant of him, the seer is warned to withdraw if afraid; he is urged to be careful not to dissipate himself; he is commanded to still every activity. Even the desire to be eternal or to seek the incomprehensible One will obstruct the project. He must finally realize that it is impossible to know the One (59.4–60.12). Thus *Allogenes* suggests that the passibility and preparation required for such a vision as Plotinus claims is virtually impossible. The seer is then told to *hear*. A long list of negative attributes follows. After he has heard these, the seer is dismissed and told not to spend more time seeking (61.22–66.24). This advice is quite different from Plotinus's suggestion that the soul can turn again into the contemplative silence. Instead, *Allogenes* has replaced the vision with hearing the divine attributes. One comes to know the highest God by hearing these praises of his incomprehensible greatness, not by vision.

In *Zostrianos*, the seer is introduced as an ascetic who has already tried other modes of salvation and has preached them before coming to Gnosis. His ascent through and baptism in the various heavenly regions is narrated at length. The treatise is so fragmentary in places that it is not always clear whether the author is describing an ascent possible in this life or the ascent of the soul through the various regions after death. We have seen that *Zostrianos* considers repeated withdrawal to the divine possible, but that passage is followed by one which describes dangers awaiting a person who withdraws from and returns to the body many times. Any ascent requires powers and glories to guard the soul (45.1–46.31) — and even the body — of the ascending seer as they are doing for *Zostrianos* (4.20–30). *Zostrianos* is clearly presented as a primordial revealer of Gnosis. It may well be that this out-of-the-body ascent in the company of angelic guides was never considered a model for the individual Gnostic to follow. Rather, it is the ultimate "evidence" for the Gnostic doctrine of salvation. Before beginning the descent to his waiting body and a mission as preacher of Gnosis, Zostrianos is told: "Behold, Zostrianos, you *have heard* all these things of which the gods are ignorant, and which are unattainable to messengers" (128.15–18). Note that it is what the seer has heard, not what he has seen, that counts. As he comes to the world to preach, the seer must deceive the lower gods, who would otherwise oppose his message — and who may be considered to be behind the rejection experienced by the Gnostics (130.10–131.25). The transcendence and unknowableness of God, then, guarantees that he is not revealed in any other philosophy or religion.

A concluding evaluation

We have thus come full circle to the Gnostic claim of divine revelation. Their revelation cannot be perceived in any other way. It is not mirrored in the order of being or in other religions. The divine is only present in this world through a deception, which only the Gnostic can unmask. The radical transcendence of God guarantees the Gnostic sole possession of Truth, since there is no other access to God. This same transcendence negates all other claims to divinity — especially of those deities who were so much a part of everyday life. Even Plotinus, who personally had little use for their ceremonies, protests the impiety of these people who challenge their glory. For the Gnostics, the combination of abstract philosophical language and the plurality of religious stories to which Hellenistic persons had access has shown up the pretensions of the intracosmic gods. God must be greater, much greater! But the social price of the Gnostic position is a high one. Gnostics depend upon a rhetoric of deception as the only way in which true revelation is present in the world. Whatever one thinks of the opposition to Gnostics by both Christians and Platonists, one must also ask whether such a rhetoric of deception could ever generate any positive symbolism of a social or cosmic order, symbolism that would be required for Gnosticism to be more than a temporary groping toward a spirituality of transcendence.

Since the Gnostic image of self correlates with its understanding of transcendence, the third-century realization of the self as locus of the divine could not serve to integrate Gnostics into a social or cosmic hierarchy. Instead, the Gnostic self transcends that "social self" which in the ancient world was proclaimed every day in one's body, dress, speech, family, name, trade. However, the Gnostic is not solitary, not engaged in some quest of individual creativity or psychological individuation as has recently been suggested. The Gnostic still lives in a highly social world of oral community tradition. Perhaps one should speak of Gnostic spirituality as "oral mysticism," since the Gnostic does pursue a self-transcendence in which personal value derives from relationship with the divine and not from social distinctions. But the failure to move to the cognitive dimension of metaphysics means more than an inability to incorporate the shared religious symbols of humanity on a lower level of truth as Plotinus does. It means that the Gnostics also run the danger of falling victim to their own deception. The Gnostic stories in books — copies of old steles, so they claimed — ran the danger of becoming artifacts themselves. They became sources of popular magic and increasingly bizarre doctrine.[44] Without a cognitively differentiated understanding of the self as the subject of interior transformation, Gnostics could hardly overcome the key hazard of the rhetoric of deception. The Gnostics remained bound in a symbiotic — if not parasitic — relationship with the very gods whose truth they denied. For example, Valentinian pneumatics live — whatever their theoretical justification for doing so — in a symbiotic relationship with the larger community of Christians, the psychics. Without some well-established system of religious symbolization that can be "unmasked" by the Gnostic hermeneutic of deception, the impulse toward its peculiar form of transcendence is lost. There must be a set body — not only physical but also cultural and religious — to be overcome and stripped off; otherwise, the narrative of deception and secret knowledge loses its power. But insofar as well-established religious and cultural symbol systems may always attract those who seek to uncover the deception that keeps them functioning, the Gnostic way of transcending those systems and their values will continue to provide its attractions — especially in situations where the structure of analytic insight such as Plotinus suggests is only weakly appropriated.

Though the Gnostic claim to have the only access to truth and divinity may seem the height of arrogance, the outsider can perhaps remember that Gnostics never claimed that they could come by this position themselves. The final requirement made of the elect is that they utter the praises of the unknown Father, and so express their own true identity. To return again to *Tripartite Tractate:*

No one can conceive or think of Him;
Or, strictly speaking, approach there, the Exalted One,
    the Pre-Existent.
But every name by which they conceive Him,
Or which they speak about Him,
        is produced for glory, like a trace of Him,
        according to the ability of each one who glorifies Him.

(CG I.65.35–66.5)

NOTES

1. Elaine H. Pagels, *The Gnostic Gospels* (New York: Random House, 1979); see also Pheme Perkins, review of *The Gnostic Gospels* by Elaine H. Pagels, *Commonweal*, 9 November 1979, p. 634.

2. John Leonard, review of *The Gnostic Gospels* by Elaine H. Pagels, *New York Times*, 14 December 1979, p. C-29.

3. Raymond E. Brown, review of *The Gnostic Gospels* by Elaine H. Pagels, *New York Times Book Review*, 20 January 1980, pp. 3, 33.

4. Peter R. L. Brown, *The Making of Late Antiquity* (Cambridge: Harvard University Press, 1978), pp. 9 ff., 65.

5. This study has been made possible through a fellowship from the National Endowment for the Humanities for which I am very grateful. A convenient translation of the Nag Hammadi materials can be had in James M. Robinson, ed., *The Nag Hammadi Library in English* (San Francisco: Harper & Row, 1977). The writings discussed in this paper are as follows: *Allogenes* 11.3; *Apocryphon of John* 2.1; *Marsanes* 10.1; *Three Steles of Seth* 7.5; *Tripartite Tractate* 1.5; and *Zostrianos* 8.1. On negative descriptions of God in Gnostic writings see Kurt Rudolph, *Die Gnosis: Wesen und Geschichte einer spätaniken Religion* (Göttingen: Vandenhoeck & Ruprecht, 1977), pp. 70–72; Jean Daniélou, *Gospel Message and Hellenistic Culture*, trans. and ed. John Austin Baker (Philadelphia: Westminster Press, 1973), pp. 324–340. Daniélou suggests that the term *anousios* and the stress on the radical unknowability of God were peculiarly Gnostic developments. His view has been confirmed by new evidence; see B. Pearson, "The Tractate *Marsanes* (NHC X) and the Platonic Tradition," in *Gnosis, Festschrift for Hans Jonas*, ed. B. Aland (Göttingen: Vandenhoeck & Ruprecht, 1978), pp. 373–384.

6. Rudolph, *Die Gnosis*, p. 72.

7. Brown, *Making of Late Antiquity*, pp. 68 ff.

8. Ibid., p. 69.

9. For example, see Arthur Darby Nock, "The Emperor's Divine Comes," in *Essays on Religion and the Ancient World*, ed. Zeph Stewart (New York: Oxford University Press, 1972), pp. 653–675.

10. Elaine H. Pagels, "The Demiurge and His Archons — A Gnostic View of the Bishop and Presbyters?" *Harvard Theological Review* 69 (July–October 1976): 301–324; idem, "Visions, Appearances and Apostolic Authority: Gnostic and Orthodox Traditions," in *Gnosis, Festschrift*, pp. 415–430. Pagels has argued that Christian Gnostics made such protests against emerging church structures, but she has not taken into account the larger social patterns of hierarchy that underlie both orthodox developments and Gnostic protests.

11. Pheme Perkins, "Gnosis as Salvation," in *Aufstieg und Niedergang der römischen Welt* (Berlin: Walter de Bruyter, forthcoming), 2:22, charts 1–3.

12. Hans Jonas, "Delimitation of the Gnostic Phenomenon — Typological and Historical," in *L'origini dello gnosticismo*, ed. Ugo Bianchi (Leiden: E. J. Brill, 1967), p. 107.

13. E. R. Dodds, *Pagan and Christian in an Age of Anxiety: Some Aspects of Religious Experience from Marcus Aurelius to Constantine* (Cambridge: At the University Press, 1965), pp. 69–96.

14. As suggested by Hans Jonas, *Gnosis und spätaniker Geist* (Göttingen: Vandenhoeck & Ruprecht, 1966), 2:1, pp. 122–170.

15. *Allogenes* and *Zostrianos* are named by Porphyry; two others from Nag Hammadi, *Marsanes* and *Three Steles of Seth*, are so similar in terminology that they must have been among the "other writings" to which he refers. *Tripartite Tractate* may also have been read in such circles, since it shows an extensive overlap in terminology as well. See Jan Zandee, *The Terminology of Plotinus and Some Gnostic Writings, Mainly the Fourth Treatise of the Jung Codex* (Istanbul: Nederlands Historisch-Archaeologisch Instituut, 1961); John H. Sieber, "An Introduction to the Tractate *Zostrianos* from Nag Hammadi," *Novum Testamentum* 15 (July 1973): 233–237; M. Tardieu, "Les Trois Stéles de Seth," *Revue des Science Religieuse* 57 (1973): 545–575; James M. Robinson, "The Three Steles of Seth and the Gnostics of Plotinus," *Proceedings of the International Colloquium on Gnosticism*, ed. George Widengren (Leiden: E. J. Brill, 1977), pp. 132–142.

16. Hans Jonas, "Myth and Mysticism: A Study of Objectification and Interiorization in Religious Thought," *Journal of Religion* 49 (October 1969): 315–329.

17. Hannah Arendt, *The Life of the Mind* (New York: Harcourt, Brace & Co., 1978), vol. 1, *Thinking*, pp. 101–119; Eric A. Havelock, *The Greek Concept of Justice: From Its Shadow in Homer to Its Substance in Plato* (Cambridge: Harvard University Press, 1978), pp. 328 ff.; Walter J. Ong, "The World as View and Word as Event," *American Anthropologist* 81 (1969): 634–647.

18. *Origins of Western Literacy* (Toronto: Ontario Institute for Studies in Education, 1976), pp. 18–21.

19. Havelock, *Greek Concept of Justice*, pp. 41–54, 88–94, 221–224, 307–329.

20. See the discussion of the varieties of "mixed literacy" situations in Jack Goody, ed., *Literacy in Traditional Societies* (Cambridge: At the University Press, 1968).

21. On the connection between philosophy and immortality, see Arendt, *Life of the Mind*, vol. 1, *Thinking*, pp. 134–139; vol. 2, *Willing*, pp. 65–67.

22. Stoic materialism may have increased the alienation between humanity and the cosmos, since, though the whole is providentially ordered toward the emergence of the wise person, such a person would be extremely rare. See A. H. Armstrong, "Gnosis and Greek Philosophy," in *Gnosis, Festschrift*, pp. 91–94. On the cosmological debates see Pheme Perkins, "On the Origin of the World (CG 2.5): A Gnostic Physics," *Vigiliae Christianae*, forthcoming.

23. Arendt, *Life of the Mind*, vol. 1, *Thinking*, pp. 152–162; vol. 2, *Willing*, p. 83.

24. Jonas, "Delimitation," p. 96.

25. From *Apocryphon of John* 2.19.25–20.28.

26. Epiphanius, *Pan* 31.5.5–7.

27. Hans Jonas, *The Gnostic Religion*, rev. ed. (Boston: Beacon Press, 1963), pp. 68–73; G. MacRae, "Sleep and Awakening in Gnostic Texts," in *L'origini dello gnosticismo*, pp. 496–507.

28. *Trimorphic Protennoia* (CG 13.1) as observed by John D. Turner, review of *La Protennoia Trimorphe* by Yvonne Janssens, *Religious Studies Review* 5 (January 1979): 66.

29. See the discussion of "word" as a reliable indicator of presence in Walter J. Ong, *The Presence of the Word: Some Prolegomena for Cultural and Religious History* (New Haven: Yale University Press, 1967), pp. 161–169.

30. A. H. Armstrong, "The Apprehension of Divinity in the Self and Cosmos in Plotinus," in *The Significance of Neoplatonism* (Norfolk: Old Dominion, 1976), pp. 93–96.

31. Plotinus characterizes their arrogance as "trying to fly," a *topos* from dream handbooks. In Artimedorus *Onir* 2.68, flying without wings implies danger for the dreamer. This topos appears in the Gnostic *Gospel of Truth* (CG 1.28. 32–29.5) in a list of nightmares.

32. Zandee, *Terminology of Plotinus*, pp. 2ff.

33. A. H. Armstrong, "Life, Eternity and Movement in Plotinus's Account of NOYC," *Le Néoplatonisme* (Paris: Centre National de la Recherche Scientifique, 1971), pp. 67–74.

34. Zandee, *Terminology of Plotinus*, pp. 13–16, stresses the analogies with Plotinus to equate Gnostic *pneuma* with Plotinus's *Nous*, but the Gnostics simply do not have an ontology finely attuned to psychological categories. His "Gnostic Ideas about the Fall and Salvation," *Numen* 11 (1964): 21–36, emphasizes the Father's responsibility for ignorance.

35. Zandee, *Terminology of Plotinus*, pp 16ff., has missed the real equation in his eagerness to identify Plotinus's Soul with the Gnos-

tic psychics, an identification which cannot be maintained in this work. He then tries to identify Logos in *Tripartite Tractate* with that in Plotinus and so overemphasizes its functional characteristics (pp. 28ff.). Jonas's interpretation of Plotinus on Soul is much closer to the Logos in this writing than it is to Plotinus; see his "The Soul in Gnosticism and Plotinus," *Néoplatonisme*, pp. 45–53 — a good example of how a Gnostic would read Plotinus?

36. Cf. Enn. 2.9.11ff. A variant of the *Tripartite Tractate* doctrine that the repentant Logos is illuminated and that shadows are the images behind this world seems to underlie the Plotinus passage.

37. By jumping immediately to the doctrine of three classes of human persons, Zandee, *Terminology of Plotinus*, pp. 19–22, has missed the philosophical point about the constitution of the individual.

38. On the relationship between the soul and inclination see A. H. Armstrong, "Plotinus," in *Cambridge History of Later Greek and Early Medieval Philosophy* (Cambridge: At the University Press, 1967), p. 225.

39. R. T. Wallis, *Neoplatonism* (New York: Charles Scribner's Sons, 1972), pp. 79–81.

40. *Allogenes* 11.61.32–67.20; *Three Steles of Seth* 7.125.23–126.16; in *Marsanes* only the Three-powered can grasp the Father, since both are *anousios*.

41. Gnostic texts vary as to whether the highest God is Three-powered or, as in *Tripartite Tractate*, beyond the Three-powered. Similar variations occur in Middle Platonism. See A. H. Armstrong, "The Eclipse of the One," *Studia Patristica* (Berlin: Akademie, 1975), 13:2, p. 77.

42. See Tardieu, "Trois Stéles," p. 564; Robinson, "Three Steles" is unclear on this point.

43. E. R. Dodds, *Elements of Theology* (Oxford: Oxford University Press, 1963), pp. 257–260. Dodds correctly rejects the view that this doctrine originates with Proclus. *Allogenes* shows that we can trace it back to Plotinus's circles. Perhaps it is earlier than Plotinus.

44. See the discussion of the "magical" use of written religious tests in traditional societies in Goody, *Literacy*, pp. 15–19.

PART III

Modes of Transcending: Will, Mind, and Praxis

8

Transcendence and the Will to Believe

LEROY S. ROUNER

I

To SPEAK OF TRANSCENDENCE is to suggest that there is a realm of reality which is beyond the immediate reach of ordinary human experience. To speak of the sacred, however, is to suggest that there are, within the reaches of our experience, certain persons, places, and things which connect with the transcendent realm of reality in some special way. These two notions are interdependent. A radical emphasis on one tends to destroy the meaning of the other. In the Protestant Reformation, for example, the emphasis on the transcendence of God was so emphatic that nothing within the realm of ordinary human experience was regarded as sacred. Even the Bible was not sacred in itself but only as it reflected the transcendent holiness of God. On the other hand, there are forms of Hindu piety which celebrate the sacred character of teachers and teachings, cows and cobras, shrines, rivers, mountains, and more, so that the ultimate religious reality is no longer beyond ordinary human experience but rather the real meaning of that experience, properly perceived.

As my illustrations suggest, the question about the nature of transcendence is a critical issue in the comparative study of religious philosophies. We usually think of this as an East-West issue, and so it is if American Protestants are confronting the Hinduism of *Advaita Vedānta*. As we become better informed and more self-aware, however, it becomes apparent that this issue is also internal to various great traditions in both East and West. For

Hindu India the qualified nondualism of Rāmānuja's *Visistad-vaita Vedānta* raises the "Protestant principle" of God's transcendent otherness over against the prevailing holism of Śaṅkara's *Advaita Vedānta* in somewhat the same way that, in the Christian West, Calvinism counters the Catholic doctrine of the analogy of being between God and the world. Cross-cultural issues in the philosophy of religion are also intra-cultural issues at the same time. An adequate doctrine of transcendence in an interreligious situation requires both understanding other traditions and re-thinking one's own tradition. Hopefully these twin adventures will provide grist for one another's mills.

Motivation for these ventures varies a good deal, from the theoretical interest of the pure scholar to the moral concern of political leaders for peace among warring religious groups. While I am a sometime purist and a sometime politician, my present motivation grows out of personal history. I was raised in Portsmouth, New Hampshire, in a Congregational parsonage, which, like most of the old homes of seacoast New England, was carpeted with rugs from the Orient. My maternal grandmother, who lived with us, had been a Baptist missionary in Burma and Japan. Pious, straitlaced, and neo-fundamentalist though she was, she brought with her an ivory statue of the Buddha which graced our dining room with a faintly benign presence. Years later, in graduate school, John Herman Randall, Jr., suggested a dissertation on William Ernest Hocking's view of the relation between Christianity and other world religions; and the dissertation was no sooner finished than I spent five years teaching philosophy in India. At the time I did not connect the dissertation or the vocational decision with the culturally mixed metaphor of my Portsmouth boyhood, but in retrospect it seems, as we Calvinists say, predestined.

Whether my grandmother ever worked out the discrepancy between her biblicism and her Buddha, I cannot say. I inherited the Buddha from her, and his presence now in my study is disconcerting. On other occasions I have worked on interreligious questions. Here, however, I am concerned with the other comparative task, which is turning homeward to rethink a critical issue which has long festered within my own tradition of Protestant Christianity. That issue is the role of the individual will in the shaping of religious truth. If, as classical Calvinism announced, transcendence is wholly other than our experience of ourselves and our world, then not only is our world essentially devoid of the sacred, but the human will is essentially impotent as a means of gaining access to the transcendent. This impotence is philosophical as well as moral. Salvation is not to be earned by our good works, nor is God to be understood by human reflection. In short, religious faith is not primarily a way of understanding the meaning of human experience. Religious faith is primarily a way of recognizing the reality of a God who is disjoined from all human experience and whose reality radically recasts the meaning of all human experience. Calvinism thus proposes its own version of the doctrine that our experience of the world is *māyā*, illusion. If, as I believe, God is the one who saves us, then God must indeed be other than we are in order to save us from our perversion of will, our misperception of what is true in ourselves and our world—in short, from our sin. But if God is both our Creator and Redeemer, then the reality of God cannot be totally alien from our inwardness and our perception of our world, or so I also believe. Consequently, there must be some good hope attending the adventure of the human will in its quest God-ward. Within human experience there must be sacred things which connect with the transcendent.

William James's brief popular essay on "The Will to Believe" is not the most substantive summary of this issue. I am not even persuaded that James was a profound religious thinker. In his genial and haphazard way, however, he touched on the issue with freshness and relevance which makes his essay—and he would like this—useful. He had a gift for cutting through scholastic niceties to the heart of the matter. Our serious concern with transcendence, after all, is how to get there. In the tradition of Pascal's "wager" and Kierkegaard's "leap of faith," James's "will to believe" has much stimulus to offer.

II

The role of the will has always been a problem for that tradition of Christian thought which is referred to, loosely, as Protestant neo-orthodoxy. Its seminal document is Paul's Epistle to the Romans, and its definitive literature runs through Augustine's *Confessions* and *City of God*, Luther's *Bondage of the Will*, Calvin's *Institutes*, Kierkegaard's *Fear and Trembling*, Reinhold Niebuhr's *Nature and Destiny of Man*, and Karl Barth's — what else? — commentary on Paul's Epistle to the Romans. Obviously this is not a single school of thought, and on any given doctrine these are often strange bedfellows. What they share is a radical notion of the transcendence of God. Protestantism is an ecclesiological and theological affirmation of the sovereignty of God over all things human and natural. It is preoccupied with the notion of God's transcendence. The battle cry of the Reformation was *Soli Gloria Deo* 'to God alone be glory'. This theme hearkened back to the radical monotheism of Israel. The God of the Covenant was transcendent over the polytheistic nature deities of the ancient Near East. These tribal gods of nature were propitiated by their devotees in order to gain protection from natural disasters and historic accidents.

The transcendent God of Israel refused to be manipulated in this way (Deut. 7:26). But precisely because he was transcendent, the God of Israel was in a position to save them from all the world-powers of nature and history. Not just in this battle or in that flood would he rescue them. Even if in his anger he flooded them out or made them lose the battle, still, flood and battle now had meaning as the universal purpose of an eternal God. He was their God and they were his people, forever. So transcendence is the key to the notion of salvation in the Old Testament, and Paul makes it central to his theology in the eighth chapter of Romans when he declares that no world-power — not even angels and principalities — can separate us from the love of God in Christ Jesus our Lord. Paul also outlines two themes which became dear to the heart of Protestant orthodoxy, the doctrine of original sin and the doctrine of faith.

Sin, said Paul, is part of the content of revelation (Rom. 5: 12ff.). We know we are sinners when we see our broken image (Rom. 3:23) reflected back from the glory of the Transcendent One. Sin is our separation from the Transcendent Holy One, and only he has the power, through his grace, to reunite us with him.

Because of sin, our wills are hopelessly ambivalent and self-seeking. In Paul's famous lament, "The good that I would do I do not, and the evil that I would not do, that I do." In his *Primitive Christianity* Rudolf Bultmann points out, "If his will is in bondage to evil, which is what the New Testament always assumes, the whole man is in bondage to evil. . . . What is needed is to bring home to the will its utter impotence; so that it can cry: 'O wretched man that I am! Who shall deliver me from the body of this death?'"[1] At the same time, because our inmost being is not *logos* ('reason' or 'spirit'), but precisely the will, the question of faith is not primarily a question of knowing but a question of doing. Faith, as a noun, is always an obscure notion in the New Testament and in the orthodox Protestant tradition. It becomes clear only as it becomes *faithfulness*, obedience to the will of God. This is why Abraham has been the model of faith from Paul to Kierkegaard, because his *obedience* to God's will was perfect.

The juxtaposition of will as impotence to will as obedience makes conversion, the transition from one to the other in Christian experience, a dramatic and critical event in this tradition, as in the lives of Paul, Augustine, and Luther. It also leads to an interpretation of God's transcendence as radical otherness and difference. Unlike the emanationist cosmologies of most Hindu and Buddhist schools, where world substance and God substance are not sharply differentiated, Protestant orthodoxy emphasizes God's creativity as *ex nihilo*. God and world, like God and humankind, are different in substance. Kierkegaard speaks of the "infinite qualitative difference between man and God." Barth announces that God is *sui generis*, or wholly other than things worldly and human.

Then how do we come to know God? Strictly speaking, we don't; God comes to make himself known to us. No effort of will can summon up God (in Calvin's doctrine of Christian vocation, the word from the Lord is "Don't call me, I'll call you"). No philosophical argument can establish the reality of God for us, because there is no *analogia entis*, no analogy of being between things human and things divine. The finite cannot contain the infinite. All human reflection on the nature of God and all human desire for the presence of God must end in a distortion of the God who is really God, because there is nothing like God in our experience of ourselves and our world. Yes, we are made in the *imago dei*, and that is why we yearn for God, but since the image is broken by our sin, human religion is always *Unglaube* 'unfaith', a pathetically misplaced trust in what T. S. Eliot calls "a heap of broken images." Yes, the mark of the Creator is everywhere in the creation, and we are surrounded by hints and guesses of the divine, but that is all, and you can't save your soul on hints and guesses. But then why are some saved so dramatically with God's power and presence and others not? God only knows. And to him alone be glory.

The price to be paid for the classical Protestant notion of transcendence is the doctrine of predestination. John Calvin said, "I confess that this decree ought to appall us." He is speaking morally in the first instance, but also philosophically, for here one must choose between the logic of one's human moral sensitivity and the logic of one's posited revelation of God's sovereignty.

The logic of God's sovereign will is that God determines all events, including the damnation of some before they are even born. In the ninth chapter of Romans, in his famous "Jacob I loved and Esau I hated" argument for double predestination, Paul echoes God's response to Job, "Who are you to ask the questions? Where were you when I formed the foundations of the earth, when the morning stars sang together and all the sons of God shouted for joy?" (Job 38:7). Augustine, Calvin, Luther, and Barth all made the same argument, in virtually the same terms. In most of us, the logic of human moral sensitivity can't accept that, so here there must be a parting of the ways concerning the uses of human reason. Calvin's dictum against speculation echoes Paul's stricture against "philosophy and vain deceit," which has been repeated in our time by Karl Barth. The issue for Barth is not for or against philosophy as such, although he often seems to say that. The issue is whether reason and human experience are an appropriate point of departure for religious reflection, or whether one must begin with revelation. In other words, must philosophy of religion be positivist, or is a broadly experiential philosophy of religion possible? Must we follow that good Calvinist John Hick—Karl Barth's philosophical alter ego—examining the God question and showing how you can't get there from here? Is it possible to avoid the appalling choice which Protestant orthodoxy at its height confronted so unflinchingly? Even more to the point, is it necessary for a Christian philosophy to have a radical doctrine of transcendence, thus forcing dualism and, as a result, falling into obscurantism? James at least opens up the possibility of an experiential philosophy of religion.

III

To move from the courage and intellectual audacity of the Predestinarians to William James's comparatively timid and tender-minded little piece may seem a bit of a comedown, but most of us will find the atmosphere more congenial. For all our recognition that warm hearts too often cohabit with soft heads, we share the modern world's instinctive trust in experience as a ground for religious authority. And while Protestant orthodoxy is steadfast and unflinching in focusing on the majestic transcendence of God, it is not very good at describing what actually goes on in the religious lives of individual believers, and that was just what James *was* good at. Curiously enough, he had no real passion for God. The author of *The Varieties of Religious Experience* never had one himself. He believed in God, but only just. James was a psychologist in the humanistic tradition, a philosopher in the ordinary and nonacademic sense of the term.

The context of "The Will to Believe" is James's three fundamental notions: radical empiricism, pragmatism, and pluralism. Pluralism is the architecture of James's universe, richly divergent in experiences and values, and not constrained or finished off with any encompassing Absolute. Like the cosmology of the Big Bang theory, James's universe is growing, open, unfinished, hospitable always to variety. The future is as yet unformed and will be, in part, what we make it. Pragmatism is the method by which we find our way in this somewhat disordered world. James did not deny the importance of that purely theoretical reason so beloved of science whereby things are named and classified into rational systems of thought. He argued only that all rationality is guided by what he called the "sentiment of rationality" which makes it serve our purposes. Philosophical reflection orders our pluralistic world so that we can feel at home in it and effect our purposes. Ideas, therefore, are not true or false in abstraction, but only in function. Truth is not a characteristic of the absolute structure of things. Truth is rather the judgment made about the successful functioning of an intention, an idea involved in some human purpose.

Radical empiricism, or the doctrine of pure experience, is the content of this pluralistic world, and the basic stuff with which philosophic method works. James's notion of experience is radical in relation to the British tradition following Hume because James denied that experience is only of singular facts — this person, that color, etc. — and that we are passive recipients of this singular, factual impression. James argued that we experience the connections among things in the same way that we experience the individual facts themselves. Hume had argued that when we see one billiard ball bump another and make it move we experience the two balls in motion; we do not experience causality as the process which relates them. For Hume, causality is an intellectual inference from what is seen. James argued that, while we cannot see causality, we are aware of it as part of the activity situation of our experience, and that the notion of separate, static objects is itself an abstraction from pure experience, which begins as "a booming, buzzing confusion." Pure experience is James's name for reality. It is what is. It is *all* that is. Consciousness, for example, is not a substance in the Idealist sense of fundamental world stuff. In this sense James argued that it does not exist. It is a function in experience which thoughts perform. Pure experience precedes the distinction between subject and object, body and mind, etc., and therefore presents what today we would call a holistic picture of reality. The process of reflection involves deciding what we need to select out of this "stream of consciousness" to shape for our own intentions.

Like everything else, God is to be known in experience, and by the same method that everything else is known, i.e., the pragmatic method. James defends the philosophic right to religious belief in general. Given our recent experience of religious fanaticism in Jonestown, an indiscriminate philosophic justification of belief in general seems the height of irrationality. Here James's bourgeois background betrays him. For all his love of the occult, his experimentalism, his delight in the bizarre varieties of individual religious experience, because he himself had no passion for God, James had no feel for the demonic possibilities of religion. If Royce's Idealism could be shattered by the sinking of the *Lusitania*, what would the Jonestown massacre have meant for James's genial religious pluralism? To be fair, he lived in a different world. He had never heard thousand-voiced Nazi choruses singing "Deutschland, Deutschland über alles" in celebration of their National Christianity, nor had he followed the logic of corrupted Calvinism as Dutch Reformed Afrikaaners transformed the theology of Covenant into a defense of apartheid. But if, ironically, this philosopher of our passional nature lacked religious passion himself, still he had a gift for sympathetic understanding. Passion is all hot immediacy; understanding also needs coolness and distance. Here James's bourgeois background was one of his strengths. His essay can also be read as a phenomenology of the will, a pragmatic examination of how believing works. This may be the most valuable aspect of the essay. At least it is the one that interests me most.

IV

James begins with the notion that certain hypotheses "may be proposed to our belief," and that these are either live or dead. That is, that some beliefs, like Judaism or Christianity, are live options for most of us, while others, like some obscure sectarianism, are not. Most of us are born believers, in some sense, not made believers. Nevertheless, insofar as we grow and change, we do come upon new *items* of belief for which James's analysis holds. The decision between hypotheses, he tells us, is an option, and options must be either live or dead, forced or avoidable, momentous or trivial. "A living option is one in which both hypotheses are live." A forced option is one in which you must decide for or against a given truth because there is no alternative to having it or not having it. A momentous choice is one concerning the meaning of your life, as when one risks social ostracism by declaring oneself homosexual, or when a white man marries a black woman and is disinherited. His thesis is this:

> Our passional nature not only lawfully may, but must, decide an option between propositions, whenever it is a genuine option that cannot by its nature be decided on intellectual grounds; for to say under such circumstances, "Do not decide, but leave the question open," is itself a passional decision — just like deciding yes or no — and is attended with the same risk of losing the truth.[2]

There can be no objective evidence for deciding the truth of a religious option. But giving up the doctrine of objective certainty in religion does not mean forsaking the truth question. The truth of a doctrine is not where it comes from, its *terminus a quo*, but what it leads to, its *terminus ad quem*. And for James religion says two things: that "the best things are the more eternal things" and that "we are better off even now if we believe [this] first affirmation to be true." The status of "being better off" is the vital good which we stand to gain or lose by the adventure of faith. Once you have grasped your "vital good," who can say it is not true for you? And since experience is all there is, and religious experience is always private and individual — James defined religion as what one does with one's solitariness — this subjective truth is all the truth there is.

His is a hardheaded subjectivism, however, with the possibility of objective truth hidden in it. He makes a distinction between knowing the truth, and knowing *that* we know the truth. In other words, what you believe may be right — there is an objective certitude to be had out there someplace — but given the world's pluralism and the booming, buzzing confusion of pure experience with which we begin, the only way to go about world shaping and truth discovering is the pragmatic one — try it; see if it works for you; see if it continues to bless you with its vital good and enables you to move into your future. If it does, then trust it, but never let your belief go unaccompanied by your empiricism and its constant reminder that others are trusting other beliefs which are as vital to them and as much of a blessing as yours. This is the best you can do if you are honest about what you really know. That appeal to honesty in regard to one's experience is what I mean by a hardheaded subjectivism.

Somewhere Luther says, "If God is not God for you then he is not God." And in his doctrine that religion is a living, forced, and momentous option I think James describes conditions under which the will to believe functions for us all. We have all finally chosen our belief—even if it has also chosen us—and we have chosen in response to our purposes and our need to be at home in a confusing and sometimes chaotic world. There is an authentic humility in James's hardheaded religious subjectivism. Protestant orthodoxy, for its part, has been so transfixed with the sovereignty of God that it has been trapped into saying more than it really knew. Calvin, obsessed with the need for clarity and logical consistency, carefully crafted an increasingly monstrous doctrine which even he found hard to believe. My teacher Wilhelm Pauck, who wrote the first book in English on Barth in 1929, once nodded toward his volumes of Barth's endless *Dogmatics* and exclaimed, "How does he know all that about God?" James, for his part, sticks to what he knows, and as far as he goes I think he is right. There is no prior confirmation for any religious belief. You have to believe it, and trust it, and live with it, before you can be assured of its truth. Even in those radical conversions such as Paul's on the Damascus road, or Augustine's in the garden, there is inevitably a history of choices and a final *willingness* to claim this dramatic moment as your "vital good."

Because of its individualism, James's pragmatism has no criteria for judgment against demonic religion. And because pragmatism allows no epistemological escape from the realm of "pure experience" there is no consistent way I can see of avoiding polytheism in a pluralistic universe. Or, to put it differently, what kind of transcendence is possible in a realm of pure experience? James believes in believing. As a psychologist he was surely right that belief always does do us *some* good, and that holds for Jonestown as well. Pragmatism is always valid in the short run. But the long-run human intention of serious belief in God is that God will save us from the bonds of our agonizing impotence in the face of sin and death. To do this God must be other than we are, for it is part of our experience — as Paul pointed out — that here we cannot save ourselves.

James's pragmatic philosophy of religion has been widely regarded as distinctively American, even provincial. Ernest Hocking, however, was quick to see that a pragmatic philosophy of religion is characteristically Oriental. In *The Meaning of God in Human Experience* Hocking has a long chapter on "The Will as a Maker of Truth" which is a defense and critique of James's view. In defense he says, "Nothing more illuminating has ever been put forward than just such interpretation of many a religious doctrine; nothing truer to the way in which religious picturing and myth-building does actually take place in human consciousness." But a sentence later he points out: "The Oriental mind realizes that the spiritual atmosphere in which either men or gods may breathe must be created; it knows nothing of empirical truth in matters of religion, truth passively taken; and postulate joins hands with poetry in constituting the medium in which all spirituality may live."[3]

My original intention in this paper — before my latent Calvinism surfaced — had been to show that the *Nyaya* logic of the orthodox systems of Hindu philosophy is also essentially pragmatic. This takes us back to my earlier comment about the distinction between Creationism in the biblical tradition, and Emanationism in the Hindu-Buddhist tradition. I am not surprised that James finally expressed dissatisfaction with Christianity, and that those process philosophers and phenomenologists who have recently rediscovered his notion of pure experience are increasingly drawn to Buddhism. To put it crudely, a philosophy of pure experience, like the classical philosophies of the Hindu and Buddhist traditions, leans to monism in finding God as a dimension of what is. This is also true of Hartshorne's process philosophy, where God is "the wholeness of the world," and it is true of Tillich's idealistic existentialism, where God is "the Ground of Being." All of these notions come perilously close to making God a way of talking and thinking about our world.

When Tillich's Calvinistic colleagues at Union Seminary raised the question of whether he really believed in God or not, they were raising a question about the nature of God's transcendence. Did he believe in a Creationist God, a God who was not simply the mind's way of giving meaning to existence but an entity which is independently real? In his personal faith, William James thought of God as objectively real; i.e., he really did believe in the aseity of God, but he seems not to have worked out the conflict between that notion and the notion of pure experience. Because so much of what the world calls "religion" equates God with the Absolute, the structure of Being, Calvinists like Barth have insisted on a radical distinction between religion and the Christian faith. The reason for this is that the idea of salvation and faithfulness as the obedience of will is inextricably tied to a notion of transcendence as otherness or difference. If you look carefully at monistic philosophies of religion, I suspect you will find that their ethical implications are Stoic, and that their notion of religious salvation is that of a mental or spiritual "realization" rather than of a historical revelation calling for obedience. Transcendence is also "spiritual" or mental.

V

If Calvin and Barth are right that the transcendence and the aseity of God require a notion of God as "other," and if James is right that the actual functioning of our will to believe means that God is who we choose him to be, then we have a problem. How are we to understand the integration of these two?

As the structure of my paper indicates, my mind is incurably dialectical, so I am persuaded that no pure philosophical solution can do justice to our experience. In fact, I think that James's notion of pure experience is as much an abstraction as Hume's doctrine of empirical particulars. The only times I have experienced a "booming, buzzing confusion" were once in my youth when I was kicked in the head during a football game and, on occasion, in my later years when introduced to the joys and sorrows of strong drink. Somewhere between James's inchoate "stream of consciousness" and Hume's pristine particulars is a realm of experience which is neither fragmented bits and pieces as in Hume, nor a muddy flow as in James, but distinctive, as Hume insists, and already partly coherent, as with James. It is waiting for further shaping by each of us. This is the world of hints and guesses which theology calls creation. God has given the fabric warp, and calls on us to give it woof, just as in the Genesis narrative he created the animals and called upon humankind to give them names. (Webster's *Dictionary* notes that the warp is usually stouter and harder twisted than the woof.) We not only name the animals, we clarify our values, and we choose the God with whom we will wrestle and to whom we will pray. All this is the will's activity, and James is right in his phenomenology of that process. But the courage to make ultimate choices, and the criteria by which we say that Jonestown represents the demonic in religion, are not something we make, but something we receive. Here our wills are passive, not active, and God comes to us, not we to him.

But the dialectic between activity and passivity in our wills is a natural dialectic. James was right, I think, that the relation between the natural and the supernatural is a natural relation. There is a comprehensible interdependence between our will and God's. Interdependence can be of two kinds. There can be a mutual interdependence, where I am as dependent upon you as you are upon me. There can be an asymmetric interdependence, where I am dependent upon an Other, who receives and is changed by that dependence without necessarily being dependent upon me in the same way. It is this latter model which reveals our relationship to God. What would this mean in the paradigm case which we have been considering, the question of will? Specifically, in what way is the will of God different from, but related to, our wills?

Protestant orthodoxy seems to me to have been anthropomorphic in speaking of God's will as though it were conditioned by time. I began thinking about this issue in a conversation with John Bennett at Union Seminary in the '50s, a time when we were all anticipating a nuclear holocaust. He said, "If that happens, then God has been defeated." I thought, No, it may mean that there never was a God after all; but if there is a God, part of what it means to be God is to have the ultimate real power, and therefore not be subject to defeat. To be theological for a moment, the meaning of the crucifixion is that God does indeed suffer; but the meaning of the resurrection is that God is not defeated. The point of the eighth chapter of Romans is that our hope is absolutely assured, no matter what. God's will, I think, is different from ours in that God does not struggle. Process philosophers like Cobb, pragmatists like James, evolutionists like Teilhard de Chardin all have a doctrine of a struggling God; but it seems to me that God speaks his Word and it is so. Our wills are teleological because we live in time, but there is no human telos in eternity, and God's will is eternal. As far as history is concerned, God makes the warp of his rain to fall on the just and the unjust, and gives us freedom in our woof-weaving.

The great weakness of the Calvinist view of God is that God is unresponsive to what we freely make of our historical future. So there must be a sense in which God does change. When, in the Holy Communion service, we offer to God ourselves, our souls and bodies, to be a reasonable, holy, and living sacrifice, that must make a difference to God. So Hartshorne's view that we contribute something to the life of God seems to me to be true. The detailed woof of history is what we will. The eschatological warp of history is what God wills. God works in history through those who serve the eschaton. And the eschaton will be whether we destroy our history or not.

NOTES

1. Rudolf Bultmann, *Primitive Christianity*, trans. R. H. Fuller (London and New York: Thames & Hudson, 1956), p. 181.

2. William James, *The Will to Believe and Other Essays in Popular Philosophy* (London and New York: Longmans Green & Co., 1927), p. 11.

3. William Ernest Hocking, *The Meaning of God in Human Experience* (New Haven, Conn.: Yale University Press, 1912), p. 149.

9

Confessions of Theory and Life

J. N. FINDLAY

I HAVE UNDERTAKEN TO give an account of my personal approach
to Transcendence under the three heads of my own life-history,
my views regarding the structure of Being, and my views regarding the structure of the Value-realm. I have certain persuasions
regarding the senses or manners in which things can be said to be,
and in the underived primacy of some of these senses or manners.
I also have certain persuasions regarding the status of various
sorts of Value, both those which I regard as merely personal, and
those which I regard as suprapersonal, valid for the choices and
preferences of everyone and in relation to everyone. And I have
persuasions which combine both of these persuasions, and it is
there that my religious persuasions are located. For Religion, I
take it, looks for what is in the supreme sense real, and on which
everything depends for its capacity to be, and it seeks to combine
this with what is in the supreme sense excellent, being that Very
Perfection itself from which all imperfect cases of excellence are
derivative. But my views on these matters would not be perfectly
understandable if I did not also tell you how I came to hold them.
For they involve all the intermixture and mutual dissolution of influences which are characteristic of our epoch and which make it
as diversified in its subtler blendings as were the later ages of
Rome. Our great modern Western cities are indeed cultural repli-
cas of Rome, Carthage, Antioch, Athens, and Alexandria. In
short, I propose to treat you to my Confessions, though with
much less claim upon your interest than those of my fellow African, Augustine. For though I have been through my Manichaean

phase, I have not abandoned its positions so utterly, nor ended up in an orthodoxy so paradigmatic, as my great African predecessor. And though my life has had its disorderly periods, they were certainly not so colorful nor prolonged, nor so worthy of scandalous mention, as those of the great saint. I shall merely tell you how I arrived at my philosophico-religious conclusions in order that they should be a little more intelligible.

I am a South African of mixed British, Dutch, German, and French-Huguenot extraction; it is possible that I have a sprinkling of Jewish blood, though I have never been able to establish this. If I have, it puts me in the upper echelons of incarnate souls, for there can be no doubt that a considerable proportion of these are the tenants of Jewish bodies. My father was a man of exemplary righteousness who lived, rather than merely recognized, human brotherhood; my mother was always serene and very, very kind. Both of my parents were vastly superior to myself in their virtues, and I also had an elder brother who was my universal educator in youth in all that was cultural and intellectual and humane. In my vain attempt to equal or surpass his versatility, I took to the study of French, of which he happily knew nothing. My father's family were, in their religious leanings, evangelical, being descended on the mother's side from a Swabian missionary called Gottlob Schreiner, who must in many ways have resembled my father. My aunts on my father's side were embarrassingly liable to fall into prayer on the most unsuitable occasions and to compel one to join them, and one of them ran a home of rehabilitation on the slopes of Table Mountain where all manner of derelicts and sinners were subjected to a regimen of mud-baths and Bible-reading, by which they were effectively rehabilitated. But my father also had an aunt who was a women's libber, who wrote a novel which anticipated Ibsen's *Doll's House*, who read Herbert Spencer, and who became a friend of Havelock Ellis. On my mother's side my religious background was Dutch Calvinist, and I underwent Dutch Scripture lessons at school and was at times made to attend services in the Dutch Reformed Church. I cannot say that I was greatly inspired by the long prayers and rhetorical sermons that I listened to. My mother's side of the family was not, however, strict in its views, and included a great-uncle who traveled to

Europe, took to opium, studied the life of baboons at close range, and became one of the founders of Afrikaans literature. Life in my family home was relaxed and comfortable, wholly permissive, though it never had anything much to permit, and always full of a delightful concourse of friends and relations on short-term or long-term or permanent visits.

Of my ethico-religious development in early youth I shall only say that I turned from meat-eating at the age of three and was completely a non-meat-eater at the age of seven. The practice of killing and eating a living creature that one might have seen walking about one day before seemed to me indescribably monstrous and horrible, and not to be tolerated at whatever cost. I have remained an abstainer from meat all my life, at considerable difficulty to myself and inconvenience to others, but I have not attempted to impose this personal ethic on my family. Of the causes of my conversion I shall not dilate: they may have been psychoanalytic — I was once terrified when a cat yawned at me in a lonely room, and I once thought that my small sister would be rather good to eat — they may have stemmed from indoctrination in a previous existence, and they may have been simple moral impulsions which others feel but manage to suppress. My abhorrence of meat has, however, colored my religious life: it made me instinctively prefer Buddha to Jesus, and shrink from a God who could prefer Abel's sacrifice of frying lambs to Cain's pure sacrifice of the fruits of the earth, and who tried to test Abraham by commanding him to sacrifice his dearly loved son Isaac. And for his admiration of this last loathsome story I shall always loathe Sören Kierkegaard. The extensive eating of one species by another — though there are indeed many herbivores, such as giraffes and zebras, who do no such thing — has always exacerbated my sense of the depth of the evil in this realm of instantial dispersion.

At the period of adolescence I underwent another mystico-religious turn which has greatly influenced my later development. I became for five years, from 1919 till 1924, a Theosophist, during which period I was also at my first South African university. Theosophists are followers of Helena Petrovna Blavatsky, a Russian lady of some genius who was said by the investigators of the Society for Psychical Research, who discredited some of her miracles, to be one of the most interesting impostors in history. She died in 1891 and was succeeded, in the leadership of the movement, by Annie Besant and C. W. Leadbeater, who both died in the early '30s. The Theosophical doctrine is a judicious amalgam of Buddhism and Hinduism, with additions allegedly derived from clairvoyant and other paranormal experiences, and which also reinterpreted Christianity and other religions on Theosophic lines.

On the Theosophic doctrine I shall only say that it held to an identity-theory of the psychic life present in all animate and supposedly inanimate things; this life was, however, imperfectly individualized in the case of inorganic beings, plants, and the lower animals but became fully individualized in human persons. Before individualization, there were only group-souls into which accumulated experience was stored; after individualization there were individual souls that persisted for countless aeons in impalpable, spiritual bodies, till they too lost their separate identity in nirvana. The moment of individualization frequently occurred in the case of the domestic animals that one cherished in one's home. Individual souls went through a long process of spiritual education in a series of bodies, with periods of disembodiment in between: a total cycle of incarnation and disembodiment was said, following Plato, to last about a thousand years. Incarnation involved an obliteration of the memory of past embodiments, but not of their *karma* or action, and this, by an eternal law of the universe, requited greedy, selfish, ignorant living with much misery, both in the flesh and in interim states, while it rewarded generous, temperate, righteous, sapient living with joy in both worlds.

Ultimately, the effect of all this education would be to school the soul out of greed, selfishness, vainglory, hatred, ambition, ignorance, and all the deadly vices, and to make it fit for membership in the great body 'of the Elder Brethren of humanity, the Masters of Wisdom and Compassion. These Masters were, as a hierarchy, entrusted with the guidance and inspiration of human affairs, and of religious, scientific, artistic, and political movements; they also acted as personal teachers of chosen disciples, who then passed, under their guidance, through successive initiations or expansions of consciousness to final Mastership. Such

Masters inhabited human bodies and lived unrecognized all over the world: T. S. Eliot, greatly influenced by Theosophy, introduces them in his *Cocktail Party*.

There were Masters particularly concerned with the Theosophical movement: two of them lived in a valley in Tibet, and one in a castle in Hungary, though he paid occasional visits to Rome. The most glorious members of the hierarchy lived, however, in the inaccessible remotenesses of Central Asia. Discipleship to a Master was a relationship of peculiar intimacy in which the thoughts of disciple and Master were continuously intertwined. I believed myself to be affiliated to one such Master, and experienced the intertwining of my thoughts with his in the most vivid and glorious manner. I learned thereby that the profoundest religious experiences are possible even when their objects are nonexistent. The Master Jesus was held to be the Master particularly concerned with Christianity, though the Virgin Mary also had an important role; the Master Jesus was, however, held to have been overshadowed at the moment of Baptism by a far more august presence, that of the Bodhisattva Maitreya, the Buddha of the future, who was identified with Christ. The whole physical world in which we lived with our bodies and our bodily senses was held, further, to be merely the lowest of a series of subtle, ethereal worlds, in each of which we had bodies. In these subtle worlds subjective changes expressed themselves in corporeal and environmental changes; the landscape was always being transformed and rearranged by the inner states of the inhabitants.

I liked to imagine that an encounter with Cézanne would be marked by a sudden restylization of the landscape. In these subtle worlds were also the heavens and hells of popular religion, though not, most happily, lasting forever, and beyond them one could ascend to supersubtle, supersensible worlds which terminated in a supra-individual nirvana. The Theosophists differed, however, from their Oriental sources in that it was not for them a supreme concern to escape from the Wheel of Birth and Death. For them it was an educational wheel in which souls were continuously being generated, educated, and perfected, and who, when perfected, were put to work in the running of the educational machine. In all these doctrines, apart from the special revelations concerning the Masters, there is nothing that is not to be found in the cosmologies of Buddhism and Hinduism, but also, let it not be forgotten, in the cosmologies of Pythagoreanism and Platonism.

I at least received a marvelous education from my experience among the Theosophists. I became familiar with a wide range of Indian religious and philosophical writings in translation, and was beginning to be able to read some of them in Sanskrit. I can still write quite prettily in Devanagari. I aspired to go on from Sanskrit to Pali, and to become an interpreter of Buddhism. I also learned practices of Raja Yoga, and had many remarkable experiences, some unutterably blissful, others involving postecstatic depression. I achieved control for the time being of my sexual proclivities, but not, however, of my ambitious tendencies. I also had remarkable experiences of what Patañjali calls "the transformations of the thinking-principle": I could never afterward be deluded into thinking of the stream of thought as a mere stream of imagery or of bodily responses. I knew and know it to be a stream of impalpable acts in which the most complex meanings, which would require pages for their elucidation, are compressed as into a nutshell.

These introspections prepared me for my subsequent discovery of the wonderful work of the Würzburg psychologists, and for the phenomenology of Edmund Husserl. I also owe my whole interest in philosophy to my Theosophic beginnings. I studied Kant and Hegel, on both of whom my brother was keen, to find intellectual underpinnings for my Theosophical insights, and I studied Descartes, Spinoza, and Leibniz, and Plato, Aristotle, and Plotinus, for similar reasons. I aspired to become a Neo-Platonist expert as an alternative to taking up Pali scholarship, and I used to carry two huge volumes of Creuzer's text to the *Enneads, emendandas potius quam emendatas* with me on my travels. The philosophy to which I adhered at this time was, of course, unshakably idealistic: everything whatever was posited by the Subject. The Subject not only constituted the world of external Nature by positing it, but even constituted itself by its own act of self-positing. I was unaware at the time of the strong strain of realism which is to be found both in Kant and Hegel, and of course also in Plato and Aristotle. I regarded them all, as was then common, as members of a single, idealistic tradition. When my professor became ill in 1923, I gave a course on Logic based on the logical writings of Bosanquet and Bradley, which borrowed much from Hegel. This, fifty-eight years ago, was my debut in philosophy.

But as time evolved I became a little shaken in my faith in idealism by a reading of Prichard's *Kant's Theory of Knowledge*, with its insistence on the evident truth, undeniable when clearly grasped, that Knowing is not Making. I was also being shaken in my faith in the Theosophic revelations, because I came to think that they involved elements of self-deception and even of fraud. Madame Blavatsky had been shown, in a large number of cases, to have used trickery to assist the impact of her revelations: bells sounding in the air, letters dropping from the ceiling, Indian servants impersonating Masters, and the like. She even confessed to the Russian philosopher Solovyoff that one had to deceive people in order to guide them, and that the more trivial a "supernatural" phenomenon, the more readily would it be believed. And Leadbeater, the hierophant who took over after she died, claimed to possess a clairvoyance which enabled him to reconstruct the past history of the world and of the souls in it, including the past lives of Theosophical members. It also enabled him to sketch the makeup of the chemical elements, of humans' subtle bodies and their thought-forms, of the invisible structures built up by the celebration of the Eucharist. Most subtle of all, he managed to convince many Theosophists, including the president, that they had had experiences on higher planes of being that they were unable to remember: in this way he was able to conjure up a multitude of confirming witnesses. Lady Emily Lutyens underwent a high initiation one night when all she remembered was that a bat flew about in her room and woke her up. Apart from a few unfortunate scandals, Leadbeater maintained a profile of modesty and probity, and was helped in his efforts by the undoubted probity of the president, Mrs. Besant. Quite apart from all this, many of the occult revelations were incredible, or have been refuted by subsequent discoveries. Mrs. Besant was alleged to have started individual life as an animal on the moon, where we now know that there never were animals; the Heads of the Hierarchy were alleged to have come here from Venus, where we now know that it is too hot and too full of CO_2 for anyone to live and breathe, and the reference in the Creed to Christ's suffering under Pontius Pilate was alleged to be a corruption of a Gnostic document which told of the descent of the Logos into the πόντος πιλητός, the 'densely packed sea', of matter, a piece of nonsense really worthy of the Gnostics.

Convinced by many such evidences, I left the Theosophical movement, and have since been effectively immunized against all sorts of revealed religion, though I tried for a time to be a High Church Anglican and still have sympathy for that undemanding persuasion. But my experiences taught me an immense amount about religions, and how there are almost always some deceivers in every religious movement who mediate the transmission of messages which do not entail deception but which are of profound spiritual worth. In Christianity Dionysius the Areopagite is acknowledged to have been such a deceiver, though his deceits were better than the narrow zeal of a Tertullian; and I am not sure that John the Evangelist did not deliberately write accounts which he knew only to have a mystical and spiritual significance, as if he were recording things that really happened. To liken small things to great, there may be spiritually valuable elements and genuine religious forces even in so tarnished a religious movement as that of the Reverend Mr. Moon.

I also still believe that the Hindu-Buddhist-Pythagorean cosmology that I learned from the Theosophists, the belief in a spiritual education embracing many incarnations and ending either in a blessed nirvana or in an indefinite life of service with struggling souls, is the *only* cosmology that makes life remotely endurable. It is infinitely superior to the heaven-and-hell eschatologies of the Christians, which have borrowed much from it, and it goes without saying that it is infinitely superior to the this-world eschatology of Marxism, which has become so sadly tarnished in practice. If anyone has cheated us all, it has been Karl Marx. And the Theosophist cosmology and eschatology is the one in which Socrates, the mentor of us philosophers, was content to die, though he also confessed that he did not know it to be true and that perpetual sleep, rather than a perpetuity of dialectic, might be our ultimate destiny.

Like Socrates, I cannot be sure that the Pythagorean cosmology is true, and there are great difficulties in believing it, especially when we consider the brevity of the human past on this earth and the immense increase in its spiritual population. Unless there is soul-transport from planet to planet, the scheme will not work, and while I am happy to think that I may once have philosophized in Nalanda or Alexandria or Paris, I cannot take kindly to the suggestion that I philosophized far from our dear earth in some unknown planet of Alpha Centauri. As regards the interim spheres of being, the objections are, however, less. What we require is a spectrum of states leading from the hard individuality and separateness of the sense-world to regions in which everything has the plasticity with which we are acquainted in imagination and thought, and the transcendence of personal otherness that we experience in sympathy and love, as well as that spanning of the gulf between what is and what ought to be that we experience in our more exalted moments. Disembodiment or the dissolution of this too, too solid flesh, can mean only a life in that freer medium in which we already partially live, and with whose lower regions we are already well acquainted, though its apical pinnacles may be hard to scale in this present life.

In 1924 I went for a three-year period to Oxford, a crucial period in my *Bildungsgeschichte*, most of whose details are irrelevant for our purposes here. Oxford is one of the terrestrial centers where Absolute Spirit, in Hegelian phrase, engenders and enjoys itself, and where one achieves touch with the best companions one will ever have in this life and also with those life-giving centers of civilization and beauty which are mainly to be found in France, in Germany, in Italy, and in Greece. During this period of my *Bildung* I not only abandoned Theosophy, but also every trace of philosophical idealism. I became convinced that Being is not constructed by the minds that think of it, but that it intimates itself to them in a variety of ontic experiences, in which it often appears in strange guises, disappointing our *a priori* expectations as often as it fulfills them. I became aware of the terrible facts of human existence, and particularly of our fantastic internal perversity as revealed by the researches of Sigmund Freud. And I began to believe in a piecemeal philosophy, one that would seek to enumerate and analyze all the queer sorts of things that one encounters in one's dealings with the world, sorts of things that are at times of the happiest internal symmetry and well-suitedness, at times of the most brutal facticity and discrepant unintelligibility. I began to doubt all speculative constructions which explained everything in terms of a single, absolute principle. I became interested in the epistemological and logico-mathematical writings of Bertrand Russell and in the Wittgenstein of the *Tractatus*, with sad consequences for my acceptance into the then Valhalla of Oxford fellowships. For were not Bertrand Russell and Wittgenstein men of the *other* University, of whom only criminal nonsense was to be expected?

In such an ambiance promotion for Findlay was not in the cards, and Findlay spent twenty years in the wilderness of South Africa and New Zealand, struggling against nationalist ebullitions in the former country and bureaucratic-imperialistic rigidities in the latter. Nonetheless, in both countries, Findlay continued to make philosophical discoveries of the utmost importance for himself: the intentionalist psychology of Brentano with its stress on the self-transcendence of even the most trivial thought-experience, the wonderful object-ontology of Alexius Meinong, on whom I wrote my first book, published in 1933 and republished in 1963, and the similar ontology and intentionalist psychology of Edmund Husserl in his early *Logische Untersuchungen*, of which I later became the privileged translator. I value the early Husserl much more than the later idealistic phenomenologist, though there are many profound insights in the declining works of the latter. But I have never been able, *pace* my friend Professor Gadamer, to make sense of that anguished existentialist Heidegger, nor of the other anguished existentialists that have been recommended to our admiration. The English language, and English thought, is for some reason not a house for that sort of *Sein*.

During this period I also spent a sabbatical year, in the middle of which the Second World War erupted, listening to Carnap and Quine and Heidegger and G. E. Moore and Wittgenstein, becoming deeply versed in the translation of the way of ideas and thought-intentions into the way of words. My reactions to Moore and Wittgenstein were expressed in a number of articles, on Time, on Wittgensteinian philosophy, and on God, all republished in my *Language, Mind, and Value*. These articles got me out of the colonial rat-race into more metropolitan rat-mazes, first in England, from 1948 to 1966, and after that in America. The article on God, published in *Mind* in 1948, deserves especial mention. There I argue that the concept of God is that of a Being which exists of necessity and not merely contingently, and that it must also possess every form of excellence not in a merely contingent but in a necessary manner. But if, following Kant, we argue that there can never be a logical bridge from a concept to its embodiment in existence and experience, and if we hold that no synthesis of all forms of excellence can be necessary, then it follows, not that God's existence is wholly beyond proof, but that it admits of a conclusive disproof. There can be no such being, since the conception of an existentially necessary, all-perfect being is intrinsically incoherent. This theologically shocking article established me in the academic firmament of England, though my well-wishers said that I was still walking humbly with my nonexistent God.

In the third period of my life, from 1948 to the present, I returned to something like my earliest philosophical convictions, though I have never been able to stomach philosophical idealism, which I regard as basically erroneous. *Esse* is not *percipi* nor *concipi*, nor even *percipere* and *concipere*, though the latter are the highest cases of *esse*, to which all other cases tend. But I have come to the view that the notion of a necessary existent, something which is, but which cannot not be, and on which all contingent existences depend, whether as its intrinsic modes or its dependent offshoots, obeys a peculiar logic: if it is internally possible, it must, being something which covers *all* possibilities, necessarily be actual, whatever is the case; but if, on the other hand, it is in any way possible for it *not* to be, then it is altogether certain and necessary that it isn't, for what is capable of not-being certainly doesn't cover all possibilities.

Kant, in his criticisms of the Ideal of Pure Reason, conclusively showed that, in the world of phenomenal contingency, where concept and intuitive fulfillment diverge, the existence of a necessary being is not doubtful, but impossible: it embodies something which contingent, phenomenal being cannot include. Kant did not, however, prove, nor did he think he was proving, that there might not be a necessary existent beyond the range of contingent, phenomenal being, and he in fact held it to be a flawless rational ideal, in terms of which we cannot but think, and in which we can and ought to believe, but of which, since knowledge is necessarily limited to phenomenal contingencies, we can never have knowledge. I accept the view of Kant, since I perceive, when I consider human ideas, that a belief in the necessary contingency of all being is held by almost no one, and seems perilously on the verge of self-contradiction, since it affirms a necessary absence of necessity.

All philosophers, as Aristotle would say, believe in the irremovable reality of something or other, whether this be brute Matter, or dialectically developing Matter, or Substance, or Space, or Space-Time, or Logical Space, or Sensibilia, or *Bewusstsein Überhaupt*, or the Transcendental Ego, or whatever. They commit themselves to the being of some great single fixture, or set of fixtures, to which everything else attaches and is wholly parasitic, it being such that *its* being requires no derivation, whereas the being of everything else requires a derivation in terms of *it*. And to the extent that such a fixture fails to explain something other than itself, what is thus other becomes a rival Absolute, regarding which the Homeric dictum, quoted by Aristotle, holds: that οὐκ ἀγαθόν πολυκοιρανίη, divided sovereignty is intolerable, and that εἰς κοίρανος ἔστω, let there be a single sovereign.

The need for an Absolute emerges from another set of considerations: that every one of our most ordinary concepts involves antinomies, often ignored, in its working, which explains the necessity of philosophy. In the case of each ordinary concept we can construct an antilogism, or inconsistent set, consisting of propositions all of which are acceptable and express the sense of the concept, but of which some are necessarily inconsistent with others, thus giving rise, according as we reject one or other of basic acceptances, to a different philosophical position or to a different analysis of a basic concept. I shall construct only one such antilogism for your benefit, the Antilogism of Knowledge, of which the members are (1) All knowledge is of the real; (2) The real is independent of knowledge; (3) Knowledge involves an inner warrant of certainty. Now if (1) and (2), not-(3): there can be no inner warrant that we are hitting upon what is independently real — Absolute Skepticism. Again, if (1) and (3), then not-(2): the real, since it is attested by an inner warrant, is not independent of knowledge — Idealism. Again, if (2) and (3), then not-(1): knowledge is not of the real — Phenomenalism. Similar antilogisms can, with a little practice, be constructed about Time, Freedom, Value, God, Causation, Negation, and in fact anything whatever.

These conflicts reveal the essential inadequacy of the sort of thought which is concerned with finite, mutually exclusive things taking in each other's washing, and which does not attempt accommodations of a more fundamental kind. And such accommodations force us toward an Absolute which will in some manner reconcile our antinomic acceptances, and show that they are in some sense different ways of regarding the same reality. The problem of knowledge, e.g., must point to some necessary accommodation of Thought and Being which I do not think is achieved in Skepticism, Phenomenalism, or Idealism, but which is not hard to find once you determine to avoid one-sided plausibilities. What will merge will astonish you by its strangeness, but after a while it will rather astonish you by its simplicity; you will have obeyed the supreme maxim of philosophy: Turn your problems into the stuff of your concepts. Thus Knowledge involves that necessary dovetailing of τὸ παντελῶς ὄν into τὸ παντελῶς γνωστὸν in which Plato believed and which Hegel followed him in believing, but which emphatically does not involve the one-sided dependence of either on the other, but on something beyond both. Everywhere philosophical problems drag us toward Absolute Being, or to the Absolute Idea, or to Unity itself, or whatever, by showing us that our familiar ideas involve strange linkages that destroy them, until at length a greater strangeness emerges, which soon reveals itself as the very truth itself.

In all this tracking down of the Absolute, notions of Value play an all-important part. For not only is knowledge shot through and through with its own peculiar values, but Knowledge of the Absolute is arguably the highest of all values. In the Absolute, however, *all* values must find a place, and be fitted into it like jewels in a crown. I am talking not just emotively but also rationally, for I believe, with Kant, that there is such a thing as Practical Reason, and that Practical Reason is characterized, not by any sort of contingent, empirical content, but by pure universality itself, its mark being that it prescribes what could and should be pursued in all cases and by all people, whatever they happen to want, and not by some only and in cases arbitrarily determined. Only, whereas Kant believes that practical universality should be applied only to the maxims of action, and not to their ends, I believe that there is a family of ends, which necessarily emerges when we strive to achieve that which, granted the endless multiplicity of concrete objects of desire, could nonetheless be desired by everyone and for everyone. I believe that the happiness of satisfied want is something that everyone could and should, all else being equal, desire for everyone. Not everyone can or should like horse-racing or polo-playing, but everyone can and should wish that all should have what they want or like, provided, of course, that it does not conflict with other wants for self or others.

Kant admits the rationality of pursuing satisfaction by making it a part of the *Summum Bonum* and a necessary complement to the Good Will. But I should contend that it is a good thing quite apart from the Good Will (though not in conflict with this), and that we should pursue it in, e.g., the case of the lower animals, where the Good Will is necessarily absent. It is also possible to deduce the theorems that certain ends such as that of reasoned knowledge and disinterested aesthetic pleasure in the contemplated structures of things are objects that should be desired by everyone for everyone, and these too are ends admitted by Kant as being parts of the Rational Good. The Good Will finally imposes itself on all the other goods, and would without them be void of all content. The Schelerian axiom that Virtue necessarily arises "on the back" of all other values, and should not, and indeed cannot, be pursued in and for itself alone, is thus a necessary codicil to the Kantian formalism. And the whole firmament of Values that has been elaborated by an intuitive value-theorist such as Nicolai Hartmann could and should be given a Transcen-

dental Deduction from the nature of the rational or universalizing Will, and this I have endeavored to do in my work *Values and
Intentions*, which has received pretty little notice, and of which I
am sure that Professor Gadamer, who has responded favorably to
some of my writings, will never have heard.

I am not, however, concerned to offer a tardy advertizement
of my seventeen-year-old book, but to consider the place of
Values in the Absolute. Mind with its infinitely ranging intentionality and essential teleology is far too remarkable and unifying a
feature of Being to be relegated to some subordinate place in the
Absolute: if not given the highest place in that structure, it must
nonetheless be given a very high one. The Absolute must at least
be credited with an inherent Purpose which is differentiated into
a large number of directions, which it must always seek to harmonize and to reconcile. This infinite endeavor necessarily involves
the presence of a great number of fundamental resistances essential to itself, which splinter it into a whole host of separate en-
deavors which are always running athwart one another, and
which Plato in the *Timaeus* calls the Works of Necessity. Against
all this splintering and mutual interference the Absolute necessarily sets itself, and the fruits of its resolution are seen in the emergence of Mind and its development toward the universal rational
values. It is not right, in my view, to regard the Absolute as a conscious, striving person, as something revealed in unconscious and
conscious being alike; but rather it should be regarded as being
more fully itself in conscious personal beings, and particularly in
those in whom aspiration assumes a religious form. For Religion
is nothing but the Absolute in its intensest expression, achieving
its fullest self-awareness and self-satisfaction. And the Absolute is
not to be conceived as something which instantiates or exemplifies the highest values, since instantiation is necessarily one-sided
and imperfect, and since the highest values also lie in different directions and cannot be instantiated all together, a point often
stressed by Nicolai Hartmann. No, the Absolute rather *is* all the
highest values, and is them all together, in a unity which transcends one-sided exemplification and one-sided comprehension.
We are forced toward a Platonic solution as the only way to make
the Absolute truly comprehensive and axiologically satisfactory.

Does my view of the Absolute mean that the Absolute is turned into something arid and abstract, not a living God active in history? No, for what people think of as concretely real is, in its transience and one-sidedness, truly abstract: only the inclusively Good is really concrete and all-embracing. One must reform one's ontology in order to have a dim understanding of the Absolute. And though the Absolute transcends all its unconsciously impersonal and consciously personal exemplifications, it is nonetheless in its essence such as to be capable of having instances, in which it will in varying degrees live and be itself. Is the view that I am advocating not wholly immanental and pantheistic? No, for it acknowledges the infinite, ontological gulf between what *is* all the species of Value themselves, and is them together, and what is merely an imperfect and perhaps deviant case of them. Do I leave place for differentiations like the Trinitarian which have been favored in many religions? I certainly do. For in addition to the dynamic Spirit of Goodness which is at work in the world and which speaks by the Prophets and Poets, there is also the timeless pattern of Goodness differentiated into all its possible species and likewise differentiated into all the knowledge — species which envisage them, and which all together make up a complex, hierarchical, articulated pattern of perfection, of which mathematicians have perhaps the best understanding. And there is also, beyond all this articulated perfection, the unarticulated principle or Organized Unity itself, in which all things, perfect and imperfect, have their source and origin. And is my view of the life of the Spirit merely a this-world affair? It need not be such. There may very well be a spectrum of states leading from sensuous, transient, spatially and temporally dispersed, embodied being, which often deviates from good form, to nonsensuous, enduring, undispersed, disembodied being, in which what is and what ought to be plainly will come together.

And do I leave place for transfigured individual persons in whom the Absolute is very specially present? I do, and I believe that human history has thrown up at least three of them, Buddha, Socrates, and Jesus. They are all very different and I do not presume to rank them. But I should regard the Tathāgata Gautama Buddha as having expressed that aspect of the Absolute which is beyond all finite, instantial being, and which formulated itself in the suprapersonal goal of nirvana and in the impersonal Dharma which silently pushes us all toward it. And I regard Socrates, the son of Sophroniscus, as having expressed and lived the timeless ideal of differentiated clarity and excellence which is the Absolute for all of us philosophers. And I should regard our Christian Master as having expressed the Absolute as a moving Spirit present in all finite, transitory things and persons, and capable of coming down from its heights and transfiguring and redeeming them all.

As Christians you may consider my three Avataras unacceptable, but I, like the Japanese, have to have a plurality of religions. And I would remind you that even Kierkegaard thought Socrates was a Saint, and that Buddha has been unwittingly canonized in the Catholic Church under the name of St. Josaphat, a corruption of Bodhisat and credited with an identical story. And above all these Avataras I am willing, at a time when the Catholic Church is trying to cut them down, to postulate any number of Hypostases, Thrones, Dominations, Princedoms, Virtues, and Powers. I am in fact sure that there are vastly many such. But I know that I am neither Pythagoras nor Aśvaghoṣa nor Augustine, and that I have made myself rather ridiculous by all my glib pronouncements on the Absolute.

10

The Religious Dimension in Heidegger

HANS-GEORG GADAMER

To INQUIRE ABOUT THE religious dimension in Heidegger seems almost a provocation, or at least a paradoxical venture. Jean-Paul Sartre comes to mind. In his admiration for Heidegger, he presented him outright, alongside Nietzsche, as one of the representative atheistic thinkers of our time. But I should like to demonstrate that such an understanding of Heidegger can only derive from an appropriation of his philosophy which remains superficial.

It is, however, quite a different question to ask whether the use of Heidegger by Christian theology is justified, and for half a century Christian theologians have been drawing on his thinking. Heidegger himself made it explicitly clear that asking the question about Being, which was his own special mission, was not to be understood as asking the question about God. His position regarding the contemporary theology of the Catholic and Protestant confessions became increasingly critical in tone as the years passed. But one has to ask oneself whether such a critique of theology does not, on the contrary, testify that "God," the revealed or the concealed, never became an empty word for him. As is known, Heidegger came from a Catholic family and was brought up in that faith. He attended the gymnasium in Konstanz, which, without being purely Catholic, was nonetheless located in an area where both Catholic and Protestant confessions enjoyed an active life. When he finished school he became a novice at the Jesuit seminary in Freiburg, but left after a short while.

Both religious commitment and philosophical inclination

193

were already strongly pronounced in Heidegger when he was quite young. He was passionately interested in philosophy during these early years, when his attachment to the Church and to religion was still unproblematic. One of his teachers at the gymnasium in Konstanz, Groeber, who later became bishop of Freiburg, recognized early on his brilliant gift and devotion to philosophy. Heidegger once told me that a teacher caught him red-handed (doubtless in a boring class) reading Kant's *Critique of Pure Reason* under his desk! That truly was a kind of free ticket for a great intellectual future! Because of Heidegger's talent, Groeber gave him a learned book on Aristotle that was "modern" for the time, although not particularly deep in its speculations: Franz Brentano's *Von der mannigfachen Bedeutung des Seienden bei Aristoteles*. In a scrupulous analysis this study developed the multiplicity of the meanings of Being in Aristotle, but without providing any answer to the question of how these meanings were connected. And it was precisely that which inspired the young Heidegger, as he has often noted. The different meanings of Being which Aristotle distinguished challenged him to ask about their hidden unity; not, to be sure, in the sense of a systematization, as Cajetan and Suarez, the Scholastics of the Counter Reformation, sought to bring into Aristotelianism. Motifs began to appear more often in Heidegger's work as evidence that for him Being was not a species, such as it was in the Scholastic doctrine of the *analogia entis*. These motifs were not developed in terms of a metaphysical doctrine, but rather for the sake of learning how to ask the open, pressing question: What does it mean to speak of Being?

Heidegger's talent brought him swift success. He wrote his dissertation on the doctrine of judgment in psychologism, under the supervision of Rickert. He mentioned this work in a Marburg lecture, saying: "when I was still playing children's games . . ." The minor subjects in which he took exams (no one would guess this) were mathematics and physics! He qualified as a university lecturer when he was twenty-seven, and became an assistant to Edmund Husserl, the successor of Rickert at Freiburg. It was Husserl, the founder of phenomenology, who taught him the splendid technique of phenomenological description. Already in these early years as an assistant, Heidegger had an unusual following for a

Privatdozent, and in no time he acquired nothing short of a magical influence on the younger students as well as on his contemporaries. Among these were Julius Ebbinghaus, Oskar Becker, Karl Löwith, and Walter Bröcker, names well-known today. Rumors about Heidegger reached me in Marburg, where I was preparing my doctoral dissertation, for students would come from Freiburg, even as early as 1920–21, with more to say about Heidegger than Husserl. They reported that his lectures were extremely individual and profoundly revolutionary. In one lecture, for example, he was said to have used the expression: "It is worlding" (*Es weltet*). We realize today that this was a splendid anticipation of his thinking after the "turn." In those days one could not hear anything like that from a neo-Kantian, nor, for that matter, from Husserl. It was young Heidegger who raised questions such as these: Whatever had become of the transcendental ego? What sort of term was it anyway? Was there even such a thing at all? Ten years before the so-called turn, when Heidegger overcame his own transcendental understanding of the self and his dependence on Husserl, he found a first expression here that did not proceed from the subject and the transcendental consciousness-in-general (*Bewusstsein überhaupt*). Instead, the 'event' (*Ereignis*) of the 'clearing' (*Lichtung*) was pronounced as a herald in the "worlding."

We have learned a good deal in the meantime about this first phase of Heideggerian thinking that took place in Freiburg after World War I. Pöggeler has written about it; in an excellent essay Karl Lehmann has reconstructed the meaning of Paul for the young Heidegger; and recently Thomas Sheehan has been able to provide us with a detailed account of a lecture Heidegger gave in 1920, "Phenomenology of Religion." From this lecture we see that Heidegger was particularly fascinated by the early Christian community's experience of time—that eschatological instant which is not experienced as anticipation, nor as a passage through time, nor as a calculation of the time that elapses before Christ's return. For Christ comes "as a thief in the night" (I Thess. 5:2). Measured time, reckoning with time, and the whole background of Greek ontology which dominates our conception of time in philosophy and scholarship, fall short before this experience of temporality. The personal letter Heidegger wrote the following

year to Karl Löwith, one of his friends and followers, demon-
strates that we are dealing with more than a philosophical challenge at this point. The basic religious concern of the young
thinker is also at issue. In that letter Heidegger wrote: "You and
Becker make a fundamental error when you measure me (hypo-
thetically or not) by the yardsticks of Nietzsche, Kierkegaard, or
any other creative philosopher. That is not forbidden, but then it
has to be said that I am not a philosopher. I do not fancy myself to
be doing anything vaguely comparable to what those others have
done." And then the letter states: "I am a Christian theologian!"

It is not wrong to recognize in this the deepest motivation of
Heidegger's way of thought. He saw himself, at that time, as a
Christian theologian. The task of disengaging himself from the
regnant Christian theology in which he was raised, in other
words, challenged all his efforts to clarify his own ideas and questions. Heidegger has said himself that he received the set of imple-
ments for this "theological" task from some of the important
teachers on the faculty of theology at Freiburg. At that same time
the young Luther above all else had acquired a decisive significance for Heidegger. And the aforementioned lecture on the phenomenology of religion teaches us that he went back with true
elective affinity to the oldest documents of the New Testament,
the epistles of Paul.

During this period there were two masters who provided
Heidegger with the proper conceptual training he needed. On the
one hand there was Husserl with his mastery of the phenomenological approach. It is significant that as Husserl's assistant Heidegger did *not* teach the neo-Kantian program of the *Ideas* (completed in 1913), but taught instead the *Logical Investigations*, a
work Husserl believed himself to have moved far beyond. And it
was the sixth investigation, which had just appeared in a revised
edition, that Heidegger taught most frequently. In it these questions had an important place: What is the meaning of "it is"?
What sort of a noetic act is it in which this formal category of "it
is" is intended? This doctrine of the categorical intuition, and certainly also Husserl's accomplished analyses concerning time-
consciousness (which Heidegger was to edit for the first time only
later), challenged Heidegger. What a detailed, analytical art

Husserl had mastered—and what a dead end. The phenomenological analysis of time-consciousness led Heidegger yet further away from the question of Christian faith which was constantly hounding him, further than Augustine's celebrated despair which arose when he tried to comprehend the enigma of time.

The idealistic elaboration of the *Ideas* was *not* what attracted Heidegger. He went to the *Ideas* to admire the consistency of Husserl's thorough encounter with the topic of transcendental subjectivity. What Heidegger learned from this undoubtedly granted him an immunity against cheap realistic escapes in the manner of the Munich phenomenologists and made him immune even to Scheler's anti-idealistic polemic as it was understood in those days. But he had always regarded the principle of the transcendental ego with suspicion. Thomas Sheehan has told me that Heidegger once showed him his offprint of Husserl's essay that appeared in *Logos*, 1910: "Philosophy as Rigorous Science." In a well-known passage of the essay Husserl says that our method and our principle must be "to the things themselves." The young Heidegger had written in the margin of his copy, "We wish to take Husserl seriously." Certainly it was a polemical statement. Instead of entangling himself with Husserl in the doctrine of transcendental reduction and in the final substantiation of the *cogito*, Heidegger obeyed this actual principle "to the things themselves" in his own way.

In order to acquire the proper distance from Husserl's transcendental idealism without slipping back into the naïveté of a dogmatic realism, Heidegger found himself another great master: Aristotle. He could hardly expect to find a blood brother for his own religiously motivated questioning, but returning to his early Aristotelian studies as an expert in phenomenology allowed Heidegger to discover a new Aristotle, who manifested aspects completely different from those preferred by Scholastic theology. Heidegger was certainly not foolish enough to overlook the fact that the Greek concept of time had been informed by Aristotle. But there had to be a more direct way leading to the conceptual clarification of the eschatological moment than Aristotelian physics. The nearness of Aristotelian thinking to factical *Dasein* in its concrete way of living and in its natural world-orientation brought indirect help. In a succession of semesters Heidegger presented his studies on Aristotelian ethics, physics, anthropology (*De anima*), and on the *Rhetoric*. Of course, he also lectured on the key passages of Aristotelian metaphysics. Heidegger wrote me in the fall of 1922, explaining that he meant to develop these lectures into a lengthy publication for the 1923 number of the *Yearbook for Philosophy and Phenomenological Research*. That enterprise, however, was never realized because meanwhile he became a full-time professor at the University of Marburg, where he was busy preparing new courses. Nevertheless, Aristotle remained one of the focal points of his teaching at Marburg.

In what way could Aristotle serve Heidegger? Was it only in contrast to the Christian experience of time and to the basic role of historicality in modern thinking? Only as a counterposition?

The opposite is true. Aristotle functioned as a chief witness for the approach "to the things themselves." And in so doing he also worked indirectly against his own ontological bias which Heidegger later was to call "Being as presence-at-hand" (*Sein-als-Vorhandenheit*). He became a critical guide for Heidegger's new questioning. The phenomenological interpretations of Aristotle which Heidegger was preparing for publication in Husserl's *Yearbook* were not aimed at the philosophical theology so dear to Scholasticism, which has its ultimate grounding in the orientation of the *Physics* and in the prime mover of Aristotelian metaphysics. His interpretations were aimed more at being close to the concrete, factical realization of *Dasein*, which could be grasped primarily in Aristotle's practical philosophy and in his *Rhetoric*. The ways of 'True-being', of ἀληθεύειν, which are considered in the *Nicomachean Ethics*, Book VI, held primarily this sense for Heidegger: the primacy of judgment, of logic, and of scientific discipline reached a critical limit for understanding the facticity of human life in these texts. An ἄλλο εἶδος γνώσεως came into its own right which does not perceive objects and does not set out to be objective knowing, but rather means to be the clarity which is possible for *Dasein* in a factically lived existence. For this reason Aristotelian rhetoric also became essential in addition to the *Ethics*, because it had to do with πράγυατα and παθήυατα — and not with objects.

The young Heidegger, moreover, could obtain in an astonishing way munitions for his "existentiell" critique of the transcendental concept of subject and object from the Aristotelian critique of Plato's idea of the Good. The Good, which differentiates itself through its manifold ways of encounter, is not some highest object or principle. So also Being (*das Sein*) is in everything that is present (*anwesend*), even though some eminent being may be standing at the end guaranteeing all presence (*Anwesenheit*). This is the metaphysical question about "Being as such" which Aristotle, and young Heidegger with him, seeks to answer. When Heidegger encountered Aristotelian physics and metaphysics, what inspired him was the fact that all understanding of Being is based on the understanding of movement, and all true assertion is based on the unconcealed presence, or, in other words, in the final analysis on the ὄν ὡς ἀληθές. Being in its movement, Being in its unconcealment, are not regions of objects about which one could make assertions. This does not imply a realism that is opposed to subjective idealism, not does it imply in any way a theory of knowledge. It describes instead the thing itself which as being-in-the-world knows nothing of the subject-object split.

Now, however, Heidegger's old question put to the Christian theologians pushed beyond this interest in an unscholastic Aristotle to ask whether there was not a more suitable Christian self-understanding than that offered by contemporary theology. In this respect his new interpretations of Aristotle are only the first step down a long path of thought. In 1922 I had the opportunity to read the introduction to these interpretations, which Heidegger had sent in manuscript form to my teacher, Paul Natorp. (The text is not yet edited but it should be preserved, at least in typescript, without the numerous handwritten additions in Natorp's copy). The introduction shows that Heidegger took these first steps consciously: he was attempting an analysis of the hermeneutic situation involved today in an interpretation of Aristotle. And where did his analysis begin? With the young Luther. It began precisely with Luther, who demanded that everyone who wished to be a genuine Christian forswear Aristotle, that "great liar." This was followed by other names which I remember in detail: Gabriel Biel, Peter Lombard the Sentence Master, Augustine, and, finally, Paul. It was undoubtedly Heidegger's old, well-testified concern for the original Christian message that stood behind his study of Aristotle.

Not that Heidegger expected to find any immediate assistance in Aristotle. On the contrary, his engagement with Aristotle's authentic thinking must have made his own theological enterprise only more difficult since the theology he had learned, which was founded to a large extent on Aristotelian metaphysics, never once concurred with the actual motives of Greek thinking. The living concept of time which Heidegger found in Paul was not Greek at all. But it was the Greek concept of time, formulated by Plato and Aristotle as measure and number of movement, which dominated the conceptual horizon of all later periods, from Augustine to Kant and on down to Einstein. As part of his most particular and deepest problem — the Christian anticipation of the end of time — this question was bound to remain active for Heidegger: Had not the pressure of Greek thinking on the Christian experience of faith made the Christian message on the whole unrecognizable, and had it not at least estranged Christian theology from the religious task which is most properly its own? Indeed, not only did Paul's and Luther's doctrine of justification become meaningful for Heidegger, but he also resumed Harnack's thesis on the fateful Hellenization of Christian theology. In the end he doubted the adequacy of his theological upbringing as a whole, and even beyond that, he recognized in the Greek heritage weighing upon all modern thought, the source of our predicament about Being as well as of modern historicism. It was that predicament which dictated the epigraph of *Being and Time* to him.

There were as well all the *aporiae* of modern thinking which Heidegger confronted in Bergson, Simmel, Lask, and especially in Dilthey. The problems of modern philosophy troubled him greatly during the decisive years of his development. Thus, around the time of World War I, when Kierkegaard's concept of existence became the new catchword for Unamuno, Haecker, Buber, Ebner, Jaspers — to name a few — it also became a concern for Heidegger. Diederich's German edition of Kierkegaard had just come out, creating a new interest in the thinker, and in Kierkegaard's brilliant essays Heidegger found once more his very own themes: existence (*Existenz*) in the new, emphatic sense of Being in the world, and an eschatological understanding of time. He found in Kierkegaard not only a polemic against Hegel from a religious viewpoint — Hegel, that last and most radical Greek of all, as Heidegger once said, who was veiling the either-or of human existence through speculative mediation. Kierkegaard's intentional confrontation with the Greek concept of memory was bound to make sense to Heidegger as well. For after all Kierkegaard's category of retrieval was coined precisely because the notion of retrieval fades into memory and into the illusion of a return of the same, if it is not experienced as the paradox of historicality, as the retrieval of the unretrievable, as time beyond all time.

This was the experience of time which Heidegger recognized in Paul's account of the return of Christ, which is neither a second coming to be expected nor is it, as *parousia*, a being present one day; rather, it is strictly a coming. Above all Kierkegaard's religious discourses (which came out in German in 1923 under the title *Leben und Walten der Liebe*) had to confirm Heidegger. In this work one finds the noteworthy distinction between understanding at a distance and understanding in contemporaneity. Kierkegaard criticized the Church, as Heidegger understood him, for not putting the Christian message into effect at the level of the individual's existence and for toning down the paradox of contemporaneity at the center of the Christian message. If Jesus' death on the cross is understood "at a distance" it has no real gravity. This also holds for speaking about God and the Christian message, as theology (and the dialectical speculations of the Hegelians) are doing. They practice the same distanciation. Is it possible to talk about God as one would about an object? Is it not the temptation of Greek metaphysics to argue over the existence and the qualities of God as one would about an object of scientific knowledge? Here in Kierkegaard lie the roots of dialectical theology which had its beginning at that time, in 1919, with Karl Barth's commentary on Paul's Epistle to the Romans. Heidegger became friends with Bultmann during his stay at Marburg, when the task at hand was above all to reckon with historicist theology and, beyond that, to learn to think the historicality and the finitude of human *Dasein* more radically.

At that time Heidegger repeatedly called upon the authority of church historian Franz Overbeck, who had been a friend of Nietzsche's. Overbeck's polemical treatise on the Christian character of theology expressed the most particular uncertainty, and this animated Heidegger. The uncertainty in Overbeck completely confirmed Heidegger's philosophical experience of the inadequacy of the Greek concept of Being for Christianity's thinking about the end of time, which is not an anticipation of a coming event. When Heidegger wrote in the letter to Löwith, "I am a Christian theologian," he meant it precisely in the sense of pitting the true lesson of theology against the arrogated Christianness of today's theology. In a theological discussion in 1923 I heard him say: "I would recommend to Christian theology that it concentrate on its authentic task, that it seek the word which is capable of calling one to faith and preserving one in faith." To do so was indeed a task of thinking.

He had learned how to think not only from Aristotle. Husserl, with his masterful analyses of time-consciousness, demonstrated the literal consequences of Greek thinking to him. As a pupil of Husserl's, he was immune from the danger of underestimating the consistency of transcendental idealism, and of simply opposing it with a naïve realism through an appeal to the passwords of phenomenology. Therefore he could not support the claims of Pfänder and the young Scheler that things are what they are and are not "produced" through thinking. Neither the Marburg concept of production nor Husserl's controversial concept of constitution has anything to do with the metaphysical idealism of Bishop Berkeley or with the epistemological problem of the reality of the outside world. Husserl's intention was precisely to make the transcendence of things, their being-in-themselves (*Ansich-sein*), transcendentally intelligible — to justify them, as it were, "immanentally" in their transcendence. The doctrine of the transcendental ego and its apodictic manifestness was nothing other than this attempt at grounding all objectivity and validity. But just that attempt entangled itself in ever more refined analyses of the temporal structure of subjectivity. Constituting the transcendental ego which is recognized to be one's inescapable task leads one to form such paradoxical concepts as self-constitution of the stream of consciousness, self-manifestation of the flow, primal present, primal change. It probably proved to the young Heidegger that neither the concept of the object, nor that of the subject, was applicable to the problem that concerned him: the facticity of human *Dasein*. In truth he began his way by proceeding from the character of realization of *Dasein's* sorrow instead of from the intentional consciousness (later he called it "care"), and by determining existence as futurity. Thus the historicality of *Dasein* came into his view guided by his theological concern, not through the influence of historicism, and directed his question toward the meaning of Being.

But how could theology consider itself a scientific discipline without losing its Christian character, and without once again coming under the spell of subjective and objective conceptualizing? In the early years at Marburg, if memory serves me correctly, Heidegger had already thought in the direction which he formulated in the Tübingen lecture of 1927: theology is a positive discipline since it deals with a certain being, namely with Christianness. Theology is designated as the conceptual explanation of faith, and indeed because of this it stands nearer to chemistry or biology than to philosophy. For philosophy, as a unique discipline, does not deal with beings (as something given — though it be merely in faith), but with Being. It is the ontological discipline.

It is easy to see the conscious provocation in handling theology as a problem of theoretical science. The thesis is: in faith one encounters that which is the object of one's faith, and the latter is also amenable to a conceptual explanation if anything in faith can be treated in such a way. But is that which is believed perchance an object or a field of objects, such as the matter of chemistry or living organisms? Or on the contrary does it concern the whole of human *Dasein* and its world, as philosophy does? Heidegger indeed had to maintain on the other hand the ontological constitutional ground of human *Dasein*, which philosophy recognizes, as a corrective for the conceptual explanation of faith. Philosophy sees the existentiality of guilt as springing from the temporality of human *Dasein*. To be sure, philosophy only makes a 'formal declaration' (*formale Anzeige*) of the guilt experienced in faith as sin.

We see that Heidegger uses at this point a concept used much earlier by him, the formal declaration, nearly as an equivalent of the Kierkegaardian 'drawing-of-attention' (*Aufmerksammachen*). And one is not wrong to recognize in the use of the term *formal declaration* that the discipline of philosophy may well be involved in a conceptual or a theological explanation of faith, but not in the realization which is a matter of faith itself. This restriction differs from the aprioristic background which Husserl's ontologies claim to prescribe to empirical disciplines. And beyond Heidegger's use of the formal declaration in his thinking about faith undoubtedly stood the far-reaching insight that the question about Being is not a question in the sense of discipline either. Instead it 'strikes back at the level of individual existence' (*ins Existenzielle zurückschlagt*).

As is known, even this cautious restriction of phenomenological apriorism was critically attacked. Is *Dasein*'s character of guilt really neutral vis-à-vis the Christian history of faith, and is it independent of it? Or is it the wish to have conscience, or the running ahead toward death? Heidegger would scarcely be able, nor would he be obliged, to deny this for himself and for the ground of his experience. He would only insist that each human is able to realize from the ground of human experience that life is finality, 'Being that moves toward death' (*Sein zum Tode*). Consequently, the conceptual explanation of the Christian experience of faith would find its application for every person.

The whole confrontation between theology and philosophy is, to be sure, on rather slippery ground. The basic question is whether theology is a scientific discipline at all, or whether, indeed, it is an obligation imposed upon faith. Still more problematic is the question of whether the actual realization of *Dasein* concretized in the form of care can truly perform the task it is intended to, namely, to cast off the ontological anticipation of transcendental subjectivity and to conceive of temporality as Being. In the final analysis care is surely as much sorrow about oneself as consciousness is self-consciousness. Heidegger has properly stressed this as the tautology of care and Being-one's-self (*Selbstsein*). In care as the primal temporalizing, he believed he had overcome the ontological narrowness of the I-saying and of the identity of the subject which constitutes itself in I-saying. But what is that authentic temporality of care? Does it not appear as a self-temporalizing? *"Dasein* is *authentically itself* in the primordial individuation of the reticent resoluteness which takes dread (*Angst*) upon itself" (*Being and Time*, #64). Listen to how the later Heidegger speaks of dread: "that is to say, clearing of Being as Being's." Would he also say that *Dasein* takes the clearing upon itself?

The later Heidegger could no longer ground the thinking of Being as time on the transcendental analytic of *Dasein*, and this led him to speak of moving into the "turn." After that he could no longer think through the relation of philosophy and theology based on the presupposition that it was a relation between two scientific disciplines. As early as the Tübingen lecture one notices that in a radical sense Heidegger meant theology not only as a historical, but also as a practical discipline. "Every theological proposition and concept addresses itself to the faithful existence of the individual man in the community and it does so according to its content and *not* only afterwards on the basis of so-called practical application." It is not surprising that later, in 1964, Heidegger — more radically — closed his comments on nonobjectivizing thinking and speaking with the question: "Can theology still be a discipline, since it presumably is not permitted to be a discipline at all?"

Thus in the end it was not with the help of theology, but in the turning away from theology and from the metaphysics and ontology which governed theology, that the religious dimension in Heidegger sought its voice. This occurred, so far as it could occur, through the renewed encounter with Nietzsche, and through the lightening of the tongue Heidegger experienced in interpreting Hölderlin's poetry.

To think that Heidegger took an interest in Nietzsche on account of the atheistic implications of his thinking is completely misleading. The opposite is the case. Heidegger's radical thinking clearly left the atheistic dogmatism behind. It was the desperate boldness with which Nietzsche asked after the whole range of metaphysics and the theoretical concept of truth, and above all with which he perceived the will to power, that attracted Heideg-

ger. Not the devaluing of all values — this seemed to him a superficial aspect of Nietzsche — but that the human was conceived
above all else as the essential being who posits and appreciates
value. This was the hour of birth for the familiar Heideggerian
expression "calculative thinking." This thinking, which reckons
everything for what it is worth, has become the fate of human
culture in the era of technology and in the technological layout of
being-in-the-world. What Nietzsche describes as the rise of Euro-
pean nihilism, Heidegger accordingly understands not as the process of a devaluation of all values, but on the contrary as the ultimate establishment of thinking in values. And he names it the forgetfulness of Being.

Nietzsche is not only the diagnostician of nihilism for
Heidegger — against the background of Nothing Being becomes
visible. Thus he cites in *Holzwege* the episode of the madman
who did not believe in God, who cried out when he entered the
marketplace among the many: "I seek God, I seek God," and who
knows, "We have killed him." The one seeking God — this is Heidegger's point — knows about God. Those who try to prove his existence are the very ones who kill him in the process. For seeking
presupposes lacking, and lacking presupposes knowing. Lacking
presupposes a knowledge of that which is absent, but indeed that
which is absent is not "not there." It is there by being absent.

The presence of the vanished gods was the message that Heidegger discovered again in Hölderlin's poems. Christ was the last
god of the ancient world for Hölderlin, the last to sojourn among
humans. Since that time we have nothing other than traces of the
fugitive gods. Nevertheless the poet can say: "But of the divine we
have yet more. . . ." What sort of having? What sort of knowing?

By this model Heidegger tried to think all over again, but
not in the sense of metaphysics, nor in the sense of science. He
tried to think thinking. As one does not know of the divine by
grasping and perceiving God, likewise the thinking of Being is
neither a grasping nor a having and dominating. Without forcing
the parallel with the experience of God and his return, which
nevertheless can be thought more properly from this point, one
could say that Being is also more than mere presence (*Präsenz*),
and certainly much more than that which has been represented

(*Vorgestelltheit*). Being is just as much absence. It is a form of "there" in which not only the "there is" is experienced, but withdrawal, retreat, and forbearance are experienced as well. Heidegger often called upon this phrase of Heraklitos: "Nature loves to conceal itself." The statement is not an invitation to aggression and attacking; rather it invites one to abide. And Rilke was right in *Malte*, in his *Elegies*, when he grieved over the inability to abide. In this way the later Heidegger speaks of remembrance as not merely a thinking of something that once was. It is just as much a thinking of something coming which causes one to think of it already—even though it came "as the thief in the night."

It is no ontology, and above all no theology, that is prepared in such thinking. And yet I should like to recall that Heidegger, in thinking through Hölderlin's poetry, once said that the question "Who is God?" is too difficult for humans. The best we can do is to ask, "What is God?" And for this reason he pointed out that the "loss of the dimension of the holy and the whole (*der Heiligen und der Heilen*), is perhaps the real unholiness (*Unheil*) of our age." With this he probably also means that we cannot reach God because we talk about God in a way that can never serve the self-understanding of faith. But that would be the task of the theologian. "My task," Heidegger could have justly said to everyone, not only to Christians and theologians, "was to warn that the traditional ways of thinking are not sufficient."

— Translated by Dennis Looney

11

Transcendence as Interruption: Theology in a Political Mode

FREDERICK G. LAWRENCE

I

I WANT TO REPORT on a trend within Christian theology known as political theology. The epithet *political* placed before the noun *theology* may indicate that while theology remains faith seeking understanding, it is in the process of changing its mode.

When Thomas Aquinas articulated theology in the Middle Ages as a *scientia subalternans*, he understood by this "(1) that the subject of theology is not a set of propositions or set of truths but a reality, (2) that theology itself as an understanding for science is a process towards a terminal understanding, (3) that this understanding is not of God himself for then the science would not be subalternated but subalternating, and (4) that an understanding of the revelation cannot be adequate for the revelation is about God and God himself is not understood."[1] This conception is a far cry from the more domesticated mode of theology that emerged from the interminable struggles of the late Middle Ages and resulted in the adaptation of the art of finding sources (*loci, topoi*) for legal arguments to the ecclesiastical task of finding authoritative grounds for theological conclusions. Both old Protestant and Roman orthodoxy became less concerned with understanding religious mystery than with certainty. However, later on under the influence of non-Christians like Rousseau, Voltaire, Lessing, and Spinoza, the work of Protestants like Arnold, Franck, von Mosheim, Spener, and Semler paved the way for Schleiermacher's historicizing of revelation and relativizing of doctrine in the light of a universal natural religion or religious consciousness. The replacement of old orthodoxy by liberal theology on the Protestant theological scene eventually called forth Karl Barth's epoch-making reaction to what he called "existentialist theological thinking and the anthropologizing of theology"[2] in his dialectical theology.

In the late nineteenth and twentieth centuries Roman Catholic theology, too, has at last pretty much given up the ahistorical orthodoxy of Bossuet, of the scholastics of the baroque period, and of the Neo-Thomist revival. Roman theologians have joined their Protestant colleagues in accommodating themselves to the academic or professional ethos of specialized knowledge.

When it has not been, in Van A. Harvey's words, "subcontracted out to the specialized disciplines of biblical study, church history, ethics, the philosophy of religion, etc.,"[3] mainline theology today seems to have settled down to one or another way of correlating the results of historical studies and the more or less unquestioned questions of modern humankind. In this way theologians try to communicate the Christian understanding of mortals before God as the structure of human existence "disclosed" by the interpretations of Jesus as an inward and usually rather private reality.

The debate among the various protagonists seems to have concentrated on a certain rehearsal of the debate between liberal and neo-orthodox theology. The liberal approach focuses not on accommodation with the cultural ethos of the day, but, as George Rupp has recently expressed it, on "the Christian ethical imperative to inform and shape the whole of life so that it realizes the ultimately religious significance which is its ground and end."[4] The neo-orthodox reaction is not to confine the relevance of the Word of God, but to preserve, clarify, and apply it to culture precisely by bringing out its *paradoxical* tension with any present moment. Still, the Barthian attempt at dialogue between text and reader does tend to be confined to the mutually disclosing relationship between the preached word, the textual word of Scripture, and the Incarnate Word of God. Similarly, the Troeltschian attempt to liberate theology from the seemingly timeless absolutes of a church dogmatics makes one wonder just what transformative influence upon culture remains.

Gershom Scholem has quoted a remark made by Malcolm Muggeridge to the effect that ours is a time of "Freudians looking for their Marx and Marxists looking for their Freud."[5] When the liberal/neo-orthodox debate became infected by this atmosphere in the countries of the industrial North, it was principally in terms of Neo-Hegelian theories of repression like those of Herbert Marcuse, Ernst Bloch, and the thinkers associated with the Frankfurt School. In the sixties and seventies theologians like Jürgen Moltmann, Johann Baptist Metz, and Wolfhart Pannenberg made their case for the idea that Rudolf Bultmann, Karl Barth, and Karl Rahner had idealistically privatized the eschatological message of Christianity. In this trend, liberalism's tendency to reduce God to a palatable imaginative construct and the Barthian emphasis on the absolute transcendence of the Word were displaced by future historical possibility. Outside the Continent, the Latin American experience of development as oppressive dependence led to the outright adoption of various species of Marxism as a structure for emancipatory critique.

II

Many of the most significant intellectual movements in the twentieth century center on Martin Heidegger. This is brought out most suggestively perhaps by Gadamer in *Truth and Method* when he asks us to consider the parallel between the revolution in theology signaled by Karl Barth's *Römerbrief* — which he labels a hermeneutic manifesto — and the revolution in philosophy Heidegger was accomplishing in the elaboration of a hermeneutics of facticity. Just as Husserl's break from Neo-Kantian foundations was enshrined in the slogan, "Back to the things themselves!" so Barth's initiative over against his liberal teachers centered upon the issue of *Sachkritik*. Heidegger dismantled the Cartesian and Kantian restrictions on phenomenological reduction and enriched Husserl's method by a fresh recovery of the great works of the

Western tradition. Barth's bombshell effect was due to his audacity in asserting that historical interpretation did not exhaust the task of coming to grips with the *subject matter* of the biblical texts; Heidegger brought the full range of the *pragmata* back to the center of his reflection by thematizing the subject matter of texts by Luther, Paul, Augustine, and Aristotle.

The most significant reception of Heidegger into Roman Catholic theology was by Karl Rahner. Rahner was a student of Heidegger at Freiburg, Germany, in the mid-thirties — during "the madness," as his colleague J. B. Lotz once put it. The Heideggerian influence comes out most clearly in his major philosophic work, *Geist in Welt*, a commentary on an article from the *Summa theologiae* of Thomas which recovers the transcendental structures of the finite human spirit in a way that is more than reminiscent of the viewpoint of *Sein und Zeit*. That motif is also present in Rahner's fundamental work in philosophy of religion, *Hörer des Wortes*. Metz,[6] as Rahner's student and disciple at Innsbruck, caught the Heidegger bug, wrote a dissertation on him,[7] brought out the definitive second editions of *Geist in Welt* and *Hörer des Wortes* and wrote a slim book named *Christliche Anthropozentrik*[8] in which he related the latent transcendental philosophy uncovered by Rahner in Thomas Aquinas to the Incarnation and to the presuppositions of modern thought.

It was not until the mid-1960s that Metz made his dramatic shift from the perspective of "hearers of the Word" to that of "doers of the Word."[9] As Moltmann wrote of Bultmann that his interpretation of the New Testament was a privatizing of the Christian message, so Metz argued that Rahner's transcendental correlation of theology and anthropology led to a privatizing of the transforming Word in history.

Scripture scholarship developed into a never-ending series of revised hypotheses, but one point attained scholarly consensus: namely, the irreducible strain of apocalyptic eschatology within the New Testament message. Imminence and futurity together with the public and cosmic character of late Jewish apocalyptic were supported by similar traits in the notion of the Kingdom of God/Heaven within the New Testament reception of prophetic eschatology. According to Moltmann and Metz, Bultmann's

Lutheran-pietist stress on intimate decision-as-gift and Rahner's transcendental anthropology were not able to take these factors sufficiently into account.[10]

Immediately following his shift in perspective, Metz consistently associated the apocalyptic-eschatological mood of liberation from the forces of evil with the human history of freedom. What specifically helpful things, asks Metz, did Bultmann and Rahner have to say about the transformation of sinful social, political, and economic structures?[11]

Metz points out that this lack on Rahner's part had to do with his typically knowledge-oriented foundations: *Geist in Welt* and *Hörer des Wortes* might do as responses to the problem of Kant's first *Critique*, but they did not really afford a sufficient acknowledgement of Kant's own concern for the primacy of praxis. Metz saw that Rahner's concern for transcendent mystery needed to be further differentiated by a concern for liberty.[12] Metz might have been suspected of reducing Christian eschatology to human emancipation according to the gospel of social criticism had he not insisted that the *terminus ad quem* of human emancipation can never be reduced to this-worldly terms.[13]

Thus there has been a tension between Metz's political theology and the thought of critical theorists of society from whom he borrows in order to locate theology within the historical and social situation of subjects—their experiences, their sorrows and struggles, and their contradictions. Even though he began to echo the secularized critical theorists at this stage, what Metz was really beginning to see was that Christian faith could not be adequately accounted for within formalized or neutral philosophic frameworks, whether they be premodern cosmological-metaphysical systems or the privatized conceptions of modernity.[14] Henceforth, the principle and end of Metz's political theology will be neither theoretical nor technical, but rather historical praxis as oriented toward eschatological promises.

III

Metz's political theology is not only an eschatologically oriented praxis but also a form of critical reflection upon praxis. He himself has called it a "practical hermeneutics of Christianity." Meanings and values are constitutive of both human praxis and human reality, especially when those meanings and values bear on what is ultimate. Central to human becoming is human self-meaning in the sense of one's own desiring, feeling, perceiving, thinking, knowing, choosing, doing, and making. Deliberation and choice constitute our human identity in a way that is not true of the workings of our metabolisms, of our biological clocks, of the growth of our hair and nails. Human subjects are more than sheer products of external force and necessity. And so political theology is concerned with the concrete becoming of each and every human being as subject.

For Metz the symbol or thought of God is correlative to one's deepest feelings, needs, and interests, and to the over-all pattern or shape of one's exercise of liberty. There is a correlation between the God of the self and the self, as Feuerbach saw. Both realities mutually disclose and transform one another in their mysteriousness. Hence, Christian reflection on this correlation actually participates in it. God constitutes the human subject not merely as the goal or *telos* of the human search for identity, but as the inner Word of love that overflows within one and as the outer Word. Jesus is not merely an external object of worship, but a Way. As Metz puts it: "Christ has always to be thought about so that he's never only *thought* about. . . . By following him we come to know with whom we've gotten involved and who it is that saves us."[15] Discipleship is a matter of practical knowledge, and to focus one's reflection on its cognitive aspect is no less practical or political.

The human subject is intrinsically social and historical; therefore the issue of God's meaning and value for the subject is a matter not simply of private conviction but of the social and political conditions for actual discipleship. This is what Metz means by the hermeneutics of Christianity. The sociopolitical dimension of Christianity requires a change in strategy from trying to legitimate Christ without actually following Jesus to reminding the Christian community of Jesus' way of standing up for the honor of God in the midst of life's contradictions. While Metz does not wish to reduce theology to a pure sociopolitical activism, he does intend a complete break with subjectless theologies of the subject.

According to Metz, for example, a theology of the Word like Barth's or Balthasar's simply evades the problem of mediating between Christian religion and post-Enlightenment culture by making history a predicate of revelation. But Metz also distinguishes his thought from a theology of history like Pannenberg's which conceives revelation as the totality of historical process in so Hegelian a fashion that the contingent acts of finite human subjects hardly make any difference: the end of history and the meaning of history are not categories of practical reason but categories of reflection. "Here," Metz objects, "praxis remains secondary, subordinate, or it runs the risk of becoming a praxis oriented towards a predetermined end."[16]

Once again what Metz labels the "transcendental-idealistic" approach of Karl Rahner comes close to being a subjectless theology of the subject. For Metz an analysis of the transcendental subject as fundamentally religious is too far from the social and political experience of persons who function within a changing world in which the relevant conditions of knowledge and conduct change too.[17] Metz finds radical shortcomings in most contemporary theologies of the subject: religious experience is privatized;[18] religious traditions are neutralized by models of commerce and technical efficiency;[19] religious authority is exercised by juridical and administrative competence at the margins of real life;[20] and the serious issues of life, liberty, and the pursuit of property actually function under the auspices of a revolt from religious truth and so a thoroughgoing critique of religion and metaphysics.[21] Metz sees both Schleiermacher's natural religion of unconditional dependence and Tillich's numinous depths of human experience as "religion tailored to the home-use of the commodity-oriented bourgeois."[22] His political theology, therefore, wants to be a critique of bourgeois religion.[23]

Metz admits that he tended to follow too closely the Kantian model of a practical philosophy of history and society. He writes: "Kant could describe the task of man's attaining maturity as an ethical one, because he had exclusively in mind men who had long since come of age socially and economically, who already existed as socially powerful and entitled."[24] And so Kant failed to take seriously the human immaturity, impotence, and oppression that were not just the result of moral weakness and laziness. "Marx," he goes on to say, "is the first to make clear the way individual ethical praxis is neither neutral socially nor innocent politically"; a purely ethical interpretation of social praxis screens out the structural dimensions of alienation.[25]

Metz sees the dominant strains of secular social thought to be ineluctably working toward the advent of what Kojeve has called the universal and homogeneous state where there will be prosperity and no friction. Even Habermas's goal of a society of communication free from domination "threatens to sink into the banal picture of mere survival or of bestially sly adaptation. . . . Its eschaton is boredom . . . the unspoken interest of its rationality is the dismantling of the world as resistant to human wish: so that it won't have to go through that anymore."[26]

But how can Metz suspect this of Habermas, who is explicitly aware of the crypto-positivism in Marx himself? Doesn't he stress the difference between production and praxis? Yes, he does, and that is why Metz borrows so freely from him and his colleagues. Still, for Metz, these thinkers share with their positivist and liberal bourgeois antagonists the master metaphor of evolution or development. As one of Metz's "Theses Out of Season" expresses it:

> Revolutionary consciousness under the spell of evolutionary timelessness: Marx who sings the praises of revolutions as the locomotive of world-history. "Maybe it is completely otherwise. Maybe the real revolutions occur when the human race travelling in this train grabs for the emergency brakes" (W. Benjamin).[27]

According to Metz, in a situation where evolution or development is the master metaphor, the shortest definition of religion is: *Unterbrechung,* interruption.[28]

Metz argues that dialectical materialism "falls prey to the subjectless logic of evolution precisely when and insofar as it can ultimately ground its emancipatory interests, its intentions of universal liberation on nothing but a teleology of freedom rooted in matter or subhuman nature."[29] Any philosophy of history oriented toward praxis which departs from or presupposes a critique of religion functions as an "anthropodicy." Since the competitor

God can no longer be made responsible for evil (which is the premise of theodicy), then the evolutionary analysis of the history of emancipation becomes an excuse mechanism for *Homo Emancipator*. The other side of the coin is that this history of freedom is just as much an "ideology of the winners" as the liberal ideology of possessive individualism. The realm of "universal justice has a relevance only for people in the future, and not for the victims of history, who still belong to the universal and solidary community of humankind."[30] According to Metz, then, liberal democratic, managerial, or Marxian versions of the history of freedom fail to come fully to terms with the history of suffering of humankind. They are a social Darwinism which relates the sufferings and degradations of the ancestors to the probability of survival and well-being of those who "make it."

Metz goes on to argue that the scientific-technological civilization which dominates liberal behaviorists, technocrats, and Marxist humanists imposes on us an experience of time which becomes an ever more homogeneous and empty continuum, a "bad infinity" free of significant surprise. The social symptoms of this timelessness are many. They range from inhibitions against any forms of conduct that have no market value, like friendship, gratitude, mourning, and melancholy, to the increasingly pervasive extremes of either fatalistic apathy or fanatical hatred.

If the pseudo-religious symbol of evolution flattens time out to an empty and homogeneous continuum, the typical apocalyptic context is "the time of crisis, the time of persecution, of overwhelming injustice and inhumanity."[31] The apocalyptic perspective arises out of a special sensitivity to the horror and misery of human suffering. Metz argues that the key to Jewish-Christian apocalyptic is not "the mythic banishing of time into a rigid cosmic scheme," but the "radical letting-be of time in the world, since the apocalyptic consciousness of catastrophe is fundamentally a time-consciousness, not of the precise moment of catastrophe, but of the catastrophic structure of time itself, of its character as discontinuity, breakdown, and of the end of time."[32]

Christian apocalyptic consciousness lives out of a saving tale about a God of the living and the dead. "The faith of Christians" Metz defines as a "praxis in history and society which understands itself as solidary hope in the God of Jesus as the God of the living and the dead who calls *everyone* into being a subject before his face."[33] Because of Jesus' passage through the strait gate of time, evolutionary time-consciousness as the reigning plausibility structure of everyday modern life can be interrupted: there can be time for suffering, pain, mourning, as well as joy, play, and celebration; there is a rationale for conduct which "takes time" but has no market value; thus friendship, love, solidarity with the dead, and mourning become timely. Christian hope has revolutionary expectations for the future because it is grounded in faith as remembrance — a dangerous or subversive memory of the passion, death, and resurrection of Jesus Christ.[34]

Remembrance, then, is perhaps the central category of Metz's political theology. Human subjectivity is constituted by acts of apprehension and choice in relation to the world, society, and God.[35] Its form is specified by its memory as the lived answer to the question, Who are you? This habitual or existential memory is what Aristotle called "character." It is the source of human action or suffering:[36] in this sense memory specifies the pattern of our expectation and our willingness because it is shaped by our loyalties and aspirations as they really operate in solving the problem of living. Metz's category of *Erinnerung* or remembrance denotes ambiguously *both* the existential memory as habitual *and* the mode of its actuation: the well-known statement, "Nothing changes like the past," suggests that our remembering is ecstatic, selective, critical, constructive, and never fully under our control.[37] Most fundamentally for Metz, our remembering can be soothing and calming, or it can also be unsettling and challenging — even dangerous.[38] Christian dogma for Metz, then, is a dangerous memory. At its core it is expressive of a solidarity in Christ Jesus which moves with him through death to life in a way which renders meaningful not only history's survivors and winners but its dead and its losers.

The intelligible unity or pattern of remembrance as existential memory and as more or less dangerous remembering has a shape or form which is open to contingency and novelty and surprise. It is never adequately expressed in strictly logical terms. It has an essentially dramatic structure of connected description

which moves to a point. One's "identity" (to use Metz's term) or
"character" (to use Aristotle's) is actually a context of unfolding
action and suffering within a narrative or story.[39] Both one's identity and the story by which one lives have a form of connectedness
that is neither systematic nor logical. Hence, Metz argues that political theology is not transcendental and idealistic (in the Rah-
nerian vein) but *narrative and practical* in nature.

Politics is the concrete elaboration of a public solution to the
problem of human living in terms of a representative regime. For
Metz modern political theory and practice imply a one-sided and
diminishing story of what life is all about. It is a praiseworthy history of emancipation which fails to make sense of human suffering and opts for what is ultimately an ideology of self-assertion
whose final truth is death. By confining knowledge to utility and
choice to the mastery of nature, these stories eliminate the spiritual from public relevance. The liberal Hobbes-Lockean story
centers upon a calculating contract which emancipated acquisi-
tiveness, self-interestedness, and the satisfactions of lower passions in order to make possible better motives.[40] Alternatively, the
Kantian vision suggests the belief that universalizing self-interest
will eventually channel power into institutional devices that will
bring about, in T. S. Eliot's phrase, "an order so perfect no one
will need to be good."

A similar outcome is projected by the Marxian story of a revolutionary process that would transfigure human nature and
eliminate the problem of evil by human means. Because these
stories of emancipation do not account sufficiently for the world's
suffering and evil, Metz says they need to be sublated to a story of
redemption. As a Christian, he locates the heart of that story in
the memory of the passion, death, and resurrection of Jesus. This
is a story that adequately responds to what he has identified as *the*
apocalyptic questions: To whom does the world ultimately belong? To whom its suffering? To whom its time?[41]

The image of the God whose dominion over the cosmic process is shown forth in "the poverty of Jesus' obedience and in his
handing over of his life to the Father is not that of a disheartening
tyrant-god; and it is not a glorified version of earthly lordship and
authority. It is the illuminating image of a God who lifts up and
liberates, who releases the guilt-ridden and discouraged into a

new future full of promise and who comes toward them with the outstretched arms of his mercy."[42] According to Metz, hope in the God of Jesus heightens one's sensitivity toward meaningless suffering and challenges one not to settle for the dominant plausibility structures of modern society which defer to nothing higher than humanity. Belief in the resurrection of the dead and hope in our passing through death to life free us to live a life of self-transcendence that goes against the grain of self-affirmation and self-aggrandizement. Jesus' identification of himself with "the least of these" (Matt. 25) — the marginal, the outcast, the hopeless — demands a dismantling of our normal notions of human leadership and points toward the Lordship of God as defenseless truth and self-sacrificial love. The dangerous memory of Jesus is a call to be present to the other and to transform the life of the other by solidary and substitutional suffering and even death. One can appreciate the superhumanness of this demand only if the issue of history is not utopia, but a God who does not condone failures of self-transcendence and guilt, but forgives them — a God to whom one can complain or sing, praise in gladness or cry out in despair.[43]

Metz believes that theologians who have transformed eschatological imminent expectation into constant expectation have sold out Christian faith to the metaphor of evolution precisely in Nietzsche's sense when he wrote: "Evolution intends not happiness but just more evolution and nothing else."[44] When Christians make their peace with Keynes's statement that "in the long run we are all dead," it is impossible for them to sustain the rigors of genuine discipleship. Only if they are seriously expecting and hoping that "the day of the Lord" has just about arrived or is just about to arrive can they even consider undertaking the radical discipleship which is really not humanly livable. For Christian praxis, the correlative to God's call, "Follow Me!" is the prayer, "Come, Lord Jesus!"[45]

IV

You will have caught from the drift of my remarks on the political theology of Metz thus far my profound esteem for his prophetic retrieval of Christian eschatology. It keeps political theology from collapsing into the political philosophic horizon of the liberalism of the right (capitalist) or left (welfare, socialist, Marxist). It is grounded in praxis as ecclesiastical and sociocultural performance in such a way that its retrieval is no mere concoction of a rival ideology in reaction to the dominant ideologies of right and left. For Metz's political theology the story is concretely and experientially located in the life of the Church as an authentic — as well as alienated — subject in and of history.[46] Moreover, as practically oriented toward performance, Metz has tried to locate political theology as reflection upon its interplay with the stories and cover stories of contemporary culture within a specifically interdisciplinary academic context. This is evident not merely from his contribution to and edition of the volume, *Theologie in der interdisziplinaren Forschung*,[47] but in his labors toward the establishing of the interdisciplinary Theological Research Center at the State University in Bielefeld,[48] and in the style of the work of his students, such as Ernst Feil,[49] Matthew Lamb,[50] and Helmut Peukert.[51]

The foundational underpinnings of Metz's work to date, however, are not sufficient in themselves.[52] As we have seen, Metz's own heightening of Christian eschatological consciousness has perhaps more in common with the respective retrievals of Jewish scholars such as Walter Benjamin and Gershom Scholem. Here I can only join Metz's student, Matthew Lamb,[53] in suggesting that Lonergan's conception of theology as a mystically grounded and functionally specialized enterprise might indeed offer the authentic transposition of practical and political philosophy as interdisciplinary collaboration in critical consciousness. "Method" in Lonergan's sense and "political theology" in Metz's have one thing — in my opinion, the crucial thing — in common — namely, the radical departure of total reflection on the human condition from the question about the right way to live, or about the good life.[54]

NOTES

1. Bernard J. F. Lonergan, "Theology and Understanding," *Collection Papers by Bernard Lonergan*, ed. R. E. Crowe (London: Darton, Longman & Todd, 1967), p. 127.

2. Karl Barth, *Kirchliche Dogmatik* (Zollikon-Zürich: Evangelischer Verlag, 1961), 1:2, pp. 19 ff.

3. Van A. Harvey, "What is the Task of Theology?" *Christianity and Crisis* 36 (1979): 119–121.

4. George Rupp, *Culture-Protestantism: German Liberal Theology at the Turn of the Twentieth Century*, American Academy of Religion Studies in Religion 15 (Missoula, Mont.: Scholars Press, 1977).

5. Gershom G. Scholem, "Reflections on Jewish Theology," in *On Jews and Judaism in Crisis: Selected Essays*, ed. W. J. Dannhauser (New York: Schocken Books, 1978), p. 290.

6. My appreciation of the significance of the work of Metz has been enhanced by Matthew Lamb (Marquette University), especially by way of the "osmosis that took place in personal conversations" and exchanges during our student days in Europe. Fortunately, there are important publications available. See "Les presuppositions méthodologiques de la théologie politique," *La pratique de la théologie politique* (Tournai, 1974); and "The Theory-Praxis Relationship in Contemporary Christian Theologies," *Proceedings of the Catholic Theological Society of America* 31 (1976): 149–178; "A Response (II) to Bernard Lonergan," *Proceedings of the Catholic Theological Society of America* 32 (1977): 22–30; and especially, *History, Method, and Theology: A Dialectical Comparison of Wilhelm Dilthey's Critique of Historical Reason and Bernard Lonergan's Meta-Methodology*, American Academy of Religion Dissertation Series 25 (Missoula, Mont.: Scholars Press, 1978).

7. The results of this work appear in Johann Baptist Metz, "Heidegger und das Problem der Metaphysik," *Scholastik* (1953): 1–23; and "Theologische und Metaphysische Ordnung," *Zeitschrift für katholische Theologie* 83 (1961): 1–14.

8. Johann Baptist Metz, *Christliche Anthropozentrik* (Munich: Kösel, 1962).

9. Johann Baptist Metz, *Zur Theologie der Welt* (Mainz: Grünewald, 1968). The transition in Metz's approach appears in this work, which is more a collection of essays than a composed whole, even though the essays do hang together thematically and form something of a connected whole. Part I (pp. 11–74) is an application of Metz's own appropriation of Rahner's hearers-of-the-word standpoint to the problems of secularization and hominization. In Parts II and III (pp. 75–146), his later perspective of doers-of-the-word is becoming prominent.

10. Ibid., pp. 75–88, which explicates the importance of eschatology.

11. Ibid., pp. 99–146.

12. Johann Baptist Metz, "Kirchliche Autorität im Anspruch der Freiheitsgeschichte," in *Kirche im Prozess der Aufklärung*, ed. Johann Baptist Metz, Jürgen Moltmann, W. Olmüller (Mainz: Grünewald, 1970), pp. 53–70; "Political Theology," *Sacramentum Mundi* 5 (New York: Herder and Herder, 1970), pp. 34–38.

13. Metz, *Zur Theologie der Welt*, pp. 75–89, 110ff.

14. Ibid., pp. 89–91, for Metz's critique of metaphysics; and pp. 99–102 on privatization.

15. See Johann Baptist Metz, *Zeit der Orden? Zur Mystik und Politik der Nachfolge*, 3rd ed. (Freiburg: Herder, 1977), p. 41 (henceforth *ZO*); also *Glaube in Geschichte und Gesellschaft. Studien zu einer praktischen Fundamentaltheologie* (Mainz: Grünewald, 1977); in this connection chap. 4: "Konzept einer politischen Theologie als praktischer Fundamentaltheologie," pp. 44–74 (henceforth *GGG*); "Der Zukünftige Mensch und der kommende Gott," *Wer ist das eigentlich — Gott?* ed. H. J. Schultz (Frankfurt: Suhrkamp, 1973), pp. 260–275.

16. *GGG*, p. 52. On Barth, *GGG*, pp. 33, 144–145 with note 145; but also see p. 12, note 18, and pp. 41–42 on the dialectical value of Barth's polemic in the context of what he had opposed. On Balthasar, *GGG*, p. 118.

17. For Metz's critical remarks on Rahner, especially *GGG*, pp. 49–51 (p. 12, note 18 on the dialectical strength of Rahner's enterprise vis-à-vis the weaknesses of the neo-scholasticism he moved away from; and p. 22 on the apologetic value of Rahner's enterprise); pp. 61–63 (n.b. note 33 on Rahner's Kantian transcendental point of departure; note 34 on a critique of the notion of transcendental experience from the standpoint of Theodore W. Adorno); pp. 117–118, where Rahner is implicated in the critique of Barth and Balthasar's theology of the cross; esp. chap. 9: "Transzendental-idealistisches oder narrativ-praktisches Christentum? Die Theologie vor der Identitätskrise des gegenwärtigen Christentums," pp. 136–148.

18. *GGG*, pp. 31–33.

19. Ibid., pp. 33–35.

20. Ibid., pp. 36–38.

21. Ibid., pp. 38–42.

22. Ibid., p. 41.

23. Ibid., pp. 29–43.

24. Ibid., p. 51.

25. Ibid., p. 50.

26. Ibid., p. 81.

27. This is the twelfth of Metz's "Theses Out of Season," from

chap. 10, entitled, "Hoffnung als Näherwartung oder der Kampf um die verlorene Zeit, Unzeitgemässe Thesen zur Apokalyptik," *GGG*, pp. 149–158, esp. p. 152. For me this was the high point of this book, maybe because Metz's acute intellect is more aptly expressed in the meditative style of the aphorism. Metz is notoriously (and mercifully, in the light of the heaps of sheer verbiage published by so many mediocrities) short-breathed.

28. *GGG*, p. 150: Thesis VI, "Kürzeste Definition von Religion: Unterbrechung."

29. Ibid., p. 7.

30. Ibid., p. 73. On this theme also see J. B. Metz, "Erlösung und Emanzipation," *Stimmen der Zeit* 191 (1973): 171–184.

31. *GGG*, p. 155.

32. Ibid.

33. *GGG*, p. 70.

34. Johann Baptist Metz, "*The Future ex memoria Passionis,*" *Hope and the Future of Man*, ed. E. Cousins (Philadelphia: Westminster Press, 1972), pp. 117–131; "The Future in the Memory of Suffering," *Concilium* 76 (1972): 9–25.

35. On the intelligibility of subjectivity, see Bernard Lonergan, "Christology Today," in *Le Christ, hier, aujour d'hui et demain*, ed. R. Laflamme, M. Gervaise (Quebec: Les Presses de L'Universite Laval, 1976), pp. 45–65, esp. pp. 61–65.

36. I am dependent here on the work of Stanley Hauerwas with David B. Burrell, "From System to Story: An Alternative Pattern for Rationality in Ethics," *Truthfulness and Tragedy, Further Investigations in Christian Ethics* (Notre Dame: University of Notre Dame Press, 1977), pp. 15–39, esp. pp. 28–31.

37. Bernard J. F. Lonergan, *Method in Theology* (New York: Herder and Herder, 1972), pp. 188–189.

38. *GGG*, pp. 61–175; also Johann Baptist Metz, "Erinnerung," *Handbuch philosophischer Grundbegriffe, Bd.* 2, ed. H. Krings, H. M. Baumgartner, Chr. Wild (Munich: Herder, 1973); idem, "Glaube als gefährliche Erinnerung," *Hilfe zum Glauben* (Theologische Meditationen 25), ed. Hans Küng (Zürich: Benziger, 1971), pp. 23–38; and *GGG*, pp. 176–194.

39. Hauerwas with Burrell, "From System to Story," pp. 28–31; Johann Baptist Metz, "A Short Apology of Narrative," *Concilium* 85 (1973): 84–96; and *GGG*, pp. 136–148, 181–194.

40. James Madison, for instance, who was convinced that "neither moral nor religious motives can be relied on as an adequate

control: over factions or the majority of propertyless men." And so he formulated for Americans instead a "policy of supplying, by opposite and rival interests, the defect of better motives." Alexander Hamilton, James Madison, and John Jay, *The Federalist*, ed. Clinton Rossiter (New York: New American Library, 1961), nos. 10–51.

41. *GGG*, p. 60.

42. Johann Baptist Metz, "Unsere Hoffnung. Die Kraft des Evangeliums zur Gestaltung der Zukunft," *Concilium* (German ed.), vol. 11, no. 12 (1975): 712–720. What follows in the text is also particularly inspired by this praxis and hope-oriented reformulation of the Creed.

43. Johann Baptist Metz, "Voraussetzungen des Betens. Ein Gespräch mit Johann Baptist Metz," *Herderkorrespondenz* 32 (1978): 125–133.

44. Cited by Metz, *GGG*, p. 151. See also his "For a Renewed Church before a New Council: A Concept in Four Theses," in *Toward Vatican III: The Work That Needs to be Done*, ed. David Tracy, Hans Küng, and Johann Baptist Metz (New York: Concilium, Seabury Press, 1978), pp. 135–145.

45. *ZO*.

46. The ecclesiological emphasis was central to *Zur Theologie der Welt* and no less so in the recent work. See *GGG*, chap. 8: "Kirche und Volk. Vom vergessenen Subjekt des Glaubens," pp. 120–135; and chap. 13: "Solidarität," pp. 204–211.

47. Johann Baptist Metz, ed., *Theologie in der interdisziplinaren Forschung* (Düsseldorf: Bertelsman, 1971). Metz's contribution is "Zu einer interdisziplinaren orientierten Theologie auf bikonfessioneller Basis. Erste Orientierungen anhand eines Konkreten Projekts," pp. 10–23.

48. Lamb, *History, Method, and Theology*, p. 535.

49. Ernst Feil, *Die Theologie Dietrich Bonhöffers: Hermeneutik, Christologie, Weltverständnis* (Munich: Kaiser, 1971). "Von der 'politischen Theologie' zur 'Theologie der Revolution'" in *Diskussion zur "Theologie der Revolution*," ed. Ernst Feil and R. Weth (Mainz: Grünewald, 1969).

50. See note 6 above. Also: "Towards a Synthetization of the Sciences," *Philosophy of Science* 32 (1965): 182–191; and "The Production Process and Exponential Growth," *Lonergan Workshop* I (1978): 257–307.

51. Helmut Peukert, "Zur formalen Systemtheorie und zur hermeneutischen Problematik einer 'politischen Theologie'," in *Diskussion zur "Politischen Theologie*," ed. Helmut Peukert, (Mainz: Grünewald,

1969), 82–95; "Zur Frage einer 'Logik der interdisziplinaren Forschung'," in *Theologie in der interdisziplinaren Forschung*, ed. Johann Baptist Metz (Düsseldorf: Bertelsman, 1971), pp. 65–71; and his recent book, *Wissenschaftstheorie — Handlungstheorie — fundamentale Theologie* (Düsseldorf: Bertelsman, 1976).

52. Frederick G. Lawrence, "Political Theology and the 'Longer Cycle of Decline,'" *Lonergan Workshop* I (1978): 223–555; "The Horizon of Political Theology," in *Trinification of the World*, ed. Frederick E. Crowe, T. A. Dunne and J. M. Laporte (Toronto: Regis College Press, 1978), pp. 46–70.

53. Lamb, *History, Method, and Theology*, chap. 4, "History and Method in Theology," pp. 459–536.

54. Frederick G. Lawrence, "A Response to Gerald McCool," *Proceedings of the Catholic Theological Society of America* 32 (1977): 90–96.

Author Index

Subject Index

Absolute, 60, 128, 187–192
Alienation, 23–24
Analytic philosophy, 26
Anxiety, 8, 33

Being, 5, 10, 92, 194
Brahman, 83ff.
Buddhism, 2, 8, 40, 45, 46, 70, 83ff., 100ff.

Calvinism, 163ff.
Christianity, 11–12, 40, 46, 118, 149, 161ff., 193ff., 208ff.
Civilizational perspective, 5–7, 58ff.
Comparative philosophy, 1ff., 26
Consciousness, 85, 120
Conversion, 42–43

Dasein, 203–205
Deception, 142ff.
Degenerate Age, 125ff.
Dharma, 8

Emptiness, 20–21, 140ff.
Enlightenment, 100ff., 120
Epistemology, 20–21, 140ff.
Experience, 41, 120, 168

Faith, 8, 11, 40ff., 84, 123, 131–132, 204

Gnosis, 3–4, 26–30, 97, 138ff.
Gnosticism, 10–11, 138ff.
God, 32–33, 42–43, 60, 66, 71, 90, 118, 150–151, 165ff., 186

Hierophany, 117
Hinduism, 2, 8, 83ff.
Holy, 48ff., 104–105, 112–113
Humility, 15, 43

Idealism, 181–182, 202
Interruption, 15, 208ff.

Jesus Christ, 42–44, 118, 180

Living option, 169ff.
Logos, 8–9, 93–94, 147ff.

Manichees, 43
Marxism, 14, 183
Middle Way, 9, 100ff.
Mysterium tremendum, 48ff., 104–105, 112–113
Mysticism, 139ff.

229

BL51 .T62
NXWW

Randall Library – UNCW

Transcendence and the sacred

3049002732850